The Life Story of an Old Rebel

JOHN DENVIR

THE LIFE STORY
OF
AN OLD REBEL

Introduction by
LEON Ó BROIN

IRISH UNIVERSITY PRESS
Shannon · Ireland

This IUP reprint is a photolithographic facsimile of
the first edition and is unabridged, retaining the
original printer's imprint

© 1972

Irish University Press Shannon Ireland

All forms of micropublishing

© *Irish University Microforms Shannon Ireland*

ISBN 0 7165 0012 4

Irish University Press Shannon Ireland

T. M. MacGlinchey Publisher

PRINTED IN THE REPUBLIC OF IRELAND AT SHANNON
BY ROBERT HOGG PRINTER TO IRISH UNIVERSITY PRESS

INTRODUCTION

In his autobiography, first published in 1910, John Denvir, a builder become journalist, author, revolutionary and political organizer, looks back benignly over the period of more than seventy years when he was intimately bound to Irish and Catholic life in England, mostly in the city of Liverpool. It is an important and valuable source book. Through it and Denvir's *The Irish in Britain* we can perceive how a community of Catholic Irish in their British outpost cherished, as Thomas Wall points out, the memory of their native land much as the Israelites in bondage remembered Zion. Denvir was born almost by chance in Ireland—in Bushmills, County Antrim to be exact—but he saw very little of the country thereafter, and for a time his impression of its shape was derived from a map on the back of a Repeal Card. Physical dissociation took nothing, however, from his essential Irishness. It may have increased it, for, with exiles of every generation, Denvir shared the Faith-and-Fatherland ideals of the homeland and enthusiastically associated himself with all the movements, political, social and religious, that originated under the stress of specifically Irish conditions.

He was fortunate, and this adds to the quality of his story, in seeing with his own eyes most of the great Irish figures of his time and in knowing many of them personally. He received the pledge from no less a person than the great Father Mathew himself. As an altar boy he saw the Liberator, O'Connell, more than once at Mass. He saw him again, 'a big man in a long cloak wearing the Repeal Cap', speaking from a hotel balcony; and his blood boiled when at the time of the Famine he came across a *Punch* cartoon in which Dan was portrayed as 'the real Potato Blight'. He was a horrified observer of the direst consequences of the Great Hunger. The port of Liverpool became the main artery through which the Irish people poured in tens of thousands in an effort to escape from their doomed land.

While secretary of a boys' refuge in the sixties and manager of a Catholic newspaper Denvir joined the Fenian or Irish Republican Brotherhood (I.R.B.), smuggled arms to Ireland and was lucky to escape arrest when other men who had engaged in similar enterprises in Lancashire were taken and sentenced to long terms of imprisonment. He became acquainted with such Fenian celebrities as John Breslin who had helped James Stephens escape from Richmond Jail, Captain Michael O'Rourke (otherwise Beecher), Captain John McCafferty, John Flood, J. F. X. O'Brien, General Halpin who was in command of the district around Dublin on the night of the 1867 rising, Stephen J. Meany and Colonel Thomas J. Kelly. The north of England was a vital area in Fenian strategy, but it was there that the overthrow of Fenian plans was achieved by the informer John Joseph Corydon whom Denvir describes on his appearance in a Liverpool police court. 'At first sight you might set him down as a third-rate actor or circus performer. He wore a frock coat, buttoned tightly, to set off a by no means contemptible figure, and carried himself with a jaunty, swaggering air.'

Denvir, having recounted the dramatic happenings at Chester, Manchester and Clerkenwell in 1867, displays a surprising optimism in spite of all the disasters. Things could so easily have gone better, he suggests, if arms had been more freely available and if England had become involved in a war with the United States as it seemed at times likely she might. The Fenians, however, had lost that particular round—of that there was no doubt whatever—and many of them turned from the use of force to peaceful persuasion. Denvir takes pains to explain that he never thought the worse of any one on that account, though he could never bring himself in conscience to take the oath of allegiance, as some of his colleagues did on their way to the palace of Westminster. He became a constitutionalist himself nevertheless, and devoted a great deal of his life to the organization of political parties and to securing the election to parliament of nationalists and Gladstonian Liberals. To that extent his remarks are rather inconsistent as indeed is his justification of Fenianism and Home Rule on the grounds that they were both just and practical.

During a lull in his early career Denvir and some friends

formed a travelling group, the Emerald Minstrels, with the idea of spreading interest in what they conceived as the very stuff of Irish nationality—the music, poetry, drama, customs and traditions of Ireland. In this venture they were, of course, under the continuing influence of the Young Irelanders of the forties who had stressed the importance of all cultural links with the past. Charles Gavan Duffy's *Spirit of the Nation*, a widely read book of ballads, was a unique source of inspiration to the group; and, in further imitation of the Young Irelanders, Denvir in 1870 began to issue from his own printing press an 'Irish Library' consisting chiefly of short biographies, stories, songs and 'stirring episodes'. Some distinguished writers helped to swell the list of these 'penny books' of which nearly a million copies were sold. In 1902 he commenced a second series.

When the Home Rule Confederation of Great Britain was formed in the early 1870s Denvir, then editing the *Catholic Times*—he later edited nationalist papers also published in Liverpool—became its first general secretary. The appointment naturally brought him into contact with the genial Isaac Butt. He liked the man and extolled what he had done for his country, but he reserved his special regard for a local leader on the English scene. This was John Barry of Manchester—'the ablest man of Irish blood in Britain', Tim Healy called him—who was practically the founder of the general organization which, under various titles, had been in existence since 1873, working in accordance with and taking the name of whatever was the recognized organization for the time being in Ireland. Barry was very much more than a party organizer, however: he was a species of king-maker, and had much to say on the rise and fall of Butt and Parnell. Another man who played a somewhat similar role in Parnell's career was Patrick Egan to whom Denvir also devotes some admiring paragraphs. Egan, he says, was Parnell's 'political god-father'; he had worked energetically to secure the faltering young squire's first election to parliament and subsequently as treasurer of the Land League he kept the agitation going with drafts of money from his Paris headquarters when Parnell and other national leaders were in prison. Barry—to return to him—was an I.R.B. man but, in Denvir's words, he 'was always a practical patriot and would use every legitimate method to save Ireland'. His practicality consisted in becoming a 'Fenian parliamentarian', favouring 'the New Departure', the association of underground Fenianism with an 'open movement'. He was subjected on that account to violent criticism as no doubt Denvir was for aligning himself with men who had abandoned the 'official' line.

It was the successful employment of a policy of deliberate and sustained obstruction in the House of Commons for the purpose of focusing attention on Ireland's problems that made alignment with constitutionalists attractive to so many of the physical force men. Denvir knew Joseph Gillis Biggar, the deformed pork butcher from Belfast, who made such original use of these tactics; later he became a friend and admirer of Parnell who, likewise as an obstructionist, first came under public notice. How well Denvir knew the enigmatic Parnell is another matter. They were drawn to each other 'because he [Parnell] looked upon me, from my life-long experience of them, as an authority upon our people in this country [England] —and I, because I was impressed by the terrible earnestness that I soon recognized underlying the young man's apparently impassive and unemotional exterior. . . . He used to speak unreservedly to me.' Denvir certainly knew Parnell well enough to be able to raise with him, as Michael Davitt did, the difficult question of his joining the I.R.B. To both men Parnell gave the same answer. He would never join any political secret society, oath-bound or otherwise, and he was satisfied that useful work for the Cause could be done in the British Parliament. He would have liked Denvir to join him there but this Denvir was not prepared to do because of his scruple over the oath.

Parnell grievously embarrassed Denvir and the Liverpool Irish when in the 1885 general election he asked them to back the candidature of Captain O'Shea for whom they had nothing but contempt, and with whose wife the Irish leader was then cohabiting though this was still hidden from them. Their half-hearted response ensured O'Shea's defeat, but that did not prevent Parnell from repeating the performance some months later in Galway, when he thrust a worthless fellow who, within five years, was to destroy him, upon a loyal and un-suspecting people. Denvir found other men more to his liking: T. P. O'Connor, for instance, whom he helped into the Liverpool seat that he held for many years. In the Carnarvon boroughs in 1900 he put the Irish vote, such as it was, behind 'a thoroughgoing Home Ruler' named David Lloyd George, and the successful partnership ripened into a close friendship. Lloyd George's majority was a mere eighteen votes, so that Denvir could claim that the Welsh wizard, who was later to play so sensational a role in Irish affairs, would not have got to Westminster without the Irish.

Denvir scarcely mentions in this book the appalling political split that followed Parnell's divorce, although we know from *The Irish in Britain* that he became a severe critic of his leader and friend on national and religious grounds. He saw him as 'a self-disgraced man, not repentant for the crime he had committed, but standing up, unblushing and audacious, determined in his selfish pride to maintain to the last his claim to the leadership, reckless of the risk of ruin to the cause of Ireland.' His struggle against Ireland, he wrote, was as fierce and as hopeless as that of Lucifer and the fallen angels against Heaven. That was in 1894. By 1910, the 'family feud' had become an unhappy memory for Denvir. He preferred to forget it if he could, to jump forward in his autobiography to the reunion of the Parliamentary party and to fill in the period between with an account of two neutral bodies that had appeared with which he was wholly in sympathy. One was the Gaelic League whose special preoccupation was the revival of the Irish language; the other was the Irish Literary Society which concerned itself with Ireland's cultural and educational needs. In the Gaelic League branches in London, where he had come to live as organizer of the Irish National League and afterwards of the United Irish League, Denvir met the songwriter Francis Fahy, William P. Ryan who contributed a life of Thomas Davis to the second series of Denvir's Irish Library, and Dr Mark Ryan, an old Fenian comrade. Among his acquaintances in the Irish Literary Society were Alfred P. Graves, the author of 'Father O'Flynn', R. Barry O'Brien, Parnell's biographer, and Charles Gavan Duffy, to whose compilation of ballad poetry he owed so much in the way of inspiration. Duffy had returned from Australia at the close of a spectacular public career and, through the publication of his New Library series, had begun to reformulate an old thesis that Denvir had long since made his own—'educate that you may be free'. The two patriots were thus linked at the end, as they were in their youth, by a common national purpose.

Denvir died in Wimbledon on the first of December 1916 and was buried in Kensal Green cemetery. He was eighty-two.

Leon Ó Broin

SELECT BIBLIOGRAPHY

Davitt, Michael. *The Fall of Feudalism in Ireland; or, The Story of the Land League Revolution.* London and New York 1904. Reprint, Shannon 1970.

Duffy, Charles Gavan. *My Life in Two Hemispheres.* 2 vols. London 1898. Reprint, Shannon 1968.

——. *Young Ireland.* London 1896.

Healy, Timothy M. *Letters and Leaders of My Day.* 2 vols. London 1928.

Irish Book Lover, VIII, no. 7–8, p. 73. Obituary of John Denvir.

O'Brien, William, and Ryan, Desmond, eds. *Devoy's Post Bag, 1871–1928.* 2 vols. Dublin 1948, 1953.

Ó Broin, Leon. *Charles Gavan Duffy, Patriot and Statesman.* Dublin 1967.

——. *Fenian Fever.* London 1971.

O'Connor, Thomas Power. *The Parnell Movement.* London 1886.

O'Hegarty, Patrick Sarsfield. *A History of Ireland under the Union, 1801 to 1922.* London 1952.

Ryan, Mark. *Fenian Memoirs.* Dublin 1945.

Thornley, David. *Isaac Butt and Home Rule.* London 1964.

Wall, Thomas. 'John Denvir'. *Journal of the County Kildare Archaeological Society,* XIV, no. 3.

White, Terence de Vere. *The Road of Excess.* Dublin 1946.

THE LIFE STORY

OF

AN OLD REBEL

John Devoir, 1910

THE
LIFE STORY
OF
AN OLD REBEL

BY

JOHN DENVIR

AUTHOR OF "THE IRISH IN BRITAIN" "THE BRANDONS" ETC.

DUBLIN
SEALY, BRYERS & WALKER
86 MIDDLE ABBEY STREET
1910

PRINTED BY
SEALY, BRYERS AND WALKER,
MIDDLE ABBEY STREET,
DUBLIN.

CONTENTS.

CHAP.   PAGE

I.—Early Recollections — " Coming Over " from
Ireland 1

II.—Distinguished Irishmen—" The Nation " Newspaper—" The Hibernians " 10

III.—Ireland Revisited 27

IV.—O'Connell in Liverpool — Terence Bellew
MacManus and the Repeal Hall—The Great
Irish Famine 48

V.—The "No-Popery" Mania—The Tenant League
—The Curragh Camp 58

VI.—The Irish Revolutionary Brotherhood—Escape of
James Stephens—Projected Raid on Chester
Castle—Corydon the Informer 73

VII.—The Rising of 1867—Arrest and Rescue of Kelly
and Deasy—The Manchester Martyrdom .. 89

VIII.—A Digression—T. D. Sullivan—A National
Anthem — The Emerald Minstrels—" The
Spirit of the Nation " 113

IX.—A Fenian Conference at Paris—The Revolvers
for the Manchester Rescue—Michael Davitt
sent to Penal Servitude 123

X.—Rescue of the Military Fenians 139

XI.—The Home Rule Movement 148

XII.—The Franco-Prussian War—An Irish Ambulance
Corps—The French Foreign Legion.. .. 160

XIII.—The Home Rule Confederation of Great Britain 170

XIV.—Biggar and Parnell—The "United Irishman "—
The O'Connell Centenary 179

CONTENTS

CHAP.   PAGE

XV.—Home Rule in Local Elections—Parnell succeeds
Butt as President of the Irish Organisation
in Great Britain   185

XVI.—Michael Davitt's Return from Penal Servitude
—Parnell and the " Advanced " Organisation   199

XVII.—Blockade Running—Attempted Suppression of
"United Ireland "—William O'Brien and his
Staff in Jail—How Pat Egan kept the flag
flying   209

XVIII.—Patrick Egan   219

XIX.—General Election of 1885—Parnell a Candidate
for Exchange Division—Retires in favour of
O'Shea—T. P. O'Connor elected for Scotland
Division of Liverpool   227

XX.—Gladstone's " Flowing Tide "   233

XXI.—The "Times" Forgeries Commission   246

XXII.—Disruption of the Irish Party—Home Rule
carried in the Commons—Unity of Parliamentary Party Restored—Mr. John Redmond
becomes Leader   252

XXIII.—The Gaelic Revival—Thomas Davis—Charles
Gavan Duffy—Anglo-Irish Literature—The
Irish Drama, Dramatists, and Actors   ..   256

XXIV.—" How is Old Ireland and how does She Stand ? "   268

THE LIFE STORY OF AN OLD REBEL

CHAPTER I.

EARLY RECOLLECTIONS—"COMING OVER" FROM IRELAND.

I OWE both the title of this book and the existence of the book itself to the suggestion of friends. I suppose a man of 76 may be called " old," although I have by no means given up the idea that I can still be of use to my country.

And a Rebel ? Yes ! Anything of the nature of injustice or oppression has always stirred me to resentment, and—is it to be wondered at ?—most of all when the victims of that injustice and oppression have been my own people. And why not ? If there were no rebels against wrong-doing, wrong-doing would prosper. To an Irishman, who is a fighter by temperament, and a fighter by choice against those in high places, life is sure to provide plenty of excitement ; and that, no doubt, is why my friends have thought my recollections worth printing. The curious thing is that my share in the struggle for Irish self-government has been almost entirely what I might call outpost work, for I have lived all my life in England.

Indeed, it seemed but a stroke of good luck that I was born in Ireland at all. My father (John, son of James Denvir, of Ballywalter, Lecale) came to England in the early part of the last century, and settled in Liverpool, where my eldest brother was born. It was during a brief period, when our family returned to Ireland, that I and a younger brother were born there. My father was engaged for about three years as clerk of the works for the erection of a castle for Sir Francis Macnaghten, near Bushmills, County Antrim. This must be one of the least Catholic parts of Ireland, for there was no resident priest, and I had to be taken a long distance to be christened. There was a decent Catholic workman at the castle, James MacGowan, who was my god-father, and my Aunt Kitty had to come all the way from " our own place " in the County Down to be my god-mother.

Brought to England, my earliest remembrances are of Liverpool, which has a more compact and politically important Irish population than any other town in Great Britain.

Anyone who has mixed much among our fellow-countrymen in England, Scotland and Wales knows that, generally, the children and grandchildren of Irish-born parents consider themselves just as much Irish as those born on " the old sod " itself. No part of our race has shown more determination and enthusiasm in the cause of Irish nationality. As a rule the Irish of Great Britain have been well organised, and, during the last sixty years and more, have been brought into constant contact

with a host of distinguished Irishmen—including the leaders of the constitutional political organisations—from Daniel O'Connell to John Redmond.

I have taken an active part in the various Irish movements of my time, and it so happens that, while I know so little personally of Ireland itself, there are few, if any, living Irishmen who have had such experience, from actual personal contact with them, as I have had of our people in every part of Great Britain. As will be seen, too, in the course of these recollections, circumstances have brought me into intimate connection with most of the Irish political leaders.

My father came to England in one of the sloops in which our people used to " come over " in the old days. They sometimes took a week in crossing. The steamers which superseded them, though an immense improvement as regards speed, had often less accommodation for the deck passengers than for the cattle they brought over.

Most of the Irish immigration to Liverpool came through the Clarence Dock, where the steamers used to land our people from all parts. Since the Railway Company diverted a good deal of the Irish traffic through the Holyhead route, there are not so many of these steamers coming to Liverpool as formerly.

The first object that used to meet the eyes of those who had just " come over," as they looked across the Clarence Dock wall, was an effigy of St. Patrick, with a shamrock in his hand, as if welcoming them from " the old sod." This was placed high upon the wall of a public house kept by a retired Irish pugilist, Jack Langan. In the thirties and forties of the last century, up to 1846, when he died, leaving over £20,000 to his children, Langan's house was a very popular resort of Irishmen, more particularly as, besides being a decent, warm-hearted, open-handed man, he was a strong supporter of creed and country.

I am old enough to remember hearing Mass in what was an interesting relic in Liverpool of the Penal days. This was the old building known to our people as " Lumber Street Chapel." Of course, the present Protestant Church of St. Nicholas (known as " the old church ") is a Catholic found-ation. Lumber Street chapel was not, however, the first of our places of worship built during the Penal days, for the Jesuits had a small chapel not far off, erected early in the eighteenth century, but destroyed by a No-Popery mob in 1746. St. Mary's, Lumber Street, too, was originally a Jesuit mission, but, in 1783, it was handed over to the Benedictines, who have had charge of it ever since. Father John Price, S.J., built a chapel in Sir Thomas's Buildings in 1788. I can recollect this building since my earliest days, but Mass was never said in it during my time.

Lancashire is the only part of England where there are any great number of the native population who have always kept the faith. I once spent a few weeks in one of these Catholic districts. My employer had an alteration to make in the house of a gentleman at Lydiate, near Ormskirk. I used to come home to Liverpool for the Sundays, but for the rest of the week I had lodgings in the house of a Catholic family at Lydiate.

There was an old ruin, which they called Lydiate Abbey, but I found it was the chapel of St. Catherine, erected in the fifteenth century. The priest of the mission had charge of the chapel which, though unroofed, was the most perfect ecclesiastical ruin in Catholic hands in South Lancashire. During the time I was at Lydiate there came a Holiday of Obligation, when I heard Mass in the house of a Catholic farmer named Rimmer. This was a fine old half-timbered building of Elizabethan days, and here, all through the Penal times, Mass had been kept up, a priest to say it being always in hiding somewhere in the district.

The priest in charge of Lydiate at the time I was there told me he was collecting for a regular church or chapel, and hoped soon to make a commencement of the building. Some years later he was able to do so. Our church choir at Copperas Hill, Liverpool, was then considered one of the best in the diocese. The choirmaster and organist, John Richardson, was a distinguished composer of Catholic church music, and held in such high esteem that, for any important celebration, he could always secure the services of the chief members of the musical profession in and about Liverpool. In this way, on one occasion Miss Santley came to help us. She was accompanied by her brother, then a boy, who has since risen to the highest position in the musical world—the eminent baritone, Sir Charles Santley.

St. Nicholas' was, as it is yet, the pro-Cathedral of the diocese, and whenever a new church had to be opened, or there was any important ceremonial anywhere in Lancashire, our choir was generally invited. In this way I was delighted to go to the opening of the new church at Lydiate, so that I was taking part in the third stage of the Catholic history of the diocese—having said a prayer in the old ruin, and attended Mass in Rimmer's, and now assisting at the solemn High Mass at the opening of the Church of our Lady, not far from the old chapel of St. Catherine.

At the time I went to Mass in Lumber Street Chapel, Liverpool, which is nearly 70 years since, there were but four other *chapels*, as they were generally called then, in the town—Copperas Hill (St. Nicholas'), Seel Street (St. Peter's), St. Anthony's and St. Patrick's. It must have been a custom acquired in the Penal days to call the older Catholic places of worship rather after the names of the streets in which they were situated than of the saint to whom they were dedicated. During the Famine years the bishops and clergy must have found it extremely difficult to provide for the tremendous influx of our people. I have seen them crowded out into the chapel yards and into the open streets; satisfied if they could get even a glimpse of the inside of the sacred building through an open window. I see by the Catholic Directory there are at the time I now write thirty-nine churches and chapels in Liverpool. The schools have increased in a like proportion.

The progress in numbers, wealth and influence of the Irish people may be pretty well marked by the gradual increase in the number of churches and schools, which have been built for the most part by the Irish and their descendants. All honour to the noble-hearted, hard-handed toilers who have contributed to such work, and greater glory still to the humble men who, after a hard week's work in a ship's hold at the docks, or perhaps in the "jigger loft" of a warehouse eight stories high, turn out every Sunday morning to act as "collectors," and go in pairs from door to door, one with the book and the other with the bag in hand, to raise the means of erecting the noble churches and schools that everywhere meet our view in Liverpool to-day.

With regard to the social position our people occupy in Liverpool, there have been many Irishmen who have come well to the front in the race of life, some of whom have occupied the foremost positions in connection with the public life of the town. On the other hand, a large number of our fellow-countrymen in Liverpool are by no means in that enviable condition. Many of them have set out from Ireland, intending to go to America, but, their little means failing them, have been obliged to remain in Liverpool. Here they considered themselves fortunate if they met someone from the same part of the country as themselves to give them a helping hand, for it is a fine trait in the Irish character—and "over here in England" the trait has not been lost—that, however poor, they are always ready to befriend what seems to them a still poorer neighbour. Those who have lived here some time are glad to see someone from their " own place," and, amid the squalor of an English city, the imaginative Celt—as he listens to the gossip about the changes, the marriages, and the deaths that have taken place since he left " home "—for a brief moment lives once more upon " the old sod," and sees visions of the little cabin by the wood side where dwelt those he loved, of the mountain chapel where he worshipped, of a bright-eyed Irish girl beloved in the golden days of youth. These and a host of other associations of the past come floating back upon his memory, as he hears the tidings brought by Terence, or Michael, or Maurya, who has just " come over." It often so happens that, from the very goodness of the Irish heart, the newcomers are frequently drawn into the same miserable mode of life as the friends who have come to England before them may have fallen into.

Irish intellect and Irish courage have in thousands of cases brought our people to their proper place in the social scale, but it is only too often the case that adverse circumstances compel the great bulk of them to have recourse to the hardest, the most precarious, and the worst paid employments to be found in the British labour market.

In the large towns, in the poorer streets in which our people live, a stranger would be struck by the swarms of children, and of an evening, at the number of grown-up people sitting on the doorsteps of their wretched habitations. John Barry once told me that a friend of his asked one of these how they could live in such places? "Because," was the reply, "we live so much *out* of them." The answer showed, at any rate, that their lot was borne cheerfully.

Nevertheless, there are Irishmen too—men who know how to keep what they have earned—who, by degrees, get into the higher circles of the commercial world, so that I have seen among the merchant princes "on 'Change" in Liverpool men who, themselves, or whose fathers before them, commenced life in the humblest avocations.

Liverpool has, on the whole, been a "stony-hearted stepmother" to its Irish colony, which largely built its granite sea-walls, and for many years humbly did the laborious work on which the huge commerce of the port rested. But, perhaps, in years to come Liverpool will realise the value of the wealth of human brains and human hearts which it held for so long unregarded or despised in its midst.

CHAPTER II.

DISTINGUISHED IRISHMEN—" THE NATION " NEWS-
PAPER—" THE HIBERNIANS."

I HAVE met, as I have said elsewhere, most of the
Irish political leaders of my time in Liverpool, but
I will always remember with what pleasure I listened
to a distinguished Irishman of another type, Samuel
Lover, when he was travelling with an entertainment consisting of sketches from his own works
and selections from his songs. Few men were more
versatile than Lover, for he was a painter, musician,
composer, novelist, poet, and dramatist. When I saw
him in one of the public halls he sang his own songs,
told his own stories, and was his own accompanist.

His was one of a series of performances, very
popular in Liverpool for many years, called the
" Saturday Evening Concerts." He was a little
man, with what might be called something of a
" Frenchified " style about him, but having with
it all a bright eye and thoroughly Irish face which,
with all his bodily movements, displayed great
animation. I can readily believe his biographers,
who say he excelled in all the arts he cultivated,
for his was a most charming entertainment.

Lover undoubtedly had patriotism of a kind,
and some of his songs show it. It certainly was

not up to the mark of the "Young Irelanders," one of whom attacked him on one occasion, when he made the clever retort that "the fount from which *he* drew his patriotism was a more genuine source than a fount of Irish type"—alluding to the plentiful use of the Gaelic characters in "The Spirit of the Nation," the world-famed collection of songs by the Young Ireland contributors to the "Nation" newspaper. There are passages in Lover's novel of "Rory O'More" and his "He Would be a Gentleman" that show he was a sincere lover of his country. I agree in the main with what the "Nation" said of him in 1843—"Though he often fell into ludicrous exaggerations and burlesques in describing Irish life, there is a good national spirit running through the majority of his works, for which he has not received due credit."

One of his stories, "Rory O'More," achieved universal popularity also as a play, a song and an air. In it there is a passage which, when I first read it, I looked upon as an exaggeration, and as somewhat reflecting upon the dignity of a great national movement like that of the United Irishmen. Lover brings his hero, Rory, into somewhat questionable surroundings in a Munster town—intended for Cork or some other seaport—to meet a French emissary. One would think that a struggle for the freedom of Ireland should be carried on amongst the most lofty surroundings. But I found in after life that the incidents described by Lover were not so exaggerated as might be supposed, for, as "necessity has no law," during a later revolutionary

struggle we had often to meet in strange and un-
romantic places, as I shall describe later, for most
important projects.

Lover's wit was spontaneous, and bubbled over
in his ordinary conversation with friends. An
English lady friend, deeply interested in Ireland,
once said to him—" I believe I was intended for
an Irishwoman." Lover gallantly replied—" Cross
over to Ireland and they will swear you were intended
for an Irishman."

A famous Irishman, whom I saw in Liverpool
when I was a boy, was the Apostle of Temperance,
Father Mathew.

At this time he visited many centres of Irishmen
in Great Britain, and administered the pledge of
total abstinence from intoxicating drink to many
thousands of his fellow-countrymen. In London
alone over 70,000 took the pledge. As in Ireland,
this brought about a great social revolution. The
temperance movement certainly helped O'Connell's
Repeal agitation, which was in its full flood about
this time.

My remembrance of Father Mathew was that of
a man of portly figure, rather under than above
the middle height, with a handsome, pleasant face.
He had a fine powerful voice, which could be heard
at the furthest extremity of his gatherings, which
often numbered several thousands. As he gave
out the words of the pledge to abstain, with the
Divine assistance, from all intoxicating liquors,
he laid great emphasis on the word "liquors,"
pronouncing the last syllable of the word with

almost exaggerated distinctness. After this he would go round the ring of those kneeling to take the pledge, and put round the neck of each the ribbon with the medal attached.

I ought to remember his visit to Liverpool, for I took the pledge from him three times during his stay in the town.

My mother took the whole family, and, wherever he was—at St. Patrick's, or in a great field on one side of Crown Street, or at St. Anthony's—there she was with her family. She was a woman with the strong Irish faith in the supernatural, and in the power of God and His Church, that can " move mountains." A younger brother of mine had a running in his foot which the doctors could not cure. She determined to take Bernard to Father Mathew and get him to lay his hands on her boy.

At St. Patrick's, with her children kneeling around her, she asked the good Father to touch her son. He, no doubt thinking it would be presumptuous on his part to claim any supernatural gift, passed on without complying with her request. Father Mathew's next gathering was in the Crown Street fields. I was a boy of about nine years, attending Copperas Hill schools. Mr. Connolly, who was in charge, was a very good master, but there was nothing very Irish in his teaching. Some idea of this may be formed when I mention that— though there were not a dozen boys in the school who were not Irish or of Irish extraction—the first map of Ireland I ever saw was on the back of one of O'Connell's Repeal cards.

It was not until the Christian Brothers came, a few years afterwards, that this was changed. I shall always be grateful to that noble body of men, not only for the religious but for the national training they gave. We had Brothers Thornton and Swan— the latter since the Superior of the Order in Ireland.

Under them we not only had a good map of Ireland, but they taught us, in our geography lessons, the correct Irish pronunciation of the names of places, such as (spelling phonetically) " Carrawn Thooal," " Croogh Phaudhrig," and similar words.

But our old master, Mr. Connolly, was a good man too, according to his lights. Hearing of Father Mathew's visit, he asked how many of the boys would go to Crown Street to " take the pledge " —their parents being willing ? Out of some 250 boys there were about a dozen who did not hold up their hands.

It is unnecessary for me to say that my mother was there again with her afflicted boy and the rest of her children, and again she pleaded in vain. She was a courageous woman, with great force of character—and a *third* time she went to Father Mathew's gathering. This was in St. Anthony's chapel yard, and amongst the thousands there to hear him and to take the pledge she awaited her turn. Again she besought him to touch her boy's foot. He knew her again, and, deeply moved by her importunity and great faith he, at length, to her great joy, put his hand on my brother's foot and gave him his blessing. My mother's faith in

the power of God, through His minister, was re-
warded, for the foot was healed.

I had an aunt—my mother's sister—married to
a good patriotic Irishman, Hugh, or, as he was
more generally called, Hughey, Roney, who kept
a public house in Crosbie Street. The street is
now gone, but it stood on part of what is now the
goods station of the London & North Western
Railway. Nearly all in Crosbie Street were from
the West of Ireland, and, amongst them, there was
scarcely anything but Irish spoken. I have often
thought since of the splendid opportunity let slip
by O'Connell and the Repealers in neglecting to
revive, as they could so easily have then done, so
strong a factor in nationality as the native tongue
of our people. My Aunt Nancy could speak the
Northern Irish fluently, and, in the course of her
business, acquired the Connaught Irish and accent.

After a time Hughey Roney retired, and the
house was carried on by his daughter and her
husband, John McArdle, a good, decent patriotic
Irishman, much respected by his Connaught neighbours, though he was from the " Black North."
It used to be a great treat to hear John McArdle,
on a Sunday night, reading the " Nation," which
then cost sixpence, and was, therefore, not so easily
accessible, to an admiring audience, of whom I
was sometimes one, and his son, John Francis
McArdle, another. This younger McArdle, originally
intended for the Church, became in after life a
brilliant journalist, and was for a time on the staff
of the " Nation," the teaching of which he had so

early imbibed. The elder McArdle was a big, imposing looking man, with a voice to match, who gave the speeches of O'Connell and the other orators of Conciliation Hall with such effect that the applause was always given exactly in the right places, and with as much heartiness as if greeting the original speakers.

After Father Mathew's visit, their trade fell away to such an extent that John McArdle, determined to hold his ground—while still keeping the public house open, though the business was all but gone— broke another door into the street, and made his parlour into a grocery and provision store. This enterprise on his part was only necessary for a short time, as the abnormal enthusiasm in the cause of temperance which, for the time being, had swept all before it, had subsided to such an extent that McArdle, after a time, turned the room to its original purpose, and was able to resume his readings from the " Nation " to admiring audiences, as heretofore.

Yet, though so many fell away from their temporary exaltation, there were still large numbers who remained firm, and the lasting good from Father Mathew's work was undeniable.

So popular was John McArdle's house, that it was used as one of the lodges of the Ancient Order of Hibernians—then very strong in Liverpool, and stout champions of country and creed. In regard to this organisation, I find in the " Irish World " of New York a high tribute paid to them by the Very Rev. Thomas J. Shahan, of the Catholic University of America. In his paper on " Hibernian-

ism " he said there was a tradition in the Ancient
Order that they first started in Ireland in the Penal
days as a bodyguard to their poor parish priest
when he said Mass in the open air. Anyone who
has spent most of his life in England, as I have done,
can well understand that this is not simply an effort
of this good priest's imagination, for, over and over
again I have seen the Hibernians among the first
to come forward in defence of their priests and
churches when these were threatened. In the
course of his paper Dr. Shahan quoted a letter from
the Brethren in Ireland, Scotland and England to
the Brethren in New York. It sent instructions
and authority to the few brothers in New York to
establish branches of their Society in America.

These were the qualifications laid down : Members must be Catholic and Irish, or of Irish descent.
They must be of good moral character, and were
not to join in any secret societies contrary to the
laws of the Catholic Church. They were to exercise
hospitality towards their emigrant brothers and to
protect their emigrant sisters from all harm and
temptation, so that they should still be known for
their chastity all over the world. The members
of the Order in America were to be at liberty to
make laws for the welfare of the Society, but these
must be in accord with the teaching of the Church,
and their working must be submitted to a Catholic
priest. The letter says—" We send you these
instructions, as we promised to do, with a young
man that works on the ship and who called on you
before." Directing that a copy of the document

should be sent to another friend, then working in Pennsylvania, the letter concluded—" Hoping the bearer and this copy will land safe and that you will treat him right, we remain your brothers in the true bond of friendship this 4th day of May, in the year of our Lord, 1837 "—

" PATRICK M'GUIRE, County Fermanagh.
" JOHN REILLY, County Cavan.
" PATRICK M'KENNA, County Monaghan.
" JOHN DURKIN, County Mayo.
" PATRICK REILLY, County Derry.
" PATRICK DOYLE, County Sligo.
" JOHN FARRELL, County Meath.
" THOMAS O'RORKE, County Leitrim.
" JAMES M'MANUS, County Leitrim.
" JOHN M'MAHON, County Longford.
" PATRICK DUNN, County Tyrone
" PATRICK HAMILL, County Westmeath.
" DANIEL GALLAGHER, Glasgow.
"JOHN MURPHY, Liverpool."

It will be noticed that of the twelve Irish counties represented above, six are in the province of Ulster, three in Connaught, and three in Leinster, so that the Hibernians appear to have had their stronghold in the Northern province and the adjoining counties in Connaught and Leinster. This is exactly as one might expect, seeing the necessity for a defensive organisation against the Orangemen of Ulster. The Order took deep root in Glasgow and Liverpool on account of the convenience of access by sea from Ireland to these cities.

I was too young to have known John Murphy, who signed the letter for the Liverpool Hibernians, but, from what I knew of these afterwards, it is likely that he was a dock labourer. As I will show, these men, over and over again, to my own knowledge, gave splendid proofs of their courage and love of creed and country. Their love of learning, too, has been equal to that of their fathers in the days when our country was " The Island of Saints and Scholars." Some of these poor men may not have had much learning themselves, but they made great and noble sacrifices that their children should have it. I noted with interest in the Irish papers recently that the name of the Secretary of the Hibernian Order at the Bridge of Mayo, County Down, was " Brother Denvir."

Our country sent over to Liverpool, besides sterling Nationalists, as bitter a colony of Irishmen—I suppose we can scarcely deny the name to men born in Ireland—as were, perhaps, to be found anywhere in the world. These were the Orangemen. If there was one place more obnoxious to them than another it was the club room of the Hibernians in Crosbie Street. But though in their frequent conflicts with the " Papishes " they wrecked houses and even killed several Irishmen—for they frequently used deadly weapons against unarmed Catholics—they were never able to make a successful attack on McArdle's. One of my earliest experiences was being on the spot on the occasion of a contemplated assault on the Hibernian club room on the day of an Orange anniversary. This was in 1843.

Parallel to Crosbie Street, where the club room was situated, was Blundell Street, where my uncle,

Hughey Roney, lived in a house immediately behind McArdle's—the back door of the one house facing the back door of the other. This side of the street, with the whole of Crosbie Street, has long since been absorbed by the railway company before mentioned.

I cannot imagine why my mother chose this particular day to take me to see our relatives, except it was the inveterate longing which her early surroundings and training had given her to assist at the " batin' of an Orangeman," or why I should have been the chosen one of the family to come, unless it was that she thought I was the one most after her own heart in her warlike propensities. However this may have been, there we were in the first-floor front room of my Uncle Hughey's. Every room, from cellar to garret, was crowded with stalwart dock labourers—at that time these were almost to a man Irish—prepared to support another contingent of Hibernians who garrisoned McArdle's in a similar manner. Hearing outside the cry— " The Orangemen ! " I looked out of the window and up the street, and there, sure enough, was a strong body of them marching down, armed with guns, swords, and ship carpenters' hatchets. At once the word was passed to the contingent in Crosbie Street to be prepared to meet the threatened attack.

Nearer and nearer the Orangemen came. They had got within some thirty yards of Roneys when, between them and the object of their attack, out of Simpson street, which at this point crosses

Blundell Street at right angles, there intervened the head of a column of police, under the Liverpool Chief Constable, an Irishman, Michael James Whitty. There was a desperate engagement, but, notwithstanding their murderous weapons, the Orangemen were utterly routed, flying before the disciplined charge of the police, who freely used their batons on their retreating opponents.

A few words about Michael James Whitty, who led the charge with right good will, may not be inappropriate here. Many years afterwards, when we were both engaged in the profession of journalism, I had the pleasure of making his acquaintance through my reviewing in the " Catholic Times " a very able book of his, a " Life of Robert Emmet." He asked Mr. Thomas Gregson, his private secretary, a friend of mine : Who had written this review ? Upon hearing who it was, he asked Mr. Gregson to bring us together. When we met, he told me how pleased he was with my review, and that there was somebody on the " Catholic Times " who could appreciate his book.

He became Chief Constable of Liverpool in 1828. About this time Messrs. Rockliffs published a weekly newspaper called the " Liverpool Journal," which came into the hands of Mr. Whitty after he had resigned the office of head constable. An offshoot of the " Journal " was the " Daily Post," which, in Mr. Whitty's hands was (and indeed has been ever since under the direction of Sir Edward Russell, who still holds the reins) a powerful organ of Liberalism. One of Whitty's sub-editors on the " Daily

Post " was Stephen Joseph Meany, a somewhat prominent figure in the Young Ireland and Fenian movements.

As showing the power of the Press, there is no doubt that Whitty and Meany, in the " Journal " and " Post," and through their influence otherwise, did much to secure recognition of a great Irish actor. This was Barry Sullivan, who was, I think, the finest tragedian I have ever seen. He is still remembered with appreciation by many in England, and, I am sure, in Ireland too.

He was a patriotic Irishman, and once offered himself to our committee as a Nationalist candidate for the Parliamentary representation of Liverpool. This was in the days when it was a three-membered constituency. It was only the belief that the sacrifice which he thus offered to make for his country would have injured his career as an actor that prevented us from accepting his offer.

In my boyhood a great feature in Liverpool was the annual procession of one or other of the local societies.

The great Irish and Catholic procession, of which the Hibernians formed the largest contingent, was, of course, on St. Patrick's Day. A considerable portion of the processionists were dock labourers ; a fine body of men, who were at this time, as I have already said, mostly Irish.

The Orange processions in Liverpool were often the occasion of bloodshed, for in them they carried guns, hatchets, and other deadly weapons, as if they were always prepared for deeds of violence.

The ship carpenters were the most numerous body in the Orange processions. Indeed, they formed such a large proportion that, by many, the 12th of July was called "Carpenter's Day." Shipbuilding used to flourish in Liverpool, and, as none of the firms engaged in it would take a Catholic apprentice, it was quite an Orange preserve. This became somewhat changed when the Chalenors, an English Catholic family, who were already extensive timber merchants, commenced ship-building, and, of course, took Catholic apprentices.

The Orange ring was thus gradually broken up, and, as iron ships superseded wooden ones, ultimately the shipbuilding trade almost vanished from Liverpool. The ship carpenters, for the most part, found their occupation gone, and many of them ended their days in the workhouse.

A further instance of the decline of rabid Orangeism might be cited. It was not an altogether uncommon thing for people to be fired at from the windows of Orange lodges. I see, according to the "Nation" of July 20th, 1850, that "an innkeeper of Liverpool named Wright fired out of his house and wounded three people." In justification of this he stated that "a crowd of Ribbonmen assembled round his house." At one time there used to be a notorious Orange lodge held in a public house called "The Wheat Sheaf" in Scotland Road. The members of this body thought nothing of firing upon an unarmed and peaceable crowd from the windows, and I remember an Irishman being shot dead upon one of these occasions. The change that has taken place in this district can be best realized from the facts that, in after years, the landlord of " The Wheatsheaf " bore the name of Patrick Finegan, that, at the present moment, Scotland Road is, as it has been for many years, represented in the City Council by a sterling body of Irish Nationalists, and that the Scotland Division of the Borough of Liverpool is the *one* place in Great Britain where an Irish Home Ruler, *as such*, can be returned to Parliament against all comers, as Mr. T. P. O'Connor has been, ever since the Division became a separate constituency.

To return to the St. Patrick's Day processions. I used to look forward to them with delight in my childhood, and, even now, cannot help lingering lovingly on their memory. They were splendid displays, which I can remember much better than many things which occurred, so to speak, but yesterday.

" Our street," which was close to Russell Street, Rodney Street, and other thoroughfares through which the procession passed, was by no means what you would call an Irish street. Indeed, the most influential man in it was a retired sea captain named Jamieson, who, if not an Orangeman " all out," was certainly at one time an Orange sympathiser. He and my mother often had political discussions, which usually ended in fierce quarrels, and when he would swear he would have us " run out of the street," she used to threaten to bring up the men from the docks and leave not a stone upon a stone of his house. Whether it was through his being impressed by her terrible earnestness as a member of the Church militant, or whatever else was the reason, Jamieson in the end became a Catholic, and died a most edifying death.

Before his conversion, however, as well as after—Jamieson to the contrary notwithstanding—" our street " always took a lively and neighbourly interest in the St. Patrick's procession, and used to turn out to a man, to a baby it would, perhaps, be more correct to say, for was not one of the chief sights of the procession their decent neighbour, Timothy, or, as he was more generally called, " Thade " Crowley, the pork butcher, at the corner ? There were splendid pictures and devices on the banners—I can see them all most vividly now—St. Patrick, Brian Boru, Sarsfield, O'Connell, the Irish Wolf Dog, with the motto " Gentle when stroked, fierce when provoked," and harps and shamrocks *galore*, but Thade Crowley was in all our eyes the finest figure in the procession.

Among his greatest admirers were a Jewish family named Hyman, who lived next door to him. Though the Jews are supposed to hold what was Crowley's stock-in-trade in abomination, the two old ladies—Mrs. Crowley, who used to say she was of " Cork's own town and God's own people," and Mrs. Hyman, who came from Cork, too, though, needless to say, without a drop of Irish blood in her veins—were great cronies.

As a consequence, the Hymans were among the most eager of the spectators to get the first glimpse of honest Thade Crowley as he walked in front of

his own particular lodge of the Hibernians. He
was a portly, well-built man, of ruddy complexion,
and open, genial countenance. He wore buckskin
breeches, top boots, green tabinet double-breasted
waistcoat, bottle-green coat with brass buttons,
and beaver hat. The Crowleys were very popular
in the neighbourhood, as they never had but a
kindly word for everybody.

When I was a small boy, about 9 or 10 years
old, I often listened with delight to Mrs. Crowley,
who had a fluent tongue, expatiating on the glories
of her native city—

> By the pleasant waters of the River Lee.

and I have heard her exclaiming, I at the time
believing it most implicitly:

"Sin, is it? Sure, I never heard of sin till I
came to Liverpool; there's no sin in Cor-r-k!"

And she rattled the "r" with a strong rising
inflexion, greatly impressing me with the high
character of Ireland and of Cork in particular.

At that time I had never seen Ireland but as an
infant at my mother's breast.

CHAPTER III.

IRELAND RE-VISITED.

I WAS a boy of about 12 when I first re-visited Ireland ; and, as the steamer entered Carlingford Lough, which to my mind almost equals Killarney's beauty—but that, perhaps, is a Northman's pre-judice--with the noble range of the Mourne mountains on the one side and the Carlingford Hills on the other, it seemed to my young imagin-ation like a glimpse of fairy land.

Carlingford reminded me of what my old masters, the Christian Brothers, used to teach us, that those places ending in " ford " had at one time been Norse settlements. There is not the slightest trace, I should say, of people of Norse descent along this coast now, unless we accept the theory that would regard as such the descendants of the Norman De Courcy's followers, who can be recog-nised by their names, and are still to be found, side by side, and intermingling with those of the original Celtic children of the soil in the barony of Lecale. It is astonishing, by the way, how you still find in Ireland, after centuries of successive confiscations, the old names in their old tribal lands, mingled in places, as in Lecale, with the Norman names ; the two races being now thoroughly amalgamated—as distinguished from the case of King James's Planters in Ulster, who, to this day are, as a rule, as distinct from the population amongst whom they live—whether of pure Celtic strain or with a Norman admixture—as when first they came.

There was an idea in our family that I had a vocation for the priesthood, and I was being sent to my uncle, Father Michael O'Loughlin, parish priest of Dromgoolan, County Down, who placed me in charge of Mr. Johnson, a somewhat noted classical teacher in the neighbouring little town of Castlewellan.

I have seen but little of Ireland, but during the few months I was here on this occasion I made the best use of my time. I could have had no better guide and preceptor than " Priest Mick," as my mother used to call my uncle. I imagine that the term " Priest," which, in the North of Ireland, was formerly so much used as a prefix to the name of the Catholic clergyman, must have arisen amongst those not of his own flock, and was probably not intended to have exactly a respectful meaning.

Father Michael sometimes came to see his relatives in Liverpool, who were very numerous. He called them the " Tribe of Brian " (his father's name) and he made a point of visiting them all, down to the very latest arrival—indeed, I think he was the only one who knew the whole of the ramifications of " the Tribe."

He used to say that his father—the aforesaid

Brian—had one of the largest noses in the country.
There was only another man, he said, who could
approach him in that respect. If the two men
met in a very narrow " loanan "—what they call
a " boreen " in other parts of Ireland—the other
man, who was a bit of a wag, would put his hand to
his nose, and make a motion of putting it aside,
as if there was not sufficient room for two such
organs, and call out with a kind of snuffle: " Pass,
Brian ! "

The late Mgr. O'Laverty, in his " History of
the Dioceses of Down and Connor," says : " From
a government official survey in 1766 there were
fifteen families in Castlewellan, of whom two only
(Hagans and O'Donnells) were Catholics." Up
to that date there must have been, during this
century, a considerable clearance of the Catholic
population from the best land of this district, for
I should say—judging from King James's Army
List and other authorities—that the Magennises
(who, with the MacCartans, were the chief territorial
families of the old race in Down) still held land in
the neighbourhood up to the end of the seventeenth
century. As still further showing this, it will be
found that " Eiver Magennis of Castlewellan " was
one of the members for the County Down in what
Thomas Davis truly describes as " The Patriot
Parliament " of 1689.

The learned historian of Down and Connor gives
an interesting account of the only Norman colony
of any extent in the province of Ulster. I have
already spoken of this. Notwithstanding the very

small Norman admixture, in the main the Catholics of the North are the most pure-blooded Celts in Ireland. And even in the case of Lecale, the original Celtic population intermingled with the descendants of the Norman settlers, who, like the older native population have ever remained true to the old faith. The preponderance of the Celtic element in the Catholics of Ulster must be overwhelming. What is called " Protestant Ulster " is practically a foreign importation, which the native population never absorbed, as they did the earlier invaders.

Speaking of the Rev. Cornelius (or, as he was oftener called, Corney) Denvir, a relative of ours, who afterwards became Bishop of Down and Connor, Father O'Laverty says : " The Denvirs are a Norman race, brought to Lecale by De Courcy. The late bishop observed the name in several of the towns in Normandy."

I only met Bishop Denvir once, when my father —who was his second cousin—took me to see him at the Grecian Hotel, Liverpool, when he was on his way either to or from Rome. I once, when a small boy, incurred my father's displeasure by criticising adversely (from what I had read in the " Nation ") Dr. Denvir's support of what was called the " Bequest Bill." There were some strictures in the " Nation " on the favour shown to this Bill by three of the Irish Hierarchy, Archbishops Crolly and Murray, and Bishop Denvir. The last was a man of great learning. An edition of the Bible was published under his auspices by Sims and McIntyre, of Belfast.

During my stay in Ireland, I lived in the house

of my uncle, Owen (or Oiney, as he was commonly
called) Bannon, in the townland of Ballymagenaghy,
where my mother was born.

No boy could have had a better object lesson in
the part of Irish history embracing the Plantation
of Ulster than Ballymagenaghy. It is eminently
typical of the kind of rocky and barren land to
which the children of the soil were driven—land
which would hardly bear cultivation. I need
scarcely say that the people were " Papishes " to
a man.

There was a hill behind my Uncle Oiney's house
called Caᴘᴘais (pronounced " Corrig "), in English
" rock," and the name might well apply to most of
the townland, in which the chief productions seemed
to be stones and rocks. Caᴘᴘais was a kind of
shoulder of what I heard the people calling " My
lord's mountain." This was part of Lord Annesley's
domain, and separated from Caᴘᴘais and several
small farms by a wall, which ran down to a sheet
of water at the foot—Castlewellan Lough. I, as
a student of the " Nation," was not at all satisfied
that an Irish mountain should be called by such a
name, which spoke volumes for the state of serfdom
into which the people had fallen. I was not long
in finding the real name—Sliab na Slat (mountain
of Rods).

I often looked with admiration at the view from
its highest point. Underneath, the side of the
mountain was clothed with trees down to the edge
of the lough, which mirrored the wooded eminences
of exquisite beauty surrounding it. Looking east-

ward you could see Dundrum Bay and the white
sails of the fishing boats. (They used to sing a
mournful lament around the turf fires of Ballymagenaghy of " The loss of the Mourne Fishermen "
in a great storm off this coast). Further off you
might see an occasional large sailing vessel or
steamer, and, further still, in the dim distance,
you could just discern the Isle of Man. Southward
the eye took in the noble range of the Mourne
mountains, running from east to west, from where,
at Newcastle, the Irish sea comes to kiss the foot
of the lofty Slieve Donard, towering in majesty
over all his fellows—rugged sentinels of the hills
and vales of Down.

Lying, as if nestling under the Mourne range, was
a small, well-wooded hill, part of the domain of
Lord Roden, who held high rank among the Orange
ascendancy faction, and, as will be seen later, may
be said to have held the lives and liberties of his
Catholic fellow-countrymen in this district in his
hands.

In Ballymagenaghy I was oftener called by my
mother's name than my father's. In those days,
as often as not, when a girl got married she was
still called by her friends by her maiden name.
So, on the first Sunday after my arrival, when I
was taken over to Leitrim chapel, where I served
my uncle's Mass, I found myself referred to as
" Peggy Loughlin's wee boy." It did not seem at
all strange to me, for I scarcely ever heard her
called by any other name. Indeed, some forty
years afterwards—when I was organising for the

Irish National League—I met a County Down man in Cumberland. He was, as I soon found, from " our own place," as they affectionately call it. He was trying to trace out what family I belonged to. At last he had it—" Oh ! " he said, " You would be a son of Margaret O'Loughlin ? " I hesitated for a moment, when Edward McConvey, the local organiser—a County Down man, too— who had introduced us, laughed heartily as he said : " Here's a quare man ; doesn't know his own mother's name ! " In fact, I had so seldom heard my mother called anything else but " Peggy " that the proper name sounded strange for the moment. Indeed, it had evidently taken our friend some time to remember the name of " Margaret," which he, no doubt, thought the more polite one to use in speaking of my mother.

Her family did not generally use the prefix " O " in her younger days. It was only after her two brothers, Bernard and Michael, became priests, and always called and signed themselves " O'Loughlin," that the prefix was resumed. This is a common experience in other Irish families.

Many of the small holdings in Ballymagenaghy would not support in anything approaching to comfort the large families with which the sturdy and industrious people were blessed. This was certainly the case with the Bannons, but they were not entirely dependent on the land they tilled, as several of the family were employed in weaving in a portion of the house, the looms being their own. I have often admired the beautiful damask table-cloths produced in the homes of these "mount-tainy" people, the webs, when finished, being taken to Banbridge, to the warehouses of the manufacturers, and the yarn and the patterns for the next lot being brought back on the return journey.

I believe that these cottage industries no longer exist, and that the beautiful fabrics, for which our northern province is famous, are now produced by steam power in Banbridge and other Ulster towns.

As the young men and boys of the Bannons worked at their looms, and the women and girls at their spinning and "flowering," when not wanted to help on the land, the father, Oiney, would oc-casionally go over to England as a travelling pack-man, and so increase the family store. I have known in late years other Ulstermen doing this—amongst others my old friend Bernard MacAnulty, of whom I shall have more to say later.

I had often, at my home in Liverpool, heard of Irish hospitality. Here in Ballymagenaghy I had many practical illustrations of this in the way they treated the "poor man" or "poor woman" as they called them—they never called them beggars—who came to their doors. Indeed, it seemed to me that these had no occasion to *ask* for help, for more than once I have seen a "poor woman" coming in with her bed upon her back, putting it down in the warmest corner behind the chimney breast, and making herself at home as a matter of course, without going through the formality of asking for a night's lodging.

Of the enormous number of harvestmen who passed every year through Liverpool, except from the County Donegal, there were not so many from the northern province. The majority were from Connaught. They generally landed at the Clarence Dock, Liverpool, a wiry, hardy-looking lot, with frieze coats, corduroy breeches, clean white shirts with high collars, and blackthorn sticks. I have seen them filling the breadth of Prescot Street, as they left the town, marching up like an army on foot to the various parts of England they were bound for. This was before special cheap trains were run for harvestmen.

At night, in my Irish mountain home, after I had prepared my Latin lessons for the following day, and my uncle, aunt, and cousins had left off work, I joined with great enjoyment in the family group around the turf fire, and listened with rapt attention to songs and stories ; my favourite among the latter being the adventures of Barney Henvey among the fairies in the old rath, or "forth," as they called it, of Ballymagenaghy.

I may say that, up to this moment, I have a certain liking for such stories—of course *as* fairy stories. But, being a boy of enquiring mind, I wanted to get at the whole theory of the existence of these beings, and, accordingly, this is what I gathered as to the origin, present existence, and future state of the " good people," as they called them. In " The Irish Fairy Legends," a number of my " Penny Irish Library," I find I have dealt with the subject. As the passage gives the explanation

I got at my uncle Oiney's more correctly than I can trust to my memory to give it now, after a lapse of some sixty years, I may be excused for giving the following extract :—

> The belief is that, in the great rebellion of Lucifer, of the spirits who fell from heaven, some, not so guilty as those who " went further and fared worse," fell upon our earth, and into the air and water that surround it. These are the *Fairies*, who have their various dispositions, like mortals, and like them, at the day of judgment, will be rewarded or punished according to their deserts.

In the " Fairy Legends " I have also given the story of " Barney Henvey " mentioned above. There is something like it in the " Ingoldsby Legends," and, no doubt, in the fairy mythologies of other nations, but my story is of Irish origin. Heaven only knows through how many ages it has been handed down to us. It is one of the fairy stories my mother and grandmother used to tell us as long ago as I can remember. I have a little grandson who, when smaller, used sometimes to insist when put to bed after he had said his " lying-down prayers," upon hearing " Barney Henvey " before he went to sleep ; and so it will, no doubt, go on, and such stories may be told in ages to come, not only in Ireland—" A Nation once again "— but in every settlement of the Clan-na-Gael throughout the world.

Friends and neighbours would come to my uncle Oiney's from beside Castlewellan Lough, and over from Dolly's Brae and Ballymagrehan, who, after

the day's work, enjoyed going " a cailey." I hope
my Gaelic League friends will forgive me if I don't
give the correct sound of this word, but that is my
remembrance of how they pronounced it some sixty
years ago in the County Down.

Sometimes at our little gatherings, the "wee boy
from England," as the neighbours called me, would
be asked to read from the " Nation " a speech of
the Liberator—the title his countrymen gave
O'Connell after Catholic emancipation. I was always
delighted with this ; entering as fully and enthusiastically into the spirit of what I read as any of the
company.

As often as not, in Ballymagenaghy there would
be sung, to the accompaniment of fiddle, flute or
clarionet, one of those stirring songs which, week
after week, appeared about this time in the " Nation"
from the pens of Thomas Davis, and the brilliant
young men in O'Connell's movement known as the
" Young Irelanders "—songs " racy of the soil,"
like the " Nation " itself, which stirred the hearts
of the Irish race like the blast of a trumpet, songs
which are still sung by Irish Nationalists the world
over.

On the Sundays, the Bannons and their next
neighbours, the Finegans, MacCartans, and MacKays,
with their fiddles, flutes, and clarionets, supplied
the chief part of the instrumental music of the
choir—for there was no organ—at the little mountain
chapel at Leitrim, where my uncle, Father
Michael, officiated. The happy remembrances of
those Sundays of my boyhood are always brought

back to me whenever I read T. D. Sullivan's " Dear
Old Ireland," which is equally characteristic of
this corner of the " black North " as of the raciest
part of Munster—more especially where he sings :—

And happy and bright are the groups that pass
    From their peaceful homes for miles,
O'er fields, and roads, and hills to Mass,
    When Sunday morning smiles ;
        And deep the zeal their true hearts feel
        When low they kneel and pray !
            Oh, dear old Ireland !
            Blest old Ireland !
        Ireland, boys, hurrah !

But nothing excited my boyish enthusiasm more
than the stories of the Insurrection of 1798. I was
too young to understand much of what my grandmother used to tell us about these times before she
died. My mother was born in 1799, and was the
youngest daughter of her family, but her eldest
sister, my Aunt Mary, wife of Oiny Bannon, was
12 or 14 years old at the time of the Rising, and
could describe more vividly what she saw connected
with it than I can now recall incidents in the Repeal
and Young Ireland Movements.

Listening to her, I could almost fancy I could
see my grandfather, Brian O'Loughlin, leaving his
home with the other Ballymagenaghy men, with
their pikes and such guns as they could muster,
to join the United Irish forces previous to the battles
of Saintfield and Ballinahinch. At the time of
my visit to my mother's birthplace, my grandfather's house was in the occupation of the family
of his youngest son, Edward, and, as a pilgrim

visiting a sacred spot, I have stood on its floor, as I afterwards did on the field of Ballinahinch itself.

My Aunt Mary used to speak of an incident which I have never read of in any account of the battle, but I am inclined to believe there was some foundation for what she used to tell us. In one part of the engagement it seemed as if the bravery of the insurgents would have been crowned with a victory as decisive as they had gained at Saintfield, when, by some untoward circumstance, the fortunes of the day turned, and, in the end, the United Men were defeated. Perhaps what my Aunt Mary told me may be some explanation of the turn in the tide of battle. She used to say that when it looked as if the United Men were carrying all before them, a portion of their forces called out for a " Presbyterian (' Prispatairan ' she used to call it) Government," that this caused some hesitation among the Catholics, that after this the battle went against them, and that the day ended in disaster.

The story seems somewhat improbable, as it might be asked how, in the excitement of a battle, men of one religion could be distinguished from those of another ? But this will not seem so unlikely if the circumstances arising out of the Ulster Plantation of King James I. be remembered. As a consequence of this you will find townlands and parishes and whole districts, where the soil is poorest, where the people are almost exclusively Catholic, and others where the non-Catholic population are in an overwhelming majority. In the United forces

the men of each locality would have been drilled
and trained together, and, in the same way would,
no doubt, act together on the field of battle, so that,
without any actual arrangement for that purpose,
the Catholic or the Presbyterian would, most likely,
find himself among his own co-religionists.

It is wonderful how the memories of '98 were
handed down from one generation to another,
not only in Ireland, but wherever our people have
made their homes.

This has been brought home to me in the most
forcible possible manner by a circumstance which has
come to my knowledge only a few months since—so to
speak—after a lapse of over a hundred years.

This is that General James William Denver—
after whom, for his distinguished career, the capital
of the State of Colorado was called Denver City—
had for his grandfather Patrick Denvir, who did
a man's share in the insurrection of '98, and, for
his connection with it, had to fly from his native
Down to America.

This information I had from General Denver's
daughter, replying on behalf of her brother, to
whom I had written to find if the family were of
Irish origin. I had some doubt about this, seeing
that they spell their name with an " e " in the last
syllable, whereas we and all of the name in the
County Down use an " i." The lady's letter was
not only interesting but most welcome, as showing
that they were not only of Irish but of patriotic
origin. They evidently continue to take an interest
in the land from which they have sprung, for the

lady made some enquiries about the late Bishop Denvir, of whom I have already spoken.

Most of the United Irish leaders and a large proportion of the rank and file in the '98 Rising were Presbyterians, and fought and bled for Ireland with the same heroism as their Catholic neighbours, amongst whom no name is more cherished in the County Down than that of the Protestant General Monroe, who, my Aunt Mary used to tell us, was hanged at his own door in 1798. How is it that the sons of the men of 1782 and of Grattan's Parliament, and of 1798 were not as good Irishmen as their fathers? I think I can give a kind of explanation.

It must be remembered that the era of Grattan's Parliament and of the Volunteer movement of 1782, of which present-day Nationalists are so proud, was also the era of the Penal laws. Since then the Protestants have seen the Irish Catholic rising from the dust of serfdom and standing in the attitude of manhood. They have seen him gradually obtaining a share in the making of the laws of the land, and, naturally, becoming the predominant political power in Ireland—the Catholics being the majority of the population. I may be wrong, but I have a theory that many of the Protestants of Ireland— who once had all the political power in their hands, and did not always use it too mercifully in their treatment of the rest of their countrymen—are afraid that if they assisted in getting self-government for Ireland the power in the hands of the enfranchised majority might be used against them.

That this is a groundless fear is shown from the fact that no men have been more honoured in Ireland than such Protestant leaders as William Smith O'Brien, Thomas Davis, John Mitchel, John Martin, Isaac Butt, and Charles Stewart Parnell. The same feeling is constantly shown at this moment towards distinguished Protestants among the present Irish Parliamentary Party.

What has fostered the Anti-Irish feeling among Irish Protestants for the last hundred years has undoubtedly been the fell system of Orangeism, which has caused so much hatred and bloodshed among men who, whatever their race or creed, are now children of the one common soil. The Orangeman looked upon himself as part of a foreign garrison, holding the " Papishes " in subjection. He was armed with deadly weapons ; consequently, the defenceless Catholic was almost entirely at his mercy, and the Orangeman was but too often backed up in his lawlessness by the law and its administrators.

This almost necessitated the existence, as a kind of defence against Orangeism, of a body I used to hear them speaking of when I was a boy in Ballymagenaghy, called the " Thrashers," which, I imagine, must have been some kind of a secret society.

It must have been a sort of survival of these " Thrashers " that my friend, Michael Davitt, many years afterwards, came across somewhere in the North of England. The incident, as described by him, was both amusing and saddening. He addressed them in his capacity as a Fenian Organiser. After they had heard him patiently, an old man, the spokesman, said :

" Tell me—do you have Prodestans in this Society of yours ? "

" Certainly," Davitt answered. " We invite all Irishmen."

" Then we'll have nothing to do with yez ! "

As my Aunt Mary could relate thrilling stories of '98, so could my own mother tell me all about the savagery of Orangemen in her days. She used to describe to me the attempts of an Orange procession to pass through Dolly's Brae, when she was a young girl, before she left Ireland. Dolly's Brae is a kind of rugged defile through which passes the road from the town of Castlewellan, which, running westward, divides the townlands of Bally-magenaghy and Ballymagrehan. It is an entirely Catholic district, and not at all on the ordinary route by which the processionists would reach their homes. Yet, in a spirit of aggression, and well-armed, as usual, with Orange banners waving, drums beating, and bands playing " Croppies lie down," " The Boyne Water," and similar airs, this was the district they sought to march through.

It so happened that the proposed hostile parade was not altogether unexpected. In any case, their approach was heralded by the firing over " Papish " houses, as the processionists came towards Dolly's Brae. From the heights above they were seen— my mother being one of the watchers—in sufficient time to have the people of the immediate neighbour-hood warned of the threatened Orange incursion:

The defenders of Dolly's Brae had no firearms, as their opponents had, but they gathered up any weapons they could to repel the invaders. The Orangemen came on, expecting an easy victory. They had got well into the defile, and were firing at their opponents, who were in sight before them at some distance on the road, and into the houses on each side, when they were thrown into confusion by a storm of large stones and pieces of rock hurled down the steep sides of the defile upon them by assailants who had been up till then invisible.

According to the description of my mother, who was always a militant Catholic of the most orthodox description, and a strong physical force Irishwoman as well, the Dolly's Brae engagement must have borne some resemblance to the battle of Limerick, as described by Thomas Davis :—

> " The women fought before the men ;
> Each man became a match for ten ;
> So back they pushed the villains then
> From the city of Luimneaċ Lionnꜱtar."

She ought to know, for she was in the thick of the fight. The confusion of the Orangemen was turned into a complete rout, and they fled, leaving their banners and other trophies in the hands of the mountainy men.

For many years the Orangemen never attempted to go near the place, but, with the connivance and active aid of the guardians of the peace, they did at last, many years afterwards, appear on the scene again. The Orange anniversary was celebrated at

Tollymore Park, the seat of Lord Roden, who was a sort of Orange deity at the time. Tollymore Park is some four or five miles south-east of Dolly's Brae, which is in the heart of the Catholic district, and, as I have said, far out of the direct road of the Orangemen returning to their own homes.

Yet they deliberately took this route. They were a formidable body, well armed with guns. At their head was one Beers, the agent of Lord Roden, and a magistrate who, for the " protection " of the Orangemen, had under his command a strong body of the constabulary and a detachment of soldiers. The ordinary Englishman, who knows the police as they are in his country as the guardians of the public peace, must not confound them with those in Ireland. The Irish constabulary are simply the permanent British army of occupation, well armed and drilled, and, physically, as fine a body of men as any in the world. These were the forces under the command of Lord Roden's agent, for the invasion, for such it was, of a peaceful Catholic district.

When the people sought to defend themselves from this invasion as best they could, Beers, in his capacity as a magistrate, gave the police and soldiers under his command the order to fire— which they did—upon the people and into their houses. Consequently, what followed was nothing short of a butchery, under cover of which the Orangemen wrecked the Catholic houses in the glen.

I shall never forget the grief of my mother, at this time residing in Liverpool, at reading in the newspapers the names of the victims who had been murdered outright or wounded. They were all her next door neighbours " at home "—people she had known from childhood.

The horrible outrage roused universal indignation. In Parliament the Irish members demanded a full official enquiry as to how this murderous business came to be carried out by a Government official. As a result Lord Roden and his agent were deprived of the Commission of the Peace—their offence was too glaring to be entirely overlooked. But to the friends of those who had been legally murdered, and the innocent people whose houses had been wrecked, this was a cruel mockery. Had the criminals been Catholic peasants, they would have been put upon their trial for their lives, and, at the very least, sent into penal servitude. What confidence could the Catholics of Ulster have in the administration of the law, knowing, as they did, that even where they were more than able to hold their own against the Orangemen, they were sure to be sufferers in the long run, seeing that their opponents would be backed up by the forces that should go to preserve law and order.

It is thirty-five years since I last re-visited the County Down. I took my son with me. He was nearly of the same age as I was myself when I lived in Ballymagenaghy, but I could only show him the site of Oiney Bannon's house. It was not the too common case of an eviction, for the Annesleys had the reputation of being tolerably good landlords. The land, as I have said, was very poor, in fact, if

the people got it for nothing it would hardly repay
cultivation. But it was picturesque, and therefore
Lord Annesley took some of it into his domain, and
these barren hills and rocks, when planted with
trees, added to the beauty of the scenery. The
dispossessed tenants got land from him in Clarkhill,
not far off.

Since that time, judging from the Irish newspapers, there seems to have been progress in the
right direction, for the little town of Castlewellan,
where for a short time I went to school, from being
a place where, in the Penal days, a Catholic was
scarcely allowed to live, seems to have become a
strong Nationalist centre for South Down. This
was my mother's part of the country. I have seen
similar paragraphs which proved to me that, in the
barony of Lecale, County Down, my father's part,
the people, though not so demonstrative as the
"mountainy men," can still, as ever, be relied upon
to stand as firm as Slieve Donard itself for creed
and country.

CHAPTER IV.

O'CONNELL IN LIVERPOOL—TERENCE BELLEW
MACMANUS AND THE REPEAL HALL—THE
GREAT IRISH FAMINE.

O'CONNELL, when passing through Liverpool on his way to Parliament, always made the Adelphi Hotel his headquarters, and used to hear Mass not far off at the Church of St. Nicholas, or, as it was more generally called, " Copperas Hill Chapel," where I used to serve as an altar boy. I must have been a very small boy at the time when I first remember the Liberator coming to Mass at our Church, for, on one occasion, on stretching up to the altar to remove the Missal it was so difficult for me to reach that I let it fall over my head.

Without being by any means what is termed a " votheen," O'Connell was a faithful and devout son of the Catholic Church. During the many years when he was passing through Liverpool, going to and returning from Parliament, and on other occasions when he came to Irish gatherings in the town, he attended Mass daily whenever possible, and frequently approached Holy Communion.

O'Connell spoke several times from the balcony of the Adelphi Hotel. From my earliest days I was an earnest politician, and one of my most cherished remembrances is of having been brought by my father to one of these gatherings. The Liberator addressed a great multitude, who filled the whole square in front, and overflowed into the adjoining streets. My recollection of him on this occasion is that of a big man, in a long cloak, wearing what appeared to me some kind of a cap with a gold band on it. This must have been the famous " Repeal Cap " designed by the Irish sculptor, Hogan, who, when investing O'Connell with it at the great gathering at Mullaghmast, said : " Sir, I only regret this cap is not of gold."

As in our later Irish movements, we frequently had meetings in one or other of the Liverpool theatres. O'Connell was, as often as his attendance could be secured, the central figure, and drew enormous gatherings. At one of these meetings at the Royal Amphitheatre there was an attempt by an armed body of Orangemen to storm the platform, on which were all our leading Irishmen. Among the most active of these was Terence Bellew MacManus, who had all his lifetime been a devoted follower and admirer of O'Connell. On this particular night, which was long before the unfortunate split into " Old Ireland " and " Young Ireland," he had a fine opportunity of displaying his " physical force " proclivities in defence of the " moral force " leader.

The Orange attack was of short duration. They were simply cleared out as if by an irresistible whirlwind. We have always been able to hold

our own in Liverpool, when it came to physical
encounters against all comers. We have generally
had some organisation or another—whether constitutional or unconstitutional—but, apart from
this, the nature of the employment of our working-
men, especially in O'Connell's time, brought them
together in such a way that large numbers of them
knew each other, and could act together in case of
emergency.

MacManus, who had command of the stewards
on the night of the attack, knew a number of men
like Mick Digney, who was what was called a
" lumper "—that is, a contractor in a small way
who took work in the " lump " and employed men
for loading and unloading ships. Digney and other
friends would find their way for consultation and
the making of the necessary arrangements before-
hand on occasions like this to MacManus, whose
place of business—he was an extensive forwarding
agent—was one of those half-offices, half-warehouses,
which used to be in North John Street.

Another class of men who were reliable for such
occasions were the bricklayers' labourers. Of course,
it is different now—and a sure sign that our people
are rising in the social scale—but in those years,
and long afterwards, I never knew a bricklayers'
labourer who was not an Irishman.

The frequent mention at these gatherings of
a sterling Irishman I knew well in after years,
Patrick O'Hanlon, reminds me of two friends of
my father of the same name who belonged to another
class of men, the wood-sawyers, who, at that time,

were mostly Irish. They had not exactly the same name as Patrick, for it was not so customary to use the O' or Mac in those days as it has since become. Not that Hughey and Ned Hanlon did not know that they were entitled to the honourable Gaelic prefix, but, with the good nature which is rather too characteristic of Irishmen sometimes, those who had preceded them had allowed other people to drop the O' in using their name, until it became rather difficult to resume it.

Needless to say that Hughey and Ned Hanlon, John Green, Mike Doolan, and other wood-sawyers were at the Royal Amphitheatre among MacManus's volunteers. The Hanlons, in particular, were fine lathy men, without an ounce of spare flesh, but they had sinews of iron. Hughey used to come to our house with other neighbours every week to hear the " Nation " read, and the songs in it sung to the accompaniment of Harry Starkey's or my Uncle John's fiddle. The Hanlons were North of Ireland men, and Hughey often used to proudly tell us that the O'Hanlons were the Ulster standard-bearers.

At that time, besides the Amphitheatre, where during those years several Irish demonstrations were held, a popular place for our gatherings was the Adelphi Theatre (previously the " Queen's "), which was in somewhat better standing then than afterwards, though it, too, has had within its walls most of the Irish leaders of the last half century.

I remember one occasion in particular when O'Connell was, of course, the hero of the day, which impressed itself upon my youthful mind the more forcibly on account of the presence on the platform of Jack Langan—of whom I have already spoken—a warm-hearted and generous supporter of the great Dan, and the Cause of Repeal. Indeed, we boys regarded the Irish champion boxer with the admiration we would have bestowed upon Finn MacCool or some other of the ancient Fenians, could they have appeared in bodily form amongst us.

Little we then thought that we should be welcoming on the same platform the Fenians of our own days.

That meeting in the Adelphi has also been frequently brought back to my mind since, because for a long time the " leading man " in the stock company at that theatre was Edmond O'Rourke (stage name Falconer), a sterling Nationalist, with whom I made a closer acquaintance in later years.

I was often brought by my father to the weekly gatherings in the Repeal Hall, Paradise Street, where, among the speakers on the Sunday nights I can best remember were Terence Bellew MacManus, Patrick O'Hanlon, Dr. Reynolds, George Smyth, and George Archdeacon.

MacManus and Smyth (the latter of whom I knew well in after years), besides being prominent workers in O'Connell's agitation for Repeal of the Union between Ireland and Great Britain, took active parts in the " Young Ireland " movement. Dr. Reynolds was another of the Young Irelanders. So also was Archdeacon, who, in addition, still showed his belief in physical force by his connection with Fenianism, for which he suffered imprisonment.

Young as I was, I shall never forget the days of the Famine, for Liverpool, more than any other place outside of Ireland itself, felt its appalling effects. It was the main artery through which the flying people poured to escape from what seemed a doomed land. Many thousands could get no further, and the condition of the already overcrowded parts of the town in which our people lived became terrible; for the wretched people brought with them the dreaded Famine Fever, and Liverpool became a plague-stricken city. Never was heroism greater than was shown by the devoted priests—English as well as Irish—in ministering to the sick and dying. So terrible was the mortality amongst them that several of the churches lost their priests twice over. Our own family were nearly left orphans, for both father and mother were stricken down by the fever, but happily recovered.

It will not be wondered at that one who saw these things, even though he was only a boy, should feel it a duty stronger than life itself to reverse the system of misgovernment which was responsible.

There was, no doubt, a good deal of English sympathy for the famine-stricken people, and there were some remedial measures by Parliament—totally inadequate, however, but I am afraid that the " Times " and " Punch," two great organs of public opinion, but too faithfully represented the feelings of many of our rulers. The " Times " actually gloated over what appeared to be the impending extinction of our race. Young as I then was, but learning my weekly lessons from the

" Nation," I can remember how my blood boiled one day when I saw in a shop window a cartoon of " Punch "—a large potato, which was a caricature of O'Connell's head and face, with the title—" The Real Potato Blight."

At the time of the Rising of 1848 I was commencing my apprenticeship with a firm of builders, who were also my father's employers. They were successors to the firm through whose agency he had been sent to Ireland as clerk of the works, just previous to my birth there. It was the custom of the firm, when a boy came to commence his apprenticeship to be a joiner, to keep him in the office for a time as office boy. I was employed in the office at the time of the Rising, but one of the partners in this firm of builders, who was also an architect, seeing that I had had a good education, and, through attending evening classes at the Catholic Institute and Liverpool Institute, had a considerable knowledge of mathematics and architectural drawing, gave me employment which was more profitable to the firm and congenial to me than that of an ordinary office boy or junior clerk. Besides helping in the ordinary clerical work in the office, I was put to copying and making tracings of ground plans, elevations and sections of buildings, and working drawings for the use of the artizans, besides assisting in surveying. I was about three years employed in this way before entering into the joiners' workshop. The firm was most anxious that I should remain in the office altogether, and I have often thought since that my father made a

mistake in insisting that I should learn the trade
of a joiner, which he considered a more certain living
than that of an architect or draughtsman, unless
one had influential connections.

It was from the upper window of the office where
I was at the work I have described that I could see
the men belonging to our firm drilling as special
constables in the school yard opposite, in anticipa-
tion of trouble in connection with an Irish Rising.

The authorities were evidently preparing for a
formidable outbreak in Liverpool, for there was a
large military camp at Everton—a suburb of the
city—and three gunboats in the river ready for
action, in case any part of the town fell into the
hands of the Irish Confederates. Special constables,
as in the case of our own firm, were being sworn in
all over the town, and the larger firms were putting
pressure upon their employees to be enrolled.
Indeed, some 500 dock labourers were discharged
because they would not be sworn in. My father
declined to be a special constable, but suffered no
further from this than becoming a suspect—his
services being too valuable to be dispensed with by
his employers.

He was a genuinely patriotic Irishman, steadfast
in his political creed, though unostentatious in his
professions, being more a man of action than of
words. My mother, as I think I have already
sufficiently indicated, was, on the other hand, more
demonstrative. I think she must have had a
positive genius for conspiracy. Whatever the movement was she must have a hand in it. On one

occasion—I forget exactly what it was—some compromising documents had to be got out of the way for the time being. In those days sloops used to come over from Ireland with potatoes, and the cargoes used to be sold on the quay at the King's Dock. She often bought a load of potatoes here to supply a small general shop which she kept to help out my father's earnings. It was under such a load of potatoes that she had brought home that she concealed the dangerous documents.

It was in June, 1848, in the columns of the " Nation " that I first met with the name of Bernard MacAnulty. In after years I worked in successive national movements with him, and ever found him a dear friend and most active and enthusiastic colleague. As showing that he was a man of advanced proclivities, I may mention that he wrote to the " Nation " suggesting the formation of the " Felon Repeal Club " in Newcastle-on-Tyne. From then up to the last day of his life he was the same generous whole-souled Irishman he had been from the beginning. His stalwart frame and pleasant, genial face were well known during the whole of the Home Rule movement, in which I was thrown into frequent contact with him, when we were both members of the Executive of the Home Rule Confederation of Great Britain.

He was a North man, from the County Down, a successful merchant—having started life as a packman—in Newcastle-on-Tyne, and so won the respect of all classes that he was elected a member of the Town Council, in which he served with great credit. The northern Catholic, who is so often a pure Celt, is sometimes credited with having acquired some of the qualities of his Presbyterian neighbours of Lowland Scots extraction. But this is only on the surface, and Bernard MacAnulty was a typical example of this. No braver or more generous Irishman ever breathed, and he had a fund of humour which would have done credit to the quickest-witted Connaughtman or Munsterman that ever lived. Though the Ulster accent is generally regarded as a hard one, I never thought it was so with my friend. Perhaps this is owing to my partiality as a County Down man, which, though born in Antrim, I always consider myself, Down being the native place of my people from time immemorial. I have always thought that the people born and reared, as Bernard was, among the Mourne Mountains and their surroundings have anything but an unmusical accent.

In connection with the Fenian movement my dear old friend was a strong, active, and generous sympathiser. His purse was always available for every good National object, whether " legal " or " illegal," and I know as a fact that many a good fellow " on the run " found shelter under his roof, and never went away empty-handed.

CHAPTER V.

THE restoration of the Catholic Hierarchy, September 29th, 1850, brought on what appeared to us one of John Bull's periodical fits of lunacy. I witnessed many scenes of mob violence at the time, when, in deference to the prevailing bigotry in opposing what they termed " Papal Aggression " a part of the Penal Laws were revived in Lord John Russell's Ecclesiastical Titles Act. In due course John got over his paroxysm, and the Act was repealed.

But for a time the storm of bigotry raged fiercely, and, as the following incident will show, while the mania lasted even the police were not entirely free from it.

The site of the noble Gothic edifice, Holy Cross Church, Great Crosshall Street, Liverpool, was, at this time, occupied by a ramshackle place made into a temporary chapel out of a number of old houses. It was so constructed that from any part you could see the altar, if you could not always hear Mass.

This was not, however, an unusual thing in Liverpool in the old days, particularly in the Famine

years, when our panic-stricken people came into
Liverpool like the wreck of a routed army.

The chief feature of the old Holy Cross Chapel
was a long narrow flight of stairs, leading from
Standish Street, the side street off Great Crosshall
Street, up to a higher part of the building which
served the purpose of a gallery.

The famous Dr. Cahill came to Holy Cross to
preach, and every part of the building was crowded
to suffocation. In the middle of the sermon an
alarm was raised of a broken beam or something
of the kind, and the people commenced to rush
down the narrow stairs in a state of panic.

Such of them as could crush their way out, instead
of being assisted, were set upon and assaulted with
their batons by several policemen, who were in the
street outside. So great was the indignation in the
town, that a public inquiry was held, and it was
proved that the police not only brutally struck men,
women and children, but even a blind man who was
trying to grope his way out. They also used foul
expressions about " Popery " and the " bloody
Papists," and it was afterwards proved that these
very men had themselves raised the alarm, apparently to get an excuse for breaking the heads of
the unfortunate people. An honest police official,
whose duty it afterwards became to make a report
of what had occurred, came upon the scene, and
did what he could to stop the brutality.

When Dowling, the head constable, came to the
police office next morning, and saw the official
report in the book kept for the purpose, he caused

the leaf containing it to be torn out, and another
report by one Sergeant Tomlinson to be substituted
for it. Mr. Mansfield, the stipendiary magistrate,
who conducted the inquiry, denounced Dowling
and Tomlinson for what he called " the disgraceful
and discreditable suppression of the report which,"
he added, " was no doubt true. He had never
heard of more disgraceful proceedings in his life."

Pending a fuller investigation, the police office
books were impounded, and, as a result of the
inquiry, several of the police were suspended.
Dowling was dismissed from his post as head constable of Liverpool, and lost a retiring pension
which, if all had been well with him, he would have
come in for a short time afterwards.

An amusing story is told of a Liverpool daily
paper in those days. It was struggling with ad-
versity, and the manager, a worthy Scotsman,
sat in his office on Monday morning with the weekly
statement before him, showing increasing expense
and decreasing revenue.

To him entered a Liverpool parson—very
determined and very menacing. He had asked for
the editor, but that gentleman had not yet come
down, and the manager was the only person in
authority visible, so he had to make shift with him.

" I am here," the parson said, " as the mouth-
piece of a large number of people who are not
satisfied with the attitude of the ' Liverpool —— '
on the great question of the hour—Whether Popery
is to dominate our liberties or are we to crush
Popery ? "

" Yes," said the manager, wearily, his mind
still on the balance sheet, " What do you com-
plain of ? "

" I wish to tell you, sir," said the parson, with
impressive emphasis, " that only this morning I
have heard the belief expressed by merchants on
'Change that the ' Liverpool —— ' is actually in
the pay of the Pope of Rome ! "

In a second a ray of light seemed to irradiate
the gloom of the manager's soul, as he contemplated
in a flash of thought the untold treasures of the
Vatican—

" Man ! " he exclaimed fervently, " I wish to
Heaven it was ! "

But the numerous exhibitions of bigotry stirred
up in connection with Lord John Russell's Ecclesiastical Titles Act were of trifling consequence
compared with the injury done to the Irish people
arising out of the same Act. For it led to the
ruin of the Tenant Right agitation in Ireland, in
which the Irish people, Protestant as well as Catholic,
had been united as they had not been since 1798
and the days of Grattan's Parliament.

For the Tenant League and the Irish Party in
Parliament had in their ranks some of the greatest
rascals who had ever disgraced Irish politics. These,
while posing as the champions of Catholicity in
opposing Lord John Russell's bill, were simply
working for their own base ends, and were afterwards
known and execrated as the Sadlier-Keogh gang.

Their infamous betrayal of the Irish tenantry
dashed the hopes and destroyed the union of North

and South from which so much was expected, besides
creating a distrust in constitutional agitation which
lasted for nearly a generation.

The after fate of the Sadlier-Keogh gang—
including the suicide of John Sadlier and the scarcely
less wretched end of Keogh—have ever since been
terrible object-lessons to the Irish people.

In his later years I enjoyed the friendship of one
of the most distinguished of the Tenant Right
leaders, who had also played a prominent and
honourable part in the Repeal and Young Ireland
movements. This was Charles Gavan Duffy, whom
I met after his return from Australia.

It was the Sadlier-Keogh treason, their selling
themselves to the Government after the most
solemn promises to the contrary, and the way in
which their conduct had been condoned by so many
of the hierarchy, clergy and people of Ireland, that
caused Gavan Duffy to lose heart for the time, and
to declare, as he left the country, in memorable
words—" that there was no more hope for Ireland
than for a corpse on the dissecting table."

But, as I learned from his own lips on his return
to this country, he never lost sight of the National
movement while in Australia, where he became
first Minister of the Crown in a self-governing
colony; and, on his return, his old hope for the
success of our Cause had, he assured me, revived.

Charles Gavan Duffy having sailed for Australia
on the 6th of November, 1855, John Cashel Hoey
succeeded him as editor of the " Nation," he having,
as one of his colleagues, Alexander Martin Sullivan,

who afterwards became sole proprietor and responsible editor.

"A. M." Sullivan, as he was always called, was an upright man, who had a very clear conception of his own policy in Irish matters. He frankly accepted the British constitution, and worked inside those lines. To me, when my country was concerned, the British constitution (with the making of which neither I nor my people had ever had anything to do) was a matter of very little moment. Any work for Ireland that commended itself to my conscience and was practicable was good enough. Nevertheless, it will ever be to me a source of pride that, from the moment when we first knew each other to the hour of his death, we were the closest friends.

In connexion with the "Papal aggression" mania, Cardinal Wiseman was the central figure against whom the storm of bigotry was chiefly directed. I remember with pleasure that I took part in the reception given to him in Liverpool by Father Nugent and the students of the Liverpool Catholic Institute, by whom the Cardinal's fine play of "The Hidden Gem" was performed in the Hall of the Institute during his stay in town. The bringing of the Cardinal to Liverpool was only one of the many occasions when the good Father was the medium through whom, from time to time, a number of distinguished Catholics and Irishmen were brought into intimate contact with their co-religionists and fellow-countrymen in the town for the advancement of some worthy object connected with creed or nationality—most frequently with both.

I have described the St. Patrick's Day annual processions in Liverpool. Notwithstanding some grand features in connection with them, they were, unfortunately, sometimes the occasion of rioting and intemperance. Father Nugent was of Irish parentage and sympathies, and possessed of great zeal, capacity, energy and eloquence. He determined to make a new departure in celebrating the national anniversary, for though the processions were magnificent displays, and it was not the fault of their promoters if ever there was any scandal arising out of them, still there was much that was inconsistent with a worthy celebration of the feast of the national saint of Ireland. Calling a number of young Irishmen together, of whom I was one, he, with their help, organised on a grand scale a festival which was held in one of the large public halls of the town. So successful was the first of these that they became an annual institution, which superseded the previous out-door celebrations.

On these occasions there were selections of Irish music and song, and oratory from some distinguished Irishman, with an eloquent and stirring panegyric on St. Patrick from Father Nugent himself, making a more creditable and enjoyable celebration of the national festival than had ever been held in the town before.

Such celebrations as these (which have for many years past been held under the auspices of the Irish national political organisation of the day), have become common in the Irish centres of Great Britain. Indeed, it has become one of the recognised duties of the members of the Irish Parliamentary Party to hold themselves in readiness to be drafted off to one or another of these gatherings, which are the means of keeping steadily burning the fire of patriotism in the breasts of our people. And what is of consequence from a financial point of view, the proceeds of these gatherings help to provide the sinews of war for carrying on the Home Rule campaign in Great Britain. For over half a century, from the time when I assisted Father Nugent with his first celebration, I took an active part in organising these gatherings in many places.

I said at the commencement that I knew little of Ireland from personal contact with it. Born there, I was too young to remember being brought to England. For some months I was there again, as I have already mentioned, as a boy of twelve, under the care of my uncle, the Rev. Michael O'Loughlin. I had often desired to see more of Ireland, and, singularly enough, it was the Crimean War that gave me the opportunity of spending another three months there in the summer of 1855.

A large firm in Liverpool had part of the contract for erecting the wooden houses and other buildings at the camp being erected on the Curragh of Kildare at the time of the war. I made application, and, with my brother Bernard, was employed to go there. Reaching the Curragh, we found that many of the men slept in the huts they were erecting, being supplied by the contractors with the requisite bed

and bedding. The contractors also erected a large
" canteen," to be used afterwards by the military
where the workmen could be supplied with food
and drink—too much drink sometimes. These
arrangements for food and sleeping were somewhat
necessary, as the nearest towns, Kildare, Kilcullen,
and Newbridge were each some three miles off.

But we were anxious to see as much of the country
and of the people as we could, and, besides, did not
care for the mixed company sleeping in the huts.
We therefore managed to secure lodgings with the
Widow Walsh, on the road leading from the Curragh
to Suncroft. The widow's husband had but recently
died, leaving her a pretty good farm, and, with the
aid of her family—one of them a fine, grown-up
young man—she was able to hold on to the land.
But the ready cash she got from the Curragh men
who came to lodge with her was useful too. It was
a good big house of the kind, and the widow made
use of every available inch of it, so that she had
about a dozen of us in all. Mrs. Walsh, though
an easy-going soul herself, had a fine bouncing girl
to help her, but, with a dozen hungry men coming
with a rush at night, it used to be a scramble for the
cooking utensils, as we were largely left to our own
devices. We used to leave early in the morning
for our work on the Curragh, taking with us the
materials for our breakfasts and dinners. As to
the cooking, some went to the canteen, while others
got their meals wherever they happened to be working. As there were plenty of chips and small
cuttings of wood, only fit for that purpose, we used

to make of these big fires on the short grass, and we boiled our water for tea or coffee and our eggs, and frizzled our chops or bacon at the end of a long stick.

I have mentioned before that whenever one finds work particularly laborious he is fairly certain to find Irishmen at it. It was so at the Curragh. When a carpenter or joiner lays down the boarding of a floor, if there is only a small quantity of it he planes it down himself to make an even surface. But if there is a large quantity this does not pay, and the contractor brings in another artist called a " flogger," who, in nine cases out of ten, in my time, was an Irishman. It was generally given out as " piece work " to one man, the " master-flogger," as you might term him, who employed the others. One of these, a very decent Irishman, Tom Cassidy, whom I had known in Liverpool, had the contract for the work at the Curragh Camp, and he had about a score of his fellow-countrymen working for him.

Going back to Liverpool for a holiday, while my brother and I were still at the Curragh, honest Tom called on my father and mother, who knew him well. They were glad to hear that he was lodging at the Widow Walsh's, and could tell them all about their boys. This he could do most truthfully without letting his imagination run away with him. " Aye, indeed," he said, " Barney and John are lodging in the one house with me, with a decent widow woman, and many a glass we had together at Igoe's." Tom had put in this bit of " local colouring " about Igoe's to show the good fellowship between us, but as their sons were both teetotalers, the old people knew that this could not be true, and the rest of his story was somewhat discredited in consequence.

Igoe's was a public house just on the corner of the road leading from the Curragh to Suncroft. What between the workmen at the Camp and the soldiers and the militia, Igoe's must have been doing a roaring trade at this time. Which reminds me that I one day saw John O'Connell (son of the Liberator), then a captain in the Dublin militia, trying to get a lot of his men, who were the worse for liquor, out of Igoe's. It could not be said that he did not give an edifying example to his men, for I saw him, on another occasion, going to Holy Communion, at the Soldiers' Mass, where the altar was fixed up under a verandah in the officers' quarter, the men being assembled in the open square in front. He was a well-meaning man, and tried to carry on the Repeal Association after his father's death, but it soon collapsed, for the mantle of Dan was altogether too big for John.

Although he generally showed himself bitterly opposed to the Young Irelanders, he was a poetical contributor to the " Nation," where I find him represented by two very fine pieces—" Was it a Dream ? " and " What's my Thought Like ? " In the latter piece he pictures Ireland—

No longer slave to England ! but her sister if she will—
Prompt to give friendly aid at need, and to forget all ill !
But holding high her head, and, with serenest brow,
Claiming, amid earth's nations all, her fitting station now.

I never met his brother Maurice, but I could imagine his a more congenial spirit with the " Young Irelanders " than any other of the O'Connell family. He, too, is represented in " The Spirit of the Nation " by his rousing " Recruiting Song of the Irish Brigade" which, sung to the air of " The White Cockade," has always been a favourite of mine.

A fine, genial old priest, full of gossip and old-time stories, was Father MacMahon, of Suncroft. If he met one of us on the road he would stop to have a gossip, and was always delighted when he found, as he often did, along with an English tongue an Irish heart. From him it was I heard the legend of St. Brigid's miraculous mantle and the origin of the Curragh—how the saint, to get " as much land as would graze a poor man's cow " made the very modest request from the king for as much ground as her mantle would cover ; how he agreed, and she laid her mantle down on the " short grass ; " how, to the king's astonishment, it spread and spread, until it covered the whole of the ground of what is now the Curragh ; and how it would have spread over all Ireland but that it met with a red-haired woman, and that, as everybody knows, is unlucky. Whenever, in our rambles along the country roads we afterwards met a red-haired woman, we used to wonder was she a descendant of the female who stopped the growth of the Curragh of Kildare.

Father MacMahon could also tell us of the gallant fight made by the men of Kildare, and the massacre of the unarmed people on the Curragh in 1798.

Many of the men from the Curragh used to come to Mass on Sundays at Suncroft, and often in his sermons—which were none the less edifying because they were given in the same free and easy style as his gossips with us on the road—he would tell his people of the talks he had had with the men from the Camp, and what good Irishmen he found among them. They, in their turn, were very fond of the good father, and most of them took a practical way of showing their feeling when it came to the offertory.

Dear old Father MacMahon! I took up an Irish Church Directory the other day and looked for the little village of Suncroft, in the dioceses of Kildare and Leighlin, to see if your name was still there, foolishly forgetting that it is over fifty years since we met—you an old man and I a young one. I am an old man now, and you—you dear good old soul—must have gone to your reward long ago, where you in your turn will be hearing from St. Brigid herself, and from the fine old Irish king who gave the Curragh, the true story of the miraculous mantle ; and how the king did not make such a bad bargain after all, for, in exchange for his gift, he now, doubtless, has what St. Brigid promised, a kingdom far greater than even her mantle would cover—the Kingdom of Heaven.

On Sundays we used to have long walks. We did not often go near Newbridge—it was too much like an ordinary English military station. We preferred going to Kildare, where stands the first Irish Round Tower I ever saw, and where the fine old ruined

church of St. Brigid put us in mind of the patron
saint of Ireland ; or to Kilcullen, where the brave
Kildare pikemen routed General Dundas in 1798 ;
and to others of the neighbouring places. We
reviewed, too, every part of the famous Curragh
itself, so full of memories—glorious and sad—of
Irish history.

As fast as we finished them, the huts we were
building were occupied by the military, and, whether
regulars or militia, I found among them, driven to
wear the uniform by stress of circumstances, as
good Irishmen as I ever met. Coming home from
work one evening, I met on the road to the Curragh
a party of them, carrying, for want of a better
banner, a big green bush, and singing " The Green
Flag." Then, as they came in sight of the famous
plain itself, a man struck up :—

> Where will they have their camp ?
>   Says the *Shan Van Voct* '

When, as if moved by one impulse, all joined in :—

> On the Curragh of Kildare,
> And the boys will all be there,
> With their pikes in good repair—
>   Says the *Shan Van Voct* !

" Igoe's porter ! " a cynic might say. True,
there may have been a glass or two and a little
harmless rejoicing, but this was too spontaneous
to be anything but the outpouring of the good,
honest warm hearts of the poor fellows, burning
with love for the land that bore them.

Peter Maughan, who, like myself, was a house joiner, working at the Curragh, had similar experiences. Indeed, you might say that he was then qualifying himself for the part he very efficiently filled some years later in the Irish Revolutionary Brotherhood, as recruiting officer among the soldiery of Britain. Of course, he found scoundrels amongst them too, for, as the history of the Fenian movement shows, he was himself betrayed and sent to penal servitude.

Before I returned to England I had a most interesting tour through the South of Ireland, that being, I may say, the most I have ever actually seen of my own country. Having a taste for drawing, I took sketches of the various noted places I visited, which I preserved for many years—the most cherished remembrances of my visit to the " old sod."

After returning from the Curragh to Liverpool, I married there and carried on business on my own account for several years as a joiner and builder, before taking service with Father Nugent, first as secretary of his Boy's Refuge, and then as conductor for some three years of his newspaper, the " Northern Press and Catholic Times."

CHAPTER VI.

THE IRISH REVOLUTIONARY BROTHERHOOD—ESCAPE
OF JAMES STEPHENS—PROJECTED RAID ON
CHESTER CASTLE—CORYDON THE INFORMER.

THE trials in 1859, following the arrests in connection
with the Phœnix movement, with which the name
of Jeremiah O'Donovan (called also " Rossa," after
his native place) was identified, were the first public
manifestations of what developed into the great
organisation known in America as the Fenian
Brotherhood, and, on this side of the Atlantic
as the I.R.B., or Irish Revolutionary Brotherhood.

Many years afterwards " Rossa " called at the
office of the Irish National League in London, to
see his old fellow-conspirator, James Francis Xavier
O'Brien, then General Secretary of the constitutional
organisation for the attainment of " Home Rule."
As I was chief organiser for the League in Great
Britain, and was in the office at the time, I was
introduced to his old comrade (who had, he said,
often heard of me) by " J.F.X.," as we used to
call him, and it was to me a delightful experience
to hear the two old warriors, who had done and
suffered so much for Ireland, fighting their battles
over again.

I was sitting in my office in Father Nugent's Refuge one day, about the beginning of 1866, when my old friend, John Ryan, was shown in to me.

As we had not seen each other for several years, our greeting was a most cordial one. Though we had not met, I had heard of him from mutual friends from time to time as being actively connected with the physical force movement for the freedom of Ireland.

During this time I had often wished to see him, and I found that exactly the same idea had been in *his* mind regarding me ; our object being the same—my initiation into the ranks of the Irish Revolutionary Brotherhood, of which he was an organiser.

A word perhaps is due here—for I wish to pay respect to the opinion of every man—to those Irishmen who call themselves loyalists. On close analysis their language and arguments appear to me to be meaningless. A study of the history of the world and of the origins of civil power show that there is only one thing that is recognisable as giving a good and stable title to any government, and that is the consent of the governed.

A man who is a member of a community owes a duty to the community in return for the benefit arising out of his membership, but his duty—which he may call loyalty if he pleases—is proportionate to the share which he possesses in the imposition of responsibilities upon himself. The application of this to Ireland is obvious, and it explains why in so many cases a man who has been a rebel in

Ireland has afterwards risen to the highest place in the self-governing communities which are called British colonies. To put it in another way, a community of intelligent men must be self-governing, or else it will be a forcing-house for rebels. I don't see any third way.

As I have before suggested, the two questions that have always presented themselves to me in connection with work for Ireland have been—first, is it right? Second, is it practicable? In joining the I.R.B. I had no doubt on either ground. As to the first, the misgovernment of Ireland, of which I had seen the hideous fruits in the Famine years and emigration, was ample justification. As to the second, there was every likelihood of the success of the movement. It will be remembered that during these years the great Civil War in America was going on, in which many thousands of our fellow-countrymen, were engaged on both sides, mostly, however, for the North. A great number of these had entered into this service chiefly with the object of acquiring the military training intended to be used in fighting on Irish soil for their country's freedom. Such an opportunity seemed likely to arise, for during this time the "Alabama Claims" and other matters brought America and England to the verge of war. Had such a conflict arisen, one result of it, as Mr. Gladstone and other British statesmen could not but have foreseen, would probably be the severance of the connexion, once for all, between Ireland and Great Britain.

John Ryan, knowing me so well, felt tolerably assured that no argument from him would be required to induce me to join the I.R.B.; consequently, one of the first things he did was, at my request, to administer to me the oath of allegiance to the Irish Republic, as the saying went, " now virtually established."

After this we had a long *seanchus*, I telling him of all that had happened among our friends during his frequent absences from Liverpool, and he describing to me many of the adventures of himself and other prominent men in the movement, which were to me both interesting and exciting. Among these were his assistance in the escape of James Stephens, of which I will speak later.

Before we parted, he arranged with me for my acting in Liverpool as a medium of communication in the organisation. In this way I was, for several years, brought into constant contact with the leaders, nearly all of whom I met from time to time.

I think the most capable Irishmen I ever met were the various members of the Breslin family, with several of whom I was intimately acquainted. Bravest among the brave, as they proved themselves at many a critical moment, there were none more prudent. John Breslin was hospital steward in Richmond Prison when James Stephens, the Fenian chief, was imprisoned there awaiting his trial.

John Devoy was the man who successfully carried through, under the direction of Colonel Kelly, the outside arrangements in connection with the escape of the C.O.I.R. (Chief Organiser of the Irish Republic), as he was called, in the early morning of the 24th of November, 1865.

But John Breslin it was who, with the assistance of Daniel Byrne, night watchman, actually set Stephens free. Byrne was arrested and put upon his trial for aiding the escape of Stephens, but nothing could be brought home to him, and, after two successive juries had disagreed on his case, he was released. Breslin, the chief instrument in the rescue, was not suspected. He simply bided his time until he took his annual holiday, from which he never returned, leaving the country before there was any suspicion of him. Michael Breslin, his brother, held a responsible position in the Dublin police, and was the means of frustrating many a well-laid scheme of the Castle, so that if the Government had its creatures in the revolutionary camp, the I.R.B. had agents in theirs.

Another, as I have already mentioned, who took part in the Stephens rescue was my friend John Ryan, better known in the Brotherhood as Captain O'Doherty. At our interview in Liverpool on the occasion of my initiation, he gave me a full account of this among other incidents. He was, like Peter Maughan, an old schoolfellow of mine with the Christian Brothers in Liverpool. He was one of the men picked out by Colonel Kelly to be on guard when the "old man"—one of Stephens' pet nicknames—came over the prison wall. Ryan was a fine type of an Irishman, morally, intellectually and physically. As Stephens slipped down from the wall, holding on to the rope, he came with such force on my friend's shoulders as almost to bear him to the ground. In my " Irish in Britain " I have described in detail how Breslin got a key made for Stephens' cell, and how he and Byrne helped the C.O.I.R. over the prison wall to where his friends awaited him, and also the adventures of the Fenian leader after his escape from Richmond.

The man who made the key for Stephens' cell, from a mould taken by John Breslin, was Michael Lambert, a trusted member of the I.R.B. Though his name was well known to the initiated at the time, it never was mentioned until later years, he being always referred to previously as " the optician."

After remaining in concealment several months Stephens got away from Ireland. The craft in which he escaped was one of a fleet of fishing hookers which sailed from Howth and Kinsale when engaged in their regular work. The owner, who was delighted to have a hand in such an enterprise, was a warm-hearted and patriotic Irishman, Patrick De Lacy Garton, for whom I acted as conducting agent, when he was returned by the votes of his fellow-countrymen to the Liverpool Town Council, where he sat as a Home Ruler.

I met several times, during 1866 and later, one of the most remarkable men connected with the organisation. He was known as " Beecher," and was a man of singular astuteness, as he required to be, particularly at the time when, unknown to his colleagues, Corydon was giving information to the police. If at any time Beecher had fallen into

their hands, they might have made a splendid haul,
which would have paralysed the m vement on this
side of the Atlantic, for he was the " Paymaster."
Captain Michael O'Rorke—otherwise " Beecher "—
was a well-balanced combination of sagacity,
cautiousness and daring, as you could not fail to see,
if brought into contact with him a few times.
Stephens had the most abounding confidence in
him, and it was well deserved. A native of Ros-
common, he emigrated to America when a boy of
thirteen. When the Civil War broke out he joined
the Federal Army, and served with much distinction.
He was a member of the Fenian Brotherhood, and
was greatly pleased to be called upon for active
service in Ireland, and, sailing from New York,
he reached Dublin on the 27th of July, 1865, when
he reported himself to the C.O.I.R. He was
entrusted with the payment of the American officers
then in Ireland and Great Britain, which duty, I
need scarcely say, involved his keeping in constant
touch with them. In this way I, from time to
time, came in contact with him in Liverpool, and
was much impressed with the perfect way in which
he carried out his arduous duties. Before Stephens
left for America, in March, 1866, he directed Captain
O'Rorke to send all the officers not arrested, and
then in Ireland, over to England. This was a
proper measure of prudence, as the Irish Americans
would be less objects of suspicion, and less liable
to arrest here than in Ireland. He had fifty officers,
and sometimes more, to provide for as Paymaster,
or, as the informers and detectives had it, the

" Fenian Paymaster." He had to visit in this way at various times all parts of the British organisation, sometimes paying his men personally, and at other times by letter, forwarded through trusted Irishmen in various places who had not laid themselves open to suspicion. But he had to run his head into the lion's mouth occasionally, too, for it was part of his duty to visit Dublin at least once a month. As a matter of precaution, there were but few who knew of any address where he might be found. At a time when Corydon had started to give information, but before " Beecher " actually knew of it, the informer gave an address of his where he thought the " Paymaster " was to be found to the Liverpool police. Major Greig, the chief constable, and a strong body of his men, surrounded the house, but the bird had flown. After that, he was more cautious than ever, only letting his whereabouts be known when it was absolutely necessary.

A noted man among the Fenians was " Pagan O'Leary." Jack Ryan told me of how he rather surprised the prison officials when they came to classify him under the head " Religion." Being asked what he was, he said he was a Pagan. No, they said, they could not accept that—they had headings in their books, " Roman Catholic," " Protestant," and " Presbyterian," but not " Pagans." " Well," he said, " You have two kinds, the ' Robbers' (meaning Protestants) and the ' Beggars' (Catholics), and if I must choose, put me down a ' Beggar.' "

A startling incident in connection with the Fenian movement, the daring plan to seize Chester Castle, will enable me to introduce two exceedingly interesting characters with whom I came in contact at this time. The idea was to bring sufficient men from various parts of England, armed with concealed revolvers, to overpower the garrison, which at the time was a very weak one, and to seize the large store of arms then in the Castle. In connection with this, arrangements had been made for the cutting of wires, the taking up of rails, and the seizure of sufficient engines and waggons to convey the captured arms to Holyhead, whence, a steamer having been seized there for the purpose, the arms were to be taken to Ireland, and the standard of insurrection raised. Of John Ryan, one of the leaders of this raid, I have already spoken. Another of them, Captain John McCafferty, was one of the Irish-American officers who had crossed the Atlantic to take part in the projected rising in Ireland. I met him several times in Liverpool in company with John Ryan, and, from his own lips, got an account of his adventurous career up to that time.

Most of the American officers I came in contact with during these years had served in the Federal Army, but McCafferty fought on the side of the South in the American Civil War. He was a thorough type of a guerilla leader. With his well-proportioned and strongly-knit frame, and handsome resolute-looking bronzed face, you could imagine him just the man for any dashing and daring enterprise.

I frequently met John Flood, too, whose name, with that of McCafferty, is associated with the Chester raid. He was then about thirty years of age, a fine, handsome man, tall and strong, wearing a full and flowing tawny-coloured beard. He had a genial-looking face, and, in your intercourse with him, you found him just as genial as he looked. He was a man of distinguished bearing, who you could imagine would fill with grace and dignity the post of Irish Ambassador to some friendly power. He was a Wexford man, full of the glorious traditions of '98. He took an active part in aiding the escape of James Stephens from Ireland. With Colonel Kelly he was aboard the hooker in which the C.O.I.R. escaped, and to his skill and courage and rare presence of mind was largely due the fact that Stephens did not again fall into the hands of his enemies.

From then up to the time immediately preceding the Chester raid, he frequently called on me in Liverpool in company with John Ryan.

Father McCormick, of Wigan, a patriotic Irish priest, used to tell me, too, of the men coming to confession to him on their way to Chester, and afterwards to Ireland, for the rising on Shrove Tuesday. And yet these were the kind of men for whom, according to a certain Irish bishop, " Hell was not hot enough nor Eternity long enough."

When John Ryan informed me of the plans that were being matured for the seizure of the arms and ammunition in Chester Castle, I volunteered for any duty that might be allotted to me. It was settled that I should hold myself in readiness to carry out when called upon certain mechanical arrangements in connection with the raid with a view to prevent reinforcements from reaching Chester.

These arrangements were to consist of the taking up of the rails on certain railway lines and the cutting of the telegraphic wires leading into Chester. I, therefore, surveyed the ground, and besides the required personal assistance, had in readiness crowbars, sledges, and, among other implements, the wrenches for unscrewing the nuts of the bolts fastening the fishplates which bound together the rails, end to end. I now held myself prepared for the moment when the call to action would reach me.

This, however, never came, for I found afterwards that the leaders had learned in time of Corydon's betrayal of the project, and made their arrangements accordingly.

I heard nothing further of the projected Chester expedition until Monday, February 11th, 1867.

My employment was at this time in Liverpool, but I lived on the opposite bank of the Mersey, at New Ferry. Anybody who has to travel in and out of town, as I did by the ferry boat, to his employment gets so accustomed to his fellow-passengers that he knows most of them by sight. But this morning it was different. In a sense some of those I saw were strangers to me, but I had a kind of instinct that they were my own people. They were fine, athletic-looking young men, and had a travel-stained appearance, as if they had been walking some distance over dusty roads.

When I reached the landing stage and saw the morning's papers I got the explanation—the police had heard of the projected raid.

These were our men returning from Chester, having been stopped on the road by friends posted there for the purpose, and turned back—and were now on their way through Liverpool to their homes in various parts of Lancashire and Yorkshire. It seemed that the information of the project being abandoned had not reached them in time to prevent many of the men leaving their homes for Chester.

I heard from John Ryan, whom I saw a few days afterwards, that the word had been sent round to a certain number of circles in the North of England and the Midlands to move a number of picked men, some on the Sunday night and some early on the Monday morning, and that the promptness and cheerfulness with which the order was obeyed was astonishing; so that, probably, not less than two thousand men were, by different routes, quietly converging on Chester. Among these was Michael Davitt and others, from Haslingden as well as from several other Lancashire towns.

But it was promptly discovered that information had been given to the police authorities almost at the last moment. Those, therefore, who had already reached Chester were sent back, and men were placed at the railway stations and on the roads leading to Chester to stop those who were coming. In this way the whole of the men forming the expedition dispersed as silently as they had come.

Corydon had given the information to Major Greig, the Liverpool Head Constable, who at once communicated with Chester, where prompt measures were taken to meet the threatened invasion.

According to his own evidence in the subsequent trial, Corydon had been giving information to the police since the previous September. There had been some suspicious circumstances in connection with him. A man resembling him in appearance, and evidently disguised, had been seen in company with individuals supposed to be police agents. But as there was a man belonging to the organisation named Arthur Anderson, who strongly resembled Corydon, the real informer, suspicion fell upon Anderson.

After Corydon had thrown off the mask and openly appeared as an informer, I had an opportunity of seeing him, and, so far as my memory serves me, this is what he was like: At first sight you might set him down as a third-rate actor or circus performer. He wore a frock coat, buttoned tightly, to set off a by no means contemptible figure, and carried himself with a jaunty, swaggering air, after the conventional style of a theatrical " professional." He was about the middle height, of wiry, active build, with features clearly cut, thin face, large round forehead, a high aquiline nose, thick and curly hair, decidedly " sandy " in colour, and heavy moustache of the same tinge. His cheeks and chin were denuded of beard.

It was in the Liverpool Police Court I saw John Joseph Corydon, as the newspapers spelled his name—if it were his name, which is very doubtful, for it was said in Liverpool that he was the son of an abandoned woman of that town.

There was at that time a reporter named Sylvester Redmond, whom I knew very well, a very decent Irishman, who made a special feature of giving humorous descriptions of the cases in the police court. I was told by someone in Court that the man whose hand Sylvester was so cordially shaking was the noted informer, Corydon. I was very much disgusted with the old gentleman, until I heard afterwards that some wag among the police had introduced the informer to him as a distinguished fellow-countryman.

After the collapse of the Chester scheme, McCafferty and Flood made their way to Ireland to be ready for the Rising, but were arrested in Dublin, charged with being concerned in the raid on Chester. They were both in due course put upon their trials, and sent into penal servitude.

I find, from a graphic sketch written for my "Irish Library" by William James Ryan, that in the convict ship that took John Flood into penal servitude was another distinguished Irishman, John Boyle O'Reilly, whose offence against British rule was his successful recruiting for the I.R.B. among the soldiery. Another lieutenant of John Devoy, who had charge of the organisation of the British army, was an old schoolfellow of mine with the Liverpool Christian Brothers, Peter Maughan, of whom I have already spoken as a fellow-workman at the Curragh.

Before joining the I.R.B. Peter had been a member of the " Brotherhood of St. Patrick," an organisation which furnished many members to the " Irish Revolutionary Brotherhood."

Most of the Fenian prisoners were amnestied before the completion of their full terms. I have a letter in my possession from John McCafferty to our mutual friend, William Hogan, written from Millbank Prison, 6th June, 1871. In this he regrets that the terms of his release will not allow of his paying Hogan a visit. He says :—

I know there are many who would like to shake my hand and bid me a kind farewell. God bless you before my departure. My route will afford me no opportunity of seeing the iron-bound coast of the home of my forefathers. Still God may allow me to see that isle again—Yes, and then perhaps I may meet somebody on the hills.

He concludes with love to William Hogan's family and " Kind regard to each and every friend."

McCafferty did, I know, see the " iron-bound " coast of Ireland again, for a few years after this an extremely mild and inoffensive-looking, dark-complexioned person, with black side whiskers, came into my place—I was carrying on a printing and newsagency business—in Byron Street, Liverpool, and, though I did not recognise him at first, I was pleased to find that this Mr. Patterson, as he called himself, was no other than my old friend John McCafferty.

The mission he was engaged on was one that

can only be described by the word amazing. So
daring was it, so hedged around with apparent
impossibilities, that to the ordinary man its very
conception would be incredible. But McCafferty
was perfectly serious and determined about it,
and to him it seemed practicable enough, provided
only he could get a few more men like himself:
and indeed if the collection of just such a company
of conspirators *were* practicable, no doubt the
impossible might become possible enough. But
the hypothesis is fatal, for the McCafferty strain
is a rare one indeed, so that his project never got
further than an idea. I think, however, that I
cannot be accused of exaggeration in saying that
if he had been successful in carrying out his idea,
his achievement would have formed the most
extraordinary chapter in English history—for it
was no less than the abduction of the then Prince
of Wales, afterwards King Edward VII., and the
holding of him as a hostage for a purpose of the
Fenian organisation.

The plan was to take him to sea in a sailing vessel,
and to keep him there, until the Fenian prisoners
still at that time unreleased were set at liberty.
He was to be treated with the utmost consideration
and—the recollection is not without its humorous
side—McCafferty had a memorandum to spare
no pains in finding what were the favourite amuse-
ments of the Prince, so that he might have a " real
good time " on board.

CHAPTER VII.

THE RISING OF 1867—ARREST AND RESCUE OF KELLY
AND DEASY—THE MANCHESTER MARTYRDOM.

ALTHOUGH the Rising of 1867 had somewhat the character of " a flash in the pan," there were some heroic incidents in connexion with it. With one of the Fenian leaders, James Francis Xavier O'Brien, I was brought into intimate connection many years after the Rising, when we were both officials, he as General Secretary and I as Chief Organiser, of the Home Rule organisation in Great Britain. When put upon his trial there was evidence against him in connection with the taking of a police barrack, he being in command of the insurgents. It was proved that he not only acted with courage, but with a humanity that was commended by the judge, in seeing that the women and children were got out safely before the place was set on fire.

This, however, did not save him from being condemned to death—he was the last man sentenced in the old barbarous fashion to be hanged, drawn and quartered—this sentence being afterwards commuted to penal servitude. Certainly, whether on the field or facing the scaffold for Ireland there was no more gallant figure among the Fenian leaders than James Francis Xavier O'Brien.

Few knew of his sterling worth as I did. For several years after his return to liberty I was in close daily contact with this white-haired mild-looking old gentleman—still tolerably active and supple, though—who could blaze up and fight to the death over what he considered a matter of principle. The most admirable feature in his character was that, in all things you found him *straight*.

One of the Fenian chiefs I met in Liverpool was General Halpin, who, on the night of the Rising, was in command of the district around Dublin. The first of the insurgents who reached Tallaght, the place of rendezvous on the night of the 5th of March, 1867, were received by a volley from the police and dispersed. One party had captured the police barracks at Glencullen and Stepaside, and disarmed the police, but on approaching Tallaght, and hearing that all was over, they too dispersed.

While most of the Irish-American officers bore the marks of their profession rather too prominently for safety against the observance of a trained detective, General Halpin was the last man in the world anyone would, from his appearance, take to be a soldier. He looked far more like a comfortable Irish parish priest. And yet he was, perhaps, the most thoroughly scientific soldier of all those that crossed the Atlantic at this time.

Reading the evidence of Corydon in one of the trials, I find he described Edmond O'Donovan as helping Halpin to make maps for use when the Rising would take place. Knowing both men so well, I can say that none better could be found for planning out a campaign. They were thoroughly scientific men, and always anxious to impart their knowledge to other Irishmen for the good of the Cause.

I remember Halpin one night, at what was a kind of select social gathering, giving a number of us enthusiastic young men a lecture on the construction of fortifications and earthworks.

We bade him farewell when he was leaving Liverpool after the Rising, and thought he had got safely away to America, but, unfortunately, he was identified at Queenstown in the outgoing steamer. He was arrested, put upon his trial, and met the same fate as so many of his comrades.

Among the men I knew long ago, who afterwards became connected with Fenianism, was Stephen Joseph Meany. He was for many years a journalist in Liverpool, having been sub-editor of the " Daily Post " under Michael James Whitty. He was an earnest and active Repealer and Young Irelander. When I first came in contact with him he was starting the " Lancashire Free Press," which, after passing through several hands and several changes of name, ultimately became the " Catholic Times," which was for three years, when Father Nugent became the proprietor, under my direction. Meany was a man of fine presence and handsome countenance, a brilliant writer and an eloquent speaker. He went to America in 1860, where he followed his original profession of journalism for several years. He returned to this country again, and was arrested in 1867 on a charge of Fenianism, and sentenced to fifteen years imprisonment.

Liverpool was flooded with refugees after the Rising, and it took us all our time to find employment for them, or to get them away to America. We had then in Liverpool a corps of volunteers known as " The Irish Brigade." Whatever National-ist organisation might exist in the town always strongly condemned young Irishmen for joining the corps. All we could urge against it, however, could not prevent our young men who were coming over from Ireland at this time from joining the " Brigade " for the purpose, they said, of learning and perfecting themselves in the use of arms. Colonel Bidwell and the officers must have had a shrewd suspicion of the truth, and there was a common remark in the town upon the improved physical appearance of the " Brigade." This was, of course, owing to the number of fine soldier-like young Irishmen who at this time filled its ranks.

During the two years that followed the escape of Stephens, I met Colonel Kelly several times in Liverpool. When I first saw him he would be about thirty years of age. This is my remembrance of his personal appearance : His forehead was broad and square, with the thick dark hair carefully disposed about it. He had somewhat high cheek bones, and wore a pointed moustache over a tolerably full beard. The general impression of his face seemed to me slightly cynical, and he had a constant smile that betokened self-possession and confidence. He sometimes wore a frock coat, a light waistcoat buttoned high up, a black fashionable necktie, and light well-made trousers. After surveying him in detail, you would come to the conclusion that he was a man of daring enough to involve himself in danger of life, and with sufficient address to extricate himself from the peril. He was undoubtedly a man capable of winning the confidence and even devotion of others, as was shown when, falling into the hands of the Government, he was snatched from their grasp in the open day on the streets of Manchester.

I met him some weeks after the Rising. The place of meeting reminded me of the incident in one of Samuel Lover's stories—" Rory O'More "— to which I have already alluded, for, in our later revolutionary movements, as in 1798, projects of great importance had sometimes to be discussed in public houses.

A few of the Liverpool men came to meet the leaders in a very humble beer shop, kept by a decent County Down man, Owen McGrady, in one of the poorer streets off Scotland Road. Here were met on this particular night a notable company, which included, if I remember rightly, Colonel Kelly, Colonel Rickard Burke, Captains Condon, Murphy, Deasy and O'Brien, all American officers who had crossed the Atlantic for the Rising, and still remained, hoping for another opportunity. There were about half a dozen of the Liverpool men there. Of these I can remember a tall, fine-looking young man, a schoolmaster from the North of Ireland, whom I then met for the first time, my old school-fellow,

John Ryan, and John Meagher, a tailor, possessing the amount of eloquence you generally find in Irish members of the craft.   There was also present, if I remember rightly, Tom Oates, of Newcastle.

Although the Rising had collapsed almost as soon as it commenced, the determination to fight on Irish soil had by no means been given up by the leaders in America.   That was why the American officers on this side remained at their posts, ready for active service at a moment's notice.   At the meeting we learned that there was at that moment an " Expedition," as it was termed, on the sea to co-operate with and bring arms for another Rising in Ireland, should such be found practicable.   It was notorious that, notwithstanding all the efforts of active agents, comparatively few arms had been got into Ireland.   Indeed, my friend John Ryan, who was in a position to know, estimated that there were not more than a couple of thousands of rifles in Ireland at the time of the Rising.

Let us see what became of the Expedition.   This was, of course, what has since become a matter of history—the secret despatch from New York of the brigantine " Erin's Hope," having on board several Irish-American officers, 5,000 stand of arms, three pieces of field artillery, and 200,000 cartridges.   About the middle of May the vessel arrived in Irish waters, agents going aboard at various points off the coast, including Sligo Bay, which she reached on the 20th of May, 1867.   By that time it was found that the chances of another Rising were but slender, and the " Erin's Hope " returned to America with her cargo, entirely un-molested by the British cruisers, which were plentiful enough around the Irish coast.

The expedition certainly proved that sufficient weapons to commence an insurrection with could be thrown into Ireland, providing there was the necessary co-operation at the time and places required.

I have often thought since of what became of those present in Owen McGrady's beer house the night we met there to prepare for the reception of the " Erin's Hope."

The arrest and rescue of Kelly and Deasy, two of these, in the following September, and the fate of their gallant rescuers, formed the most striking and startling chapter of Irish history during the nineteenth century.

That such a scheme as the rescue of the two Fenian chiefs should be successfully carried out, not in Ireland amid sympathisers, but in the heart of a great English city, surrounded by a hostile population, showed unexpected capacity and daring on the part of the revolutionary organisation, and produced consternation in the British Government.

At this time the organisation of the Irish Revolutionary Brotherhood in Great Britain had been placed in the hands of three of the Irish-American officers, Captain Murphy, who had charge in Scotland, Colonel Rickard Burke in the southern part of England, and Captain Edward O'Meagher Condon in the northern counties.

Previous to the arrest of the two leaders on the

morning of September 11th they, with Captain Michael O'Brien, had been staying with Condon, upon whom now devolved the command, the capture of Kelly and Deasy having taken place in his district.

He at once arranged for their food while in prison, for their defence in the law courts, and for their rescue, in which latter enterprise he was enthusiastically supported by the chief men of the Manchester circles.

But, whatever their good will and courage, they were deficient both in money and arms for such a daring undertaking. Condon had, therefore, a difficult task to accomplish. Money was soon raised, for our people are ever generous and equal to the occasion when it arises. Daniel Darragh—about whom I shall have more to say later—was sent to Birmingham, where by the aid of William Hogan he purchased and brought back with him sufficient revolvers to arm the volunteers for the rescue. These last were picked men, the cream of the Manchester circles, and there was some jealousy afterwards among many who had not been selected. I need scarcely say that the utmost secrecy was required in connection with such a perilous enterprise.

To Edward O'Meagher Condon belongs the credit of having organised, managed, and carried out the Manchester Rescue, at the cost to himself, as it turned out, of years of penal servitude, and almost of his life. Though with the aid of Michael O'Brien and his Manchester friends he had made all the arrangements, selecting the spot where the prison

van was to be stopped, assigning to every man his
post, and providing for every contingency, including
the possibility of the rescuing party being taken in
the rear from Belle Vue prison, he wired for the
assistance of Captain Murphy and Colonel Burke,
the message being that " his uncle was dying."

Murphy was from home, but Burke came on to
Manchester, and with Michael O'Brien accompanied
Condon on September 17th, the night before the
rescue, to meet the men chosen for the daring
enterprise, when the arms were distributed, each
man's post on the following day allotted to him, and
the final arrangements made.

The two Fenian chiefs stayed with Condon that
night, fighting their old campaigns over again,
e'er they retired to rest, not to meet again till eleven
years after the Manchester Rescue, when Condon
and Burke came across each other in New York,
each having suffered in the interval a long term of
imprisonment, and it was the last night that Burke
and Condon passed on earth with Michael O'Brien,
whose memory Irishmen, the world over, honour
as one of the " noble-hearted three "—the Manchester Martyrs—who died for Ireland on the
scaffold.

The secret of the intended rescue was closely
guarded, and though the Mayor of Manchester
did get a warning wire from Dublin Castle, it reached
too late, and the birds had flown. When Kelly
and Deasy were brought before the city magistrates
they were remanded. " They were," said the
" Daily News," " placed in a cell with a view to

removal to the city jail at Belle Vue. At this time
the police noticed outside the court house two men
hanging about whom they suspected to be Fenians,
and a policeman made a rush at one of them to
arrest him, in which he succeeded, but not until
the man had drawn a dagger and attempted to
stab him, the blow being warded off. The other
made his escape."

As to the incident just related, it seems that a
patriotic but imprudent man belonging to one of
the Manchester circles had got to hear of the intended
rescue, and was indignant at being left out. His
suspicious conduct outside the court house drew
the attention of the police—as we have seen—with
the result, as the paper said, that the authorities
became alarmed. Kelly and Deasy were put in
irons on their removal, and a strong body of police
were sent with the van intended to take them to
Belle Vue Prison.

It was the custom for a policeman to ride outside
the van, on the step behind, but, on this occasion,
owing to the incident just described, Brett, the
officer in charge, went *inside* the van. The door
was then locked, and the keys handed to him
through the ventilator.

It is certain that, up to this point, the Manchester
police had no suspicion of the intended rescue, and
it was only the imprudent behaviour of the man
whom the police had arrested that caused additional
precautions to be taken. Certain it is that if
the Manchester authorities had had any information
of the probability of an attempted rescue there

would have been a formidable escort of the police and military.

With so much false swearing at the trials with regard to the facts of the Manchester Rescue, it is important that the information given in books for the benefit of the present and future generations of Irishmen should be correct. It is serious that in some of our best books so important a matter as the actual scene of the rescue is incorrectly given. One book says : " The van drove off for the *County jail at Salford.*" In another description it is stated : " Just as the van passed under the arch that spans Hyde Road at Belle Vue, a *point midway between the city police office and the Salford Jail.*, etc." Following this, one of our ablest writers, apparently quoting from the previous descriptions, falls into the same error. I can readily understand how these errors have arisen—the writers concerned have confounded the place of the execution of the Manchester Martyrs, Salford Jail, with the prison, Belle Vue, to which the prisoners were being taken on being remanded.

The point chosen by Condon as the most suitable for the attack was certainly where the railway bridge crosses Hyde Road, but if the van had been going to Salford Jail it would have been in a totally different direction.

Since writing the above, I find it still more necessary I should correct the mis-statement as to the scene of the rescue, for the error seems to be getting perpetuated. I find in one of the leading Irish-American newspapers, in a description of the death of Colonel Kelly on February 5, 1909, the scene of the rescue is given as " *midway between the police office and Salford Jail.*" This is evidently taken from the erroneous statement in the books I have referred to.

After this slight digression, may I resume my narrative.

At the police court a man appointed for the purpose took a cab in advance of the van. When sufficiently close to them he waved a white handkerchief as a signal to the men in ambush. Just as the van passed under the railway arch two men with revolvers barred the way.

"Stop the van!" one cried. But the driver took no heed. A bullet fired over his head and another into one of the horses effectually stopped the van. At the sound of the shots the rest of the rescuers came from their ambush behind the walls that lined the road, and from the shadow of the abutments of the railway arch.

The police fled panic-stricken at the first volley fired over their heads by the Fenians, for these wanted to release their chiefs without bloodshed if possible. One portion of the assailants, carrying out a pre-arranged plan, formed an extended circle around the van, and kept the police and mob who had rallied to their assistance at bay, while a second party set themselves to effecting an entrance to the van. This was more difficult than had been expected, for had Brett ridden on the step behind as usual the keys could readily have been taken from him. The rescuing party were, however, equal to the occasion, and the military precision with which the work was carried out displayed the discipline of the men and the able direction of the leaders.

Indeed, the fullest testimony is borne to this by a great English newspaper, the " Daily News,' which, while showing the most intense hostility to the men and their daring act, is thus compelled to recognise the courage and discipline of the devoted band of Fenians :—" The more astonishing, therefore, is it to read of the appearance of the public enemy in the heart of one of our greatest cities, organised and armed, overpowering. wounding and murdering the guardians of public order, and releasing prisoners of state. There is a distinctness of aim, a tenacity of purpose, a resolution in execution about the Fenian attack upon the police van which is very impressive. The blow was sudden and swift, and effected its object. In the presence of a small but compact body of Fenians, provided with repeating firearms, the police were powerless, and the release of Kelly and Deasy was quickly effected.''

An unfortunate accident was the killing of Brett, the policeman, by a shot fired with the intention of breaking the lock of the van. A female prisoner then handed out the keys on the demand of the Fenians outside, and the door was quickly opened, and the two leaders brought out, their safe retreat being guarded by their rescuers.

As Captain Condon had anticipated and provided for, some of the warders from Belle Vue quickly came upon the scene, as it was but a short distance across what were then brickfields from the prison to the scene of action.   But, when they saw the determined men who were guarding the leaders' retreat, they, too, like the police, kept at a safe distance from the Fenian revolvers, and devoted themselves to picking up any stragglers who had got separated from the main body of Irishmen.

In this way a number of arrests were made, and, later on, Condon himself was taken, but the main object had been accomplished, and Kelly and Deasy got safely away, and, ultimately, as we shall see, out of the country.

Following the rescue, there was a perfect reign of terror, the police authorities striking out wildly in all directions to gather into their net enough Irish victims to satisfy their baffled vengeance. There were numerous arrests and no lack of witnesses to swear anything to secure convictions.   Every detail of the attack on the van while on the way from the courthouse to the prison, and of the release of the prisoners was sworn to with the utmost minuteness, as the witnesses professed to identify one after another of the men in the dock, some of whom had no connection or sympathy with the rescue at all.

In Liverpool, men whom I knew were arrested who were at work all that day at the docks, and yet were sworn to by numerous witnesses as having assisted in the attack on the van in Hyde Road, Manchester,   the   most   minute   details   being given.

I have mentioned a case of the kind in my " Irish in Britain." William Murphy, of Manchester, a man whom I knew well, was convicted and sent into penal servitude as having taken part in the rescue. On his liberation I was surprised to learn from his own lips that, although he would gladly have borne his part if detailed for the duty, he was not present at the rescue of the Fenian leaders. With the authorities in such a panic, it can readily be understood that it behoved any of us in Lancashire who were in any way regarded as " suspects " to be ready with very solid testimony as to where we were on the day in question.

In a recent letter I have had from Captain Condon —from whom communications reach me from all parts of America, for he is constantly travelling, holding as he does the post of Inspector of Public Buildings in connection with the Treasury Department of the U.S.A.—he tells me something about William Murphy that I never heard before. He says : " When Allen, Larkin, O'Brien, myself, and the other men were sentenced, Digby Seymour (one of the counsel for the prisoners) went down to a large cell in the court house basement where all the others were kept together. He urged them all to plead ' guilty ' and throw themselves upon the mercy of the court, declaring that, if they refused to do this all would be convicted and executed.

" There was an instant's hesitation among the prisoners, but William Murphy, who was later sentenced to seven years penal servitude, addressed his comrades, urging them to stand fast together, imitate our example, and die like men, rather than live like dogs, for as such they would be regarded by all true Irishmen if they pleaded ' guilty.'

" To a man the whole twenty-two shouted out— ' We will never plead guilty ! '

" And Seymour, baffled and irritated, went away without accomplishing his purpose."

Of the men convicted for taking part in the rescue, five—Allen, Larkin, O'Brien, Condon and Maguire— were sentenced to death. Condon was reprieved, really on account of his American citizenship, and Maguire, who was a marine, because the authorities discovered in time that the evidence against him was false. A number of others were sent to penal servitude for various terms.

The execution of Allen, Larkin and O'Brien, so far from striking terror, but gave new life to the cause of Irish Freedom, and to-day, over the world, no names in the long roll of those who have suffered and died for Ireland are more honoured than those of the " Manchester Martyrs," while the determination has become all the stronger that, in the words of our National Anthem—founded on Condon's defiant shout in the dock of " God Save Ireland ! " :—

> On the cause must go
> Amidst joy or weal or woe,
> Till we've made our isle a Nation free and grand.

It is not generally known how Colonel Kelly got out of the country after the rescue. He lay concealed in the house of an Irish professional man for some weeks, and then, all the railway stations being closely and constantly watched night and day, he was driven in a conveyance by road all the way from Manchester to Liverpool.

It was a patriotic foreman ship-joiner, whom I knew well, who actually got him away to America. My friend Egan had charge of the fitting up of the berths aboard the steamer in which Colonel Kelly sailed. In emigrant steamers the usual practice was for temporary compartments to be made and taken down at the end of the voyage. I had fitted up such berths myself, and therefore perfectly understood what my friend had done to secure Colonel Kelly's escape when he described it to me afterwards at my place in Byrom Street. Egan actually built a small secret compartment, so constructed as to attract no notice, and when Kelly was smuggled aboard at the last moment—he might be supposed to be one of Egan's men—he was put into it and actually boarded up, sufficient provisions being left with him, until the steamer got clear of British waters, when he could come out with safety.

Deasy also made his way to America.

In speaking of the after-career of those assembled that night at McGrady's, I have sufficiently accounted for Michael O'Brien.

Rickard Burke, who also assisted at the same gathering, was a remarkable personality, and one of the most astute men I ever met. He was a graduate of Queen's College, Cork, and an accomplished linguist. He was a skilful engineer, and had served with distinction in the American Civil War. When I knew him he was about thirty-five years of age, tall and of fine presence. To him was deputed the work of purchasing arms for the intended Rising in Ireland.

After many adventures, he fell into the hands of the police, was convicted, and sentenced to a long term of imprisonment. It was with the idea of effecting his rescue that the Clerkenwell Prison wall was blown up on December 13th, 1867, this insane plan causing the death and mutilation of a number of people. Burke himself would probably have been killed had he happened to be confined in that part of the jail that was blown up.

While in Chatham prison he was reported as having lost his reason, and was removed to Woking. The matter was brought before the House of Commons by Mr. McCarthy Downing, who suggested that Burke's insanity had been caused by his treatment in prison. He was released on Sunday, July 9th, 1871.

Captain Murphy, another of the company in our Scotland Road rendezvous, whom I had often met before, was a gentlemanly, genial man of portly presence, and an exceedingly pleasant companion. After some time he found his way back to America.

Edward O'Meagher Condon was one of the American officers I most frequently came in contact with in Liverpool, previous to and after the Rising. Since his return to America, after his release from penal servitude in 1878, we have frequently corresponded with each other. From a report of a Manchester Martyr's Commemoration in a newspaper which accompanied one of his letters, and conversations I had with him when I was delighted to have him as my guest during his recent visit to this country, I find he has just the same sanguine temperament as on that night at McGrady's, when the chances of another Rising were being discussed. In the report I refer to he says, " Had the Irish people been furnished with the necessary arms and munitions of war, which ought and could have been provided, they would have proved victors in the contest."

I have no doubt but that, in propounding this view, he had in his mind the probability there was at one point of England being embroiled in a quarrel with America. None knew better than he, at the time, of the enormous number of Irishmen in the American armies, on both sides, during the Civil War who, with their military training, longed for the task of sweeping English rule from the soil of Ireland. It will be remembered that it was Condon who, when sentenced to death, concluded his speech in the dock with the prayer, " God save Ireland ! " the words which have since become the rallying cry of the whole Irish race, and have given us a National Anthem.

In his letters to me since his first return to America, I have been gratified to hear that he always took a warm interest in my publications. I am pleased, too, to find from the newspaper reports he has sent me that he is, as ever, an eminently practical man, and believes in using the means nearest to hand for the advancement of the Irish Cause.

While giving his experiences in connection with the revolutionary movement, he declares that no one can blame the Irish people for having recourse

to any means which may enable them to remain on
their native soil. They have, he says, to use
whatever means have been left to save themselves
from extermination and Ireland from becoming a
desert. He, therefore, declares his sympathy with
the later movements of the Irish people—the Land
League, the National League, and the United Irish
League, while never abandoning the principles
of '98, '48 and '67.

I referred to two Liverpool men as being present
at the meeting at McGrady's. One of these, John
Ryan, my dear old schoolfellow, one of the rescuers
of James Stephens, has been dead many years—
God rest his soul! He was a noble character, and
would have risen to the top in any walk of life, but
though he had a good home—his father was a
prosperous merchant of Liverpool—he gave his
whole life to Ireland. I often heard from him of
his adventures, for he always looked me up whenever
he came to Liverpool, and how, sometimes, he and
his friends had to fare very badly indeed.

It was most extraordinary that, while constantly
running risks, for he was a man of great daring, he
never once was arrested, though he had some hair-
breadth escapes. On one occasion, about the time
of the Rising, a good, honest, Protestant member
of the Brotherhood, Sam Clampitt, was taken out
of the same bedroom in which he was sleeping with
Ryan, who was left, the police little thinking of the
bigger fish they had allowed to escape from their
net, the noted Fenian leader, "Captain O'Doherty."
I forget his precise name at this particular time,

but it was a very Saxon one, for he was supposed to be an English artist sketching in Ireland. Questioned by the police, he was able to satisfy them of his *bona fides*. He had a friend in Liverpool, an old schoolfellow like myself, Richard Richards—"Double Dick" we used to call him—a patriotic Liverpool-born Irishman. He was an exceedingly able artist, making rapid progress in his profession, and, about this time, having some very fine pictures, for which he got good prices, on the walls of the Liverpool Academy Exhibition. Richards supplied all the trappings for the part that Ryan was playing, and also sent him letters of a somewhat humorous character, which he sometimes read to me before sending off. In these he was anticipating all sorts of adventures for his friend in the then disturbed state of Ireland. As John Ryan had much artistic taste, and was himself a fair draughtsman, and well up in all the necessary technicalities, and as Richards' letters, which he always carried for emergencies like this, were strong evidences in his favour, he had not much difficulty in convincing the Dublin police he was what he represented himself to be.

Some of Jack Ryan's reminiscences had their droll sides, for he had a keen sense of humour. One of his stories was in connection with the well-known old tradition of the Gaels—both Irish and Scottish —that wherever the "*Lia Fail*" or "Stone of Destiny" may be must be the seat of Government. There is some doubt, as is well known, as to where the real stone now is. At all events, the stone which is under the Coronation Chair in Westminster

Abbey is that which was taken from Scone by King Edward, and that on which the Scottish monarchs were crowned, having been originally brought from Ireland, the cradle of the Gaelic race. The tradition is still, as it happens, borne out by the fact that Westminster is *now* the seat of Government.

Now two of John Ryan's Fenian friends, Irish-American officers, stranded in London—a not unusual circumstance—just when affairs looked very black indeed, conceived the brilliant idea of *stealing the stone*, bringing it over to Ireland, and, once for all, settling the Irish question. This, notwithstanding their oath to " The Irish *Republic* now virtually (virtuously some of our friends used to say) established," for it did not seem to strike them that they were proposing to bring to Ireland an emblem of royalty.

I never heard if they took any actual steps to accomplish their object. Perhaps they were impressed by the mechanical difficulties, as I was myself one day, when standing with David Barrett, an Irish National League organiser, in Edward the Confessor's Chapel, in front of the famous " *Lia Fail*." It is a rough-hewn stone, about two feet each way, and ten inches deep. I was telling my friend the story of the plot to carry off the " Stone of Destiny," and was making a calculation, based on the weight of a cubic foot of stone, of what might be its weight.

" We'll soon see," said David, and, in a moment, he had vaulted over the railing, and taken hold of a corner of the stone.

But, so closely is this national treasure watched, that instantaneously a couple of attendants appeared, and broke up peremptorily our proposed committee of enquiry. An archæological friend of mine suggests that, one day, when Ireland is making her own laws and able to enter on equal terms into a contract with England, a reasonable stipulation would be the restoration of that stone—unless the Scottish Gaels can prove a stronger claim to it.

From John Ryan I heard of the mode of living of many of the Fenian organisers and of the Irish-American officers,—very different from the slanderous statements of their " living in luxury upon the wages of Irish servant girls in America." John was of a cheery disposition, never complaining, but always sanguine, and loving to look at the bright side of things. Yet I could see for myself, each time I saw him, how the life of hardship he was leading was telling upon his once splendid constitution, and, I felt sure, shortening his days. John Ryan, I have often said, is dead for Ireland, for though he did not perish on the battlefield or on the scaffold, as would have been his glory, I most certainly believe he would have been alive to-day but for the hardships suffered in doing his unostentatious work for Ireland.

There is one other friend I mentioned as having been present that night at Owen McGrady's—the school master. You will ask what became of him ? Almost the last time I spoke to him—not very long before these lines were written—was in the inner lobby of the British House of Commons, for he has been for many years a member of Parliament. Now some of my most cherished friends are or have been members of Parliament, and I would be sorry to think any of them worse Irishmen than myself on that account. Their taking the oath of allegiance to the British sovereign was a matter for their own consciences, but I never could bring myself to do it. Mr. Parnell would, I know, have been pleased to see me in Parliament, but he knew that I never would take the oath, and respected my conscientious objections to swear allegiance to any but my own country.

With the exception of a few, whose names I forget, I have accounted for the whole of the company comprising the Council of War at McGrady's public house. Summed up as follows, nothing in the pages of romance could be more startling than the after fate of these men :—

CAPTAIN MICHAEL O'BRIEN.—Hanged at Manchester. R.I.P.

COLONEL RICKARD BURKE.—Sent to Penal Servitude —Returned to America.

COLONEL THOMAS KELLY, CAPTAIN TIMOTHY DEASY. —Rescued from Prison Van in Manchester.

CAPTAIN EDWARD O'MEAGHER-CONDON.—Sentenced to death for the Manchester Rescues, but reprieved and sent to Penal Servitude—-Returned to America.

CAPTAIN MURPHY.—Returned to America. Died a few years since.

THE SCHOOLMASTER.—A Member of Parliament.

JOHN RYAN.—Dead—God rest his soul.

CHAPTER VIII.

A DIGRESSION—T. D. SULLIVAN—A NATIONAL ANTHEM
—THE EMERALD MINSTRELS—" THE SPIRIT OF
THE NATION."

IF it were for nothing else, it will be sufficient fame
for T. D. Sullivan for all time that he is the author
of " God Save Ireland." He had no idea himself,
as he used to tell me, that the anthem would have
been taken up so instantaneously and enthusiastically as it was.

A National Anthem can never be made to order.
It must grow spontaneously out of some stirring
incident of the hour. Never in those days were
our people so deeply moved as by the Manchester
Martyrdom. There is no grander episode in all
Irish history. The song of " God Save Ireland,"
embodying the cry raised by Edward O'Meagher
Condon, and taken up by his doomed companions
in the dock, so expressed the feelings of all hearts
that it was at once accepted by Irishmen the world
over as the National Anthem.

I sympathise with the ground taken up by our
friends of the Gaelic League that a National Anthem
should be in the national tongue. That objection
has to some extent been met by the very fine trans-
lation of " God Save Ireland " into Gaelic by Daniel

Lynch. This appeared in one of my publications, and is the version now frequently sung at Irish patriotic gatherings.

With regard to the objection that the air—" Tramp, tramp, the boys are marching"—to which T. D. wrote the song is of American origin, I was under the impression that Patrick Sarsfield Gilmore, the famous Irish-American bandmaster, was the composer of it, and that, therefore, we could claim the air of " God Save Ireland " as being Irish as well as the words. To place the matter beyond doubt, Gilmore himself being dead, I wrote to his daughter, Mary Sarsfield Gilmore, a distinguished poetical contributor to the " Irish World," to ascertain the facts. I got from her a most interesting reply, in which she said, " I am more than sorry to disappoint you by my answer, but my father was *not* the composer of the air you mention."

I have heard it suggested that McCann's famous war song " O'Donnell Aboo !" should be adopted as our National Anthem instead of " God Save Ireland," and I have heard of it being given as a *finale* at Gaelic League concerts.

Without doubt it is a fine song, and the air to which it is generally sung is a noble one. A distinguished Irish poet tells me he is of opinion that " what will be universally taken up as the Irish National Anthem has never yet been written." My friend may be right, but let us see what claim "O'Donnell Aboo !"—song or air—has upon us for adoption as our National Anthem.

To do this I must go back in my narrative to the

time when I made the acquaintance of Mr. Michael
Joseph McCann, its author. This was a few years
before " God Save Ireland " was written, and over
twenty years after " O'Donnell Aboo ! " appeared
in the " Nation."

A party of young Irishmen from Liverpool
engaged the Rotunda, Dublin, for a week. They
called themselves the " Emerald Minstrels," and
gave an entertainment—" Terence's Fireside ; or
the Irish Peasant at Home." I was one of the
minstrels. The entertainment consisted of Irish
national songs and harmonized choruses, inter-
spersed with stories such as might be told around
an Irish fireside. There was a sketch at the finish,
winding up with a jig.

At my suggestion, one of the pieces in our programme was " O'Donnell Aboo ! " which first
appeared in the " Nation " of January 28th, 1843,
under the title of " The Clan-Connell War Song—
A.D. 1597," the air to which it was to be sung
being given as " Roderigh Vich Alpine dhu." This
was the name of the boat song commencing " Hail
to the Chief," from Sir Walter Scott's poem of
" The Lady of the Lake." This was published in
1810, and set to music for three voices soon afterwards by Count Joseph Mazzinghi, a distinguished
composer of Italian extraction, born in London.

As " Roderigh Vich Alpine " was the air given
by Mr. McCann himself as that to which his song
was to be sung, we, of course, used Mazzinghi's
music in our entertainment.

One night—I think it was our first—at the close

of our entertainment in Dublin, a gentleman came
behind to see us. It was Mr. McCann. He was
pleased, he said, we were singing his song, but
would like us to use an air to which it was being
sung in Ireland, and which *he had put to it himself.*
He also told us he had made some alterations in
the *words* of the song, and was good enough to
write into my " Spirit of the Nation " the changes
he had made. This copy is the original folio edition,
with music, published in 1845. It was presented
to me by the members of St. Nicholas's Boys'
Guild, Liverpool. I have that book still, and value
it all the more as containing the handwriting of
the distinguished poet. (I should say, however,
that most of my friends do not consider the alterations in the song to be improvements.)

The measure and style of " O'Donnell Aboo ! "
were evidently imitated from Sir Walter Scott's
boat song. Besides this strong resemblance, there
is the fact that Mr. McCann gave as the air to which
his song was to be sung, " Roderigh Vich Alpine,"
part of the burden of Sir Walter's song.

But not only is there a resemblance in the words
and general style, but in the music. Indeed, it
seems to me that most of the fine air of " O'Donnell
Aboo ! " as it is now sung is based on Mazzinghi's
music—either that for the first, second, or bass
voice, or upon the concerted part for the three
voices at the end of each verse.

Another fact is worthy of mention. Since meeting
Mr. McCann I have often noticed in Irish papers
that when the air, as adapted by him, was played

at national gatherings, it was often given by the
name of Scott's song and Mazzinghi's composition.
And when Mr. Parnell was in the height of his
popularity and attended demonstrations in Ireland,
the air used to be played as being applicable to
the Irish leader, and given in some papers as " Hail
to the Chief," while others described the same air
as " O'Donnell Aboo ! "

But if we cannot claim as an original Irish air
McCann's song as it is now sung, the same critical
examination which brings out its resemblance to
Mazzinghi's music, also shows that the Italian
composer most probably got his inspiration from
the music of the Irish or Scottish Gaels, as being
most suitable for his theme. So that, perhaps, we
may take the same pride in the present air as our
island mother might in some of her children who
had been on the *shaughraun* for a time, but had
again come back to the " old sod."

It may be that even before the era of Irish in-
dependence some inspired poet may write, to some
old or new Irish melody, a song which, by its tran-
scendent merits, may spring at once into the first
place. But until that happens, or till " we've
made our isle a nation free and grand " I think we
may very well rest content with " God Save Ireland."

It has been suggested to me that it might form
an interesting portion of these recollections if I
were to give some account of how we came to start
the " Emerald Minstrels," and what we did while
that company was in existence. I may say without
hesitation that we got our inspiration from the

teaching of Young Ireland and the "Spirit of the Nation." We called our entertainment "Terence's Fireside ; or The Irish Peasant at Home."

We had most of us been boys in the old Copperas Hill school, then in the Young Men's Guild connected with the church, and some of us members of the choir. At the Guild meetings on Sunday nights, the chaplain, Father Nugent, an Irishman, but, like most of ourselves, born out of his own country, used to delight in teaching us elocution, and encouraging us to write essays, besides putting other means of culture in our way.

After a time he founded an educational establishment, the Catholic Institute, where, when he left Copperas Hill, many of us followed him and joined the evening classes. About this good priest I shall have more to say in this narrative, and, though he was no politician, I don't think any man ever did so much to elevate the condition of the Irish people of his native town, and make them both respectable —in the best sense—and respected, as Father Nugent.

We started the "Emerald Minstrels" at a time when there was a lull in Irish politics ; our objects being the cultivation of Irish music, poetry and the drama ; Irish literature generally, Irish pastimes and customs ; and, above all, Irish Nationality.

Father Nugent's training from the time we were young boys had been invaluable. We numbered ten, the most brilliant member of our body, and the one who did most in organising our entertainments, being John Francis McArdle. Besides our main objects, already stated, we considered we were doing good work by elevating the tastes of our people, who had, through sheer good nature, so long tolerated an objectionable class of so-called Irish songs, as well as the still more objectionable "Stage Irishman."

Some items from the programme will give an idea of our entertainment. We opened with a prologue, originally written by myself, but re-cast and very much improved by John McArdle. I may say that we two often did a considerable amount of journalistic work in that way in after years. I can just remember a little of the prologue. These were the opening lines :—

> Sons of green Erin, we greet you this night!
> And you, too, her daughters—how welcome the sight!
> We come here before you, a minstrel band,
> To carol the lays of our native land.

There was one particularly daring couplet in it, the contribution of John McArdle :—

> In your own Irish way give us one hearty cheer,
> Just to show us at once that you welcome us here.

Had mine been the task to speak these lines, I must inevitably have failed to get the required response, but in the mouth of the regular reciter they never once missed fire. This was Mr. Barry Aylmer. He afterwards adopted the stage as a profession, and became recognised as a very fine actor, chiefly in Irish parts, as might be expected. He also travelled with a very successful entertainment of his own, and it is but a short time since he informed me that he spoke our identical " Emerald Minstrel " prologue in New York and other cities in America, adapting it, of course, to the circumstances of the occasion. I found that during the many years which had elapsed since I had previously seen him until I met him again quite recently he had been a great traveller, not only in this country and America, but also in South Africa and Australia.

We had a number of harmonized choruses, including several of Moore's melodies, Banim's " Soggarth Aroon," " Native Music," by Lover ; McCann's " O'Donnell Aboo ! " and others. " Killarney," words by Falconer, music by Balfe, was sung by James McArdle, who had a fine tenor voice. Richard Campbell was our principal humorous singer. He used chiefly to give selections from Lover's songs, and one song written for him by John McArdle, " Pat Delany's Christenin'."

John had an instinctive grasp of stage effect. A hint of the possibilities of an idea was enough for him. On my return from the Curragh I told him of how I had heard the militia men and soldiers singing the " Shan Van Vocht " on the road. He decided that this should be our *finale*, the climax of the first part of our minstrel entertainment.

We had a drop scene representing the Lower Lake of Killarney. When it was raised it disclosed the interior of the living room of a comfortable Irish homestead, with the large projecting open chimney, the turf fire on the hearth, and the usual pious and patriotic pictures proper to such an interior—Terence's Fireside.

Ours was a very self-contained company. Each had some special line as singer, musician, elocutionist, story teller or dancer.

John Clarke was our chief actor. He excelled in " character parts," and, when well " made up " as an old man made a capital " Terence " in the first part of the entertainment, besides giving a fine rendering of Lefanu's " Shemus O'Brien " between the parts.

In the miscellaneous part there was a rattling Irish jig by Joseph Ward and Barry Aylmer. The latter, being of somewhat slight figure and a good-looking youth, made a bouncing Irish colleen. These two made a point of studying from nature, not only in their dancing, but in their acting and singing, so that their performances were always true to life, without an atom of exaggeration. They were always received with great enthusiasm, particularly by the old people, who seemed transported back, as by the touch of a magic wand, to the scenes of their youth.

We finished the evening with a sketch, written by John McArdle, called " Phil Foley's Frolics " —he was fond of alliteration. Noticing that Joseph Ward had made a special study of the comfortable old Irish *vanithee*, and had many of her quaint and humorous sayings, he added to the characters a special part for him—" Mrs. Casey,"—to which he did full justice. Indeed, so incessant was the laughter that followed each sally, that he and Barry Aylmer, who was the Phil Foley, sometimes found it difficult to get the words of the dialogue in between.   We had another sketch, " Pat Houlahan's Ghost," which used to go very well.

The first part of the entertainment, showing old Terence in the chimney corner and the others singing songs and telling stories, almost necessitated our sitting around in a semi-circular formation. This gave us much the appearance of a nigger troupe.   To depart from this somewhat, we occasion- ally introduced a trifling plot.   We made it that one of the sons of the house entered while the family were engaged in their usual avocations, having unexpectedly returned from America.   Then came the affectionate family greeting, and the bringing in of the friends and neighbours, who formed a group sitting around the turf fire, making a merry night of it.

The services of the " Emerald Minstrels " were in great demand, and were always cheerfully given for Catholic, National and charitable objects.

While our own people mostly furnished our audiences, our entertainment was appreciated by the general public.   The best proof of this was that Mr. Calderwood, Secretary of the Concert Hall, Lord Nelson Street, gave us several engagements for the " Saturday Evening Concerts," in which, from time to time, Samuel Lover, Henry Russell, The English Glee and Madrigal Union, and other well-known popular entertainers, appeared.   Mr. Calderwood told us he was well pleased to have in the town a company like ours, upon whom he could always rely for a successful entertainment.

CHAPTER IX.

A FENIAN CONFERENCE AT PARIS—THE REVOLVERS
FOR THE MANCHESTER RESCUE — MICHAEL
DAVITT SENT TO PENAL SERVITUDE.

I HAVE referred to Michael Breslin in speaking of
his brother John. Michael was not suspected of
any complicity with the revolutionary movement
until after the rising on the 5th of March, 1867,
when he found it prudent to get out of the country.

He was, as the saying is, " on his keeping," and
stayed with me at my father's house in Liverpool
for a short time, until he found a favourable opportunity of getting away to America. This was by
no means an easy task, as all the ports were closely
watched, and as, like his brother John, he was a
fine handsome man, of splendid physique, and
well known, of course, to the Irish police, it required
all his caution successfully to run the gauntlet ;
but this eventually he did.

The next I heard from him was that he was coming
to Paris to a conference between the representatives
of the two parties of American Fenians—what were
known as the Stephens and Roberts wings. Michael
Breslin was sent as a representative of the Stephens
party. There were prominent members of the

I.R.B. in this country, also friends of Breslin, who were anxious that the two parties should join. I wrote to him on their behalf, asking him to work towards that end. For greater safety the letters for Breslin were sent under cover through my cousin, Father Bernard O'Loughlin, Superior of the Passionist Fathers in Paris. He, of course, knew nothing of the nature of the communications he was handing to Breslin, who did his best to bring about the desired unity ; but his action was repudiated by his principals in America.

He came over to England, and had a narrow escape from falling into the hands of the police. When William Hogan was arrested in Birmingham, charged with supplying the arms used in the Manchester Rescue, Michael Breslin was in the house at the time. Questioned by the police, he described himself as a traveller in the tea trade for Mr. James Lysaght Finigan, of Liverpool. As he had his proper credentials (samples, etc., from James Finigan, who, anticipating an emergency of this kind, had given them for this express purpose), he was allowed by the police to go on his way.

James Lysaght Finigan was a good type of the Liverpool-born Irishman, educated by the Christian Brothers. With other members of his family he was at the time engaged in the tea trade ; but he was of an adventurous disposition, and afterwards served in the French Foreign Legion in the Franco-Prussian War. Later still he became a member of the Irish Party in the House of Commons.

In connection with Breslin's narrow escape, the

sequel, as regards our friend Hogan, is worth relating. Those who ever met William Hogan will agree with me that a more warm-hearted and enthusiastic Irishman never lived. He was a good-looking man, of imposing presence—a director of an Insurance Company, for which he was also the resident manager in Birmingham. Living in that town, he was of great assistance to the various agents entrusted with the task of procuring arms for the revolutionary movement. It speaks much for his sagacity that a man of his impulsive and generous temperament should so long have escaped arrest in connection with such hazardous undertakings. Hogan, however, like Shemus O'Brien, " was taken at last."

Some of the revolvers brought from Birmingham by Daniel Darragh, which had been used at the Hyde Road action, had been picked up from the ground afterwards by the police. It was for supplying these that Hogan was put upon his trial. The maker of the revolvers was brought from Birmingham, and put in the witness box. He swore that a revolver produced was one of his own make, which he had sold to the prisoner. Thus, fortunately for Hogan, the whole case against him turned on this point—not a very strong one, as it was obviously possible for the Crown witness to be mistaken.

Hogan's counsel produced a similar revolver, and asked the witness if he could identify it as his manufacture ? The witness unhesitatingly did so. The counsel, when his turn came, called another witness

—a decent-looking man of the artizan class. The barrister handed him the revolver.

" Do you recognise it ? " he asked.

" I do—I made it myself."

The Court was astonished. The prosecuting counsel asked :—

" How do you know it is yours ? "

" By certain marks on it," the man replied, and these he proceeded to describe. As the description was found to be correct, and as the other witness, who had sworn that *he* had made the weapon, had not described any such marks, the case against Hogan broke down, and he was acquitted.

A few days afterwards he called on me, and explained how the thing had happened. When he was arrested, his friends in Birmingham, having still on hand some of the revolvers he had purchased, had an exact copy of one of them made by a gunsmith whom they could trust, with instructions to put his own private marks upon it, which he could afterwards identify. It was this weapon that had deceived the witness for the prosecution to such an extent that he wrongly swore to it as being his own manufacture.

Daniel Darragh, who was also put upon his trial for supplying the weapons for the Manchester Rescue, was not so fortunate as his friend Hogan, for he was convicted. He was sent into penal servitude on April 15th, 1869, but, being in delicate health, did not long survive, for he died in Portland Prison on June 28th of the following year. William Hogan, as the fulfilment of a sacred duty, brought the body of his friend home to Ireland, to be buried among his own kith and kin, in the Catholic cemetery of Ballycastle, Co. Antrim ; and Edward O'Meagher Condon, when recently visiting this country, considered it a no less sacred duty to visit the grave.

It will be seen that William Hogan, with all his acuteness, had a very narrow escape from falling into the hands of the law and suffering its penalties. Still, it has been my experience, that men like him, who have stood their ground, following their usual legitimate occupations, were. always less liable to be molested than what might be termed birds of passage, such as Rickard Burke, Arthur Forrester, or Michael Davitt.

Such, I consider, was the case of my friend, John Barry, when he was a resident in Newcastle-on-Tyne, in connection with. an incident which he related to me a short time since. Some arms were addressed to him " to be called for," under the name of " Kershaw," a well-known north-country name, not at all likely to be borne by an Irishman. By some means the police got wind of the nature of the consignment, and the arms were held at the station, waiting for Mr. Kershaw to claim them. But it was a case of plot and counterplot ; and when John was actually on the way to the railway station, he was warned in time by a railway employé, an Irish Protestant member of the I.R.B., and did not finish his journey. As " Kershaw " did not turn up, the case of arms was sent off to London to be produced at a trial then impending.

John Barry was at that time a commercial
traveller, and, strangely enough, on one of his trips,
he found himself in the same railway carriage with
two detectives who were in charge of the arms on
their way to the metropolis.   John, as everybody
acquainted with him knows, " has the music on the
tip of his tongue ; " the racy accent acquired in his
childhood in his native Wexford.   But he can put
it off when the occasion requires it ; and the two
police officers were quite charmed with the social
qualities of the genial commercial " gent " who was
their fellow-traveller, never suspecting him to be
an Irishman.   They chatted together in the most
agreeable manner, making no secret of their mission
to London, and letting drop a few facts which
proved useful to the counsel for the defence in the
subsequent trial.   Reaching London, they asked
the commercial " gent " to spend a social evening
with them and some of the witnesses in the case,
which had some connection with the arms intended
for "Mr. Kershaw."   He could not do so, he said, as
he had a previous engagement—which happened
to be with Arthur Forrester and some witnesses on
the other side.   But, he continued, he would be
glad to see them on the following day.   Where
could he see them ?   At Scotland Yard ; and at
Scotland Yard, accordingly, he met them, where
they showed him, as an evidence of the desperate
characters they had to deal with—his own case of
arms !

They told him of the pleasant evening he had
missed, the only drawback being, they said, that

one of the witnesses, named Corydon, got drunk and was very troublesome.

This reminds me of another case, in connection with which I, at the time, fully expected to be arrested. The reader can form his own conclusion, but my impression was, and is, that I owed my safety to a gentleman I shall now introduce. Detective Superintendent Laurence Kehoe, of Liverpool, was a very decent man in his way. He was by no means of the type of John Boyle O'Reilly or the Breslins, who have shown that in the British army and in the police force there have been men, mostly compelled by adverse circumstances, who have for a time worn the blue, or green, or scarlet coat of Britain without changing the Irish heart beneath.

No; Larry (as he was generally called) was nothing of the kind. Still, I believe he faithfully did his duty according to his lights, in the service in which he was engaged. He was a conscientious Catholic, and a son of his is a most respected priest in the diocese of Liverpool. He was a kind-hearted, charitable man, always ready to do a good turn, particularly for a fellow-countryman. If an Irish policeman called his attention to some poor waif of an Irish child who had lost its parents; or was in evil surroundings—having parents worse than none, or in danger of losing its faith—Laurence Kehoe would take the matter in hand. He would not always go through the formality of bringing the case of such child under the notice of the managers of one or other of the Catholic orphanages. When I was Secretary of Father Nugent's Boys' Refuge, he brought one of these waifs to the Brother Director, and claimed admittance for him. The place was full, the Brother said—it could not be done. Without another word Kehoe left the child on the doorstep, and simply saying, " Good-night," left Brother Tertullian sorely perplexed, but with no alternative but to take the child in.

Now, Laurence Kehoe must have known that I was a notorious suspect—for it was his duty to know—but we were good friends, never, however, talking politics by any possible chance. I cannot, of course, state for certain how it was, but the reader, from what I am going to describe, may possibly come to the conclusion that Detective Superintendent Kehoe may have shut both eyes and ears in my particular case.

To Rickard Burke was entrusted the critical and dangerous task of buying and distributing arms for the revolutionary movement. *Exit* Rickard Burke, in the usual way, through the prison gate. *Enter* Arthur Forrester, who, in due course, found his way also—though but for a short time—within prison walls. Then, following in quick succession, came Michael Davitt, engaged in the same task as Burke and Forrester.

Forrester was a young man of great eloquence, and, like his mother and sister, a poet. Mrs. Ellen Forrester's " Widow's Message to her Son " is, I think, one of the finest and most heart-stirring poems we possess. I have often listened with pleasure to Arthur Forrester, when he used to come to address the " boys " in Liverpool. On one of those occasions

Michael Davitt was with him, a modest, unassuming young man, with but little to say, although he was to make afterwards a more important figure in the world than his friend. Forrester was a young fellow full of pluck, and made a desperate resistance when, a boy, he was first arrested in Dublin.

One night, just before Christmas, 1869, he left fifty revolvers with me. Early next morning I read in a daily paper that he had been arrested the previous night in a Temperance Hotel where he had been staying. There were no arms found upon him or among his belongings. He had left them with me ;—indeed, as I read the account of his arrest, they were still in my possession. You may depend upon it I quickly got them into safer hands than my own. Some compromising documents were found in Forrester's possession, including a certain letter with which Michael Davitt's name was connected. This same letter was brought forward in evidence some years afterwards, in the famous "*Times* Forgeries Commission," with a view to showing that the Irish leaders had incited to murder. As I expected, I was not long without a visit from Laurence Kehoe's lieutenants. Horn and Cousens, detective officers, called upon me to make enquiries about the revolvers which, they said, "Arthur had left with me." I need scarcely say they gained nothing by their visitation. I fully expected that the matter would not end here, and that I was likely to find myself in the dock along with Forrester.

The same evening I had a visit from my sister-

in-law, Miss Naughton.   She had a friend, a Miss
Cameron, who was sister to the wife of Lawrence
Kehoe.   Miss Cameron lived in the house of the
Detective Surperintendent, along with her sister,
Mrs. Kehoe.   In the middle of the previous night—
Miss Cameron told Miss Naughton—her room being
on the same landing as Kehoe's—she heard him
called, and a man's voice saying :—

"We've taken Forrester.   Shall we go to
Denvir ? "   There was a pause ; then Kehoe said,
" No," adding some words to the effect that he did
not think that I was implicated.

I dare say, after the manner of some pious people
I know, he had persuaded himself that such was the
case.   After he had worked out his full term in
Purgatory (for he is dead many years, God rest his
soul !), I don't think St. Peter can have kept the
Heavenly gates closed on Larry Kehoe for whatever
he said about me that night.   Nay, let us hope
that it was even put down to his credit.

Forrester's explanation, when he was arrested,
as to his employment was that he was a hawker.
He had his licence, all quite regular, to show.   Under
this he could sell his revolvers.   There was nothing
illegal in that, unless a connection were established
with the revolutionary movement.

This, it appeared, they were not able to make
out ; but he was kept in custody, evidently with
a view to gain time to establish such a connection.
In fact, his case was the same as Davitt's, who took
up the work of procuring and distributing arms, after
Forrester had become too well known to the police

in connection with it. Davitt, too, had a hawker's licence ; and, at first, there was really no evidence to connect him with the Fenian movement. The farce was gone through of bringing Corydon to identify him—not a very difficult task in the case of a one-armed man—though this was the first time Corydon had ever seen Davitt.

The evident explanation of Forrester being kept in custody, and remanded, as he was, from day to day, without being charged with any offence, was that a similar connection might be established, to prove which a little perjury would not stand in the way.

Michael Davitt, who had not yet come under the notice of the police, came to me, along with Arthur Forrester's mother, on hearing of the arrest. They had tea with us, and, I need scarcely say, were warmly welcomed in our little family circle, those in the house who were but small children then being in after years proud to remember that they had had such noble characters under their roof.

Mrs. Ellen Forrester was a homely, sweet-looking, little North of Ireland woman. She was a native of the County Monaghan, and, at this time, about forty years of age. Her maiden name was Magennis. Her father was a schoolmaster, which would, no doubt, account for her literary tastes. Songs and poems of hers appeared in the "Nation" and "Dundalk Democrat." She was quite young when she came to England, and settled first in Liverpool, and then in Manchester. She married Michael Forrester, a stonemason, and had five children. It was quite evident there was a poetic strain in the Magennis blood, for two of her daughters, and her son Arthur, inherited the gift, which her brother Bernard also possessed. She produced "Simple Strains" and (in conjunction with her son Arthur) "Songs of the Rising Nation," and other poems. She was a frequent contributor to the English press, her work being much appreciated.

Arthur Forrester, whose release we were trying to effect, was, at this time, only nineteen years old, though he looked much older. Besides the poetic strain which he inherited from his mother, he must also have had that fiery and unconquerable spirit which displayed itself in the determined resistance he made against the police who came to arrest him in 1867, in Dublin, where he had found his way for the projected rising. He was a young Revolutionist truly—being then only seventeen. He was not long kept in prison that time, there being no evidence to connect him with Fenianism, nor, indeed, was there now, when he had fallen into the hands of the police in Liverpool, though they were doing their best to manufacture some.

His warlike proclivities seem to have been ever uppermost, as will be seen later, where we find him joining the French " Foreign Legion " during the Franco-Prussian War. Besides the "Songs of the Rising Nation" in connection with his mother, he produced "An Irish Crazy Quilt," prose and verse, and was a frequent contributor to the "Irish People" and other papers over the signature of " Angus " and " William Tell."

It is too bad of me to be keeping poor Arthur in durance vile while I am going into these particulars ; but I want to show what kind of people these Forresters were, and what the rebelly Ulster Magennis strain in their blood let them into.

Together, Davitt and I called upon several Liverpool Irishmen to get bail for Forrester. There was no difficulty—we could easily get the necessary security ; but, name after name, good, substantial bail, was refused by the police on one pretence or another.

Ultimately, on Christmas Eve, when the prisoner was again brought before the stipendiary magistrate, Mr. Raffles, a very just and high-minded man, Dr. Commins, barrister, acting for Forrester, claimed that no charge, but a mere matter of suspicion, being forthcoming against him, the bail offered should be accepted. The magistrate agreed to accept two sureties of £100 each, " to keep the peace for one year," and Arthur Forrester was released.

It is interesting to know that while one of the bails was William Russell, a patriotic Irishman, having an extensive business, the other was Arthur Doran, a wholesale newsagent. He was a decent Irishman, of Liverpool birth, who took no part in politics. He had been induced to go bail by one of the greatest scoundrels Ireland ever produced— Richard Pigott, Doran being an agent for Pigott's papers. the "Irishman" and "Flag of Ireland." Let this one good act, at all events, be put down to Pigott's credit.

To return to Forrester. After such a close shave

as he had in Liverpool, with the eyes of the police now upon him, his occupation was gone, and Michael Davitt took up the work. I am afraid that Davitt's visit to Liverpool on this occasion brought him under the notice of the police, and may probably have led to his arrest a few months afterwards.

This took place on May 14th, 1870, at Paddington Station, London, with him being arrested also John Wilson, a Birmingham gunsmith. Davitt had £150 in his possession, and Wilson had fifty revolvers, it being suggested that the gunsmith was about to deliver the weapons in exchange for the money. So far—Davitt having a hawker's licence, as in the case of Forrester—this would have been perfectly legitimate. What was wanted by the authorities was evidence to show a connection with the Fenian conspiracy. They really had no such evidence, but as Davitt was a marked man, and as it was necessary to have him removed, Corydon was brought to identify him, and, of course, had no difficulty, when a number of men were brought into the corridor, in picking out the one-armed man from among them.

At the trial Corydon swore, among other things, that Davitt took part in the Chester raid. Now, Michael himself told me afterwards that Corydon had never seen him before he " identified " him in prison ; and that though he really was at Chester, Corydon could not have known this. Michael Davitt and John Wilson were convicted of treason-felony. As showing the man's noble character, it should not be forgotten that the Irishman made an earnest appeal for the Englishman, declaring that Wilson knew nothing of the object for which the weapons were wanted, and asking that whatever sentence was to be passed on the gunsmith might be added to his own. This was quite worthy of Davitt's chivalrous and unselfish nature, and I can well imagine his tall and commanding figure in the dock, with his strongly marked features and dark, bright eyes—while utterly defiant of what the law might do to himself—making this appeal for the man who stood beside him. Davitt was, on July 11th, 1870, sentenced to fifteen years, and Wilson to seven years penal servitude.

Michael Davitt will appear in these pages as the founder of another organisation, the results of which seem likely to make the Irish people more the real possessors of their own soil than they have ever been since the Norman invasion.

About this time I had started a printing and publishing business in Liverpool, and commenced to realise what I had long projected as a useful work for Ireland. This was the issue of my " Irish Library," consisting chiefly of penny books of biographies, stories, songs, and stirring episodes of Irish history.

In their production and afterwards, when I continued the issue of these booklets in London, I had valuable assistance from various friends, including Rev. Father Ambrose, Rev. Father O'Laverty, Michael Davitt, Daniel Crilly, T. D. Sullivan, Timothy McSweeney, Hugh Heinrick, William J. Ryan, Francis Fahy, William P. Ryan, Alfred

Perceval Graves, Michael O'Mahony, John J.
Sheehan, Thomas Boyd, Thomas Flannery, John
Hand, James Lysaght Finigan, and other well-
known writers on Irish subjects.   Some of the
penny books were from my own pen, in addition to
which I wrote "The Brandons," a story of Irish life
in England, and other books, of which my most
ambitious work was "The Irish in Britain."

CHAPTER X.

RESCUE OF THE MILITARY FENIANS.

BEFORE concluding the section of my Recollections connected with Fenianism, I must re-introduce John Breslin, the rescuer of James Stephens.

Though the episode I am about to describe took place some six years after the commencement of the constitutional Home Rule agitation, I think it well, as it was connected with Fenianism, for the sake of compactness, to introduce it here.

My excuse for introducing it as part of *my* recollections will be seen further on.

It will be remembered that John Breslin, when a warder in Richmond Prison, was the man who actually opened the door of James Stephens's cell, and, with the aid of Byrne, another warder, helped the Head Centre over the prison wall, and left him in charge of John Ryan and other friends outside.

It was no wonder, then, that, when a similar perilous and even more arduous undertaking was projected, John Breslin should be the man chosen as the chief instrument to carry it out.

This was the rescue of six military Fenians from Freemantle, in Western Australia, which was ultimately effected on Easter Monday, 17th April, 1876.

The enterprise was projected in America, among

its most active promoters being John Devoy.
Associated with him were John Boyle O'Reilly
(himself an escaped Fenian convict) and Captain
Hathaway, City Marshal of New Bedford.   An
American barque, of 202 tons, the *Catalpa*, was
bought, and converted into a whaler, but was
intended to be used in carrying off the convicts.
She was ready for sea in March, 1875. It was more
than a year before she took the prisoners away
from Australia, and a further four months before
she reached New York with the rescued men. The
ship was taken out by Captain S. Anthony, an
American, to whom was confided the object of the
mission.   The only Irishman on board among the
crew was Denis Duggan, the carpenter, a sterling
Nationalist, to whom also was made known the
mission on which they were bound.

As John Breslin was now in America, obviously
he was the man of all others to entrust with the
command of the daring project of carrying off the
prisoners.   Happily he was available for the work,
and entered into it heartily.   He sent me the
narrative of the rescue himself—through his brother
Michael—on his return to America, after having
successfully accomplished his mission.

He and Captain Desmond sailed from San Fran-
cisco on the 13th of September, 1875, and reached
Freemantle on 16th of November. They were not
long in opening up communications with the
prisoners, so as to be in readiness for the arrival of
the *Catalpa*.   In the meantime two more men joined
the expedition—John King, who brought a supply

of money from New Zealand, which was most useful, and Thomas Brennan, who arrived at the last moment, just as the *Catalpa* appeared off the coast, and had got into communication with Breslin.

Everything being arranged, it was determined to carry off the following prisoners—Martin Harrington, Thomas Darragh, James Wilson, Martin Joseph Hogan, Robert Cranston, and Thomas Henry Hassett. They were at work outside the prison walls, or at other employment equally accessible, when they were taken away in two traps from Freemantle, about nine o'clock in the morning of the 17th of April, 1876. By the time the news of their flight, and of the direction they had taken, was known in the prison, the party had reached Rockingham, and were on the sea in the whale-boat which was to take them to the *Catalpa*.

The gunboat *Conflict*, which was usually stationed at King George's Sound, was telegraphed for by the authorities, but it was found that the wires had been cut the previous night, and by the time they were repaired the vessel had gone on a cruise.

After some hours' delay, the governor engaged the passenger steamer *Georgette* to go in pursuit. It was nine o'clock that evening before she left Freemantle. The police boat was cruising about also, looking for the whaler and her boat. The *Georgette* came up with the *Catalpa* about 8 o'clock on the following (Tuesday) morning. A demand to go on board and search the barque was refused. As it was found there was a short supply aboard the *Georgette*, she returned to Freemantle to coal, leaving the police boat to watch the *Catalpa*, and to look out for the whale boat containing the rescued men, which had not yet appeared, although, as it turned out, not far off at the time. The boat had been vainly searching for the *Catalpa* all night, and had only now discovered her. The party in the boat had actually seen the *Georgette* overhauling the *Catalpa*, and had yet themselves remained undiscovered. In order to keep clear of falling into the hands of the *Georgette* they stood off from the ship, and it was about half-past two o'clock in the afternoon before the boat containing the rescued men approached the *Catalpa* again. They then saw the police boat making for the ship at about the same distance from her on the land side as the whale boat was to the seaward. The men scrambled aboard just as the police boat was coming up on the other side.

Breslin says :—" As soon as my feet struck the deck over the quarter rail, Mr. Smith, the first mate, called out to me, ' What shall I do now, Mr. Collins (this was the name Breslin went by) ; what shall I do ? ' I replied, ' Hoist the flag, and stand out to sea ; ' and never was a manœuvre executed in a more prompt and seamanlike manner."

The police boat did not attempt to board the vessel, but made its way back to Freemantle to report. There the *Georgette* had been fully coaled and provisioned, and had taken aboard, in addition to the pensioners and police, a twelve-pounder field-piece. At 11 o'clock the same night (Tuesday) she steamed out once more. At daylight on the following morning she came came up with the *Catalpa* again, and fired a round shot across her bows. After some parleying, Captain Anthony being prompted by Breslin, the *Georgette* hailed that if the *Catalpa* did not heave to, the masts would be blown out of her.

" Tell them," said Breslin to the captain, " that's the American flag ; you are on the high seas ; and if he fires on the ship, he fires on the American flag."

Preparations were made to give the armed party on the *Georgette* a warm reception should they attempt to board the whaler. But the pursuers had a wholesome fear of coming into conflict with a vessel sailing under the Stars and Stripes, and, after some further parleying, left the *Catalpa* to pursue her homeward voyage unmolested.

I was fortunate enough to get the account of *both* expeditions—for there were two—for the rescue of the military Fenians in each case direct from the man having the command.

I have already given John Breslin's account, which, it will, perhaps, be remembered I published at the time as a number of my penny " Irish Library."

I had the pleasure of hearing John Walsh, who had charge of the expedition from this country, relating the part he and his friend bore in assisting the Irish-American rescuers. He told the story at a very select gathering in Liverpool, at which I was present. On the 13th of January, he said, two men, of whom he was one, left this country with money and clothing to carry out the rescue. They landed on the 28th of February at King

George's Sound, whence a sailing vessel took them to Freemantle.

They soon got into communication with the two men who had come from America, and had been on the spot since November, 1875—John Breslin and J. Desmond, the latter of whom worked as a coach-builder at Perth. Walsh and his friend offered their co-operation to the men from America in any capacity, and arrangements were made accordingly. They lent the Americans arms, and they cut the telegraph wires from Perth to King George's Sound, where a man-of-war was stationed.

It will be seen from Breslin's account that this was why the man-of-war was not available to deal with the *Catalpa* ; for when the telegraphic communication was restored, it was found that the gunboat *Conflict* had left on a cruise.

Walsh and his friend were on the ground on the morning when the prisoners started to escape, and if a fight took place, they were to fight and fly with their friends. If there was no fight, they were to remain behind. If the *Catalpa* failed, they were to fly to the bush, with the exception of some who were to remain behind to succour those in the bush.

John Walsh described how, when the rescued men were being driven in two traps from Freemantle to Rockingham, to be taken on the whale-boat to the *Catalpa*, which was lying off the coast awaiting them, he and his friend started with them, and remained behind to stop pursuit. He also described the attempt to recapture the escaped men, as told in Breslin's narrative, and how the attempt failed

My own connection with this incident was that the funds, or some part of them, for John Walsh's expedition passed through my hands between their collection and their distribution.

On Monday, August 21st, 1876, while we were holding the Annual Convention of the Home Rule Confederation of Great Britain, in the Rotunda, Dublin, the joyful news reached us that the *Catalpa,* having on board the rescued men and their rescuers, had safely reached New York. The news was received with the wildest enthusiasm. The terrible strain of the last four months had passed, and we were relieved from the constant dread that, after the gallant rescue, the men might again fall into the hands of the enemy.

A few more words about the Breslins before finishing this chapter. Michael went back to America after his escape from arrest in Birmingham. I have corresponded with him from time to time ever since. A letter of mine to Michael, written after he finally went to America, came back to me in a very curious manner. A gentleman came into my place of business in Liverpool one day, and presented to me, as an introduction, a letter I had sent to my friend about a month previously. I was somewhat suspicious about this. I told him there was nothing to show that my letter had ever been in Breslin's hands at all. The gentleman agreed that I was right, and said he would merely ask to be allowed to leave his luggage for a short time.

I got a careful watch kept on his movements in Liverpool, but nothing more suspicious was reported than that he had been seen to enter a Catholic church, where he had gone to Confession.

My friend William Hogan was in my place when my messenger returned, and when he heard this, exclaimed, in his usual impetuous style—" He's a spy !"

The deduction might not seem obvious, but, doubtless Hogan had in his mind one or two of the worst cases of the anti-Fenian informers, who made a parade of great piety a cloak for their treachery.

The gentleman returned and reclaimed his luggage, and I heard nothing further of him for about a month afterwards, when I had a letter from Michael Breslin, saying that his friend, whom I had treated with such suspicion and such scant hospitality, was Mr. John B. Holland, the famous submarine inventor. He was, I believe, in this country in connection with his invention.

It may be asked, after all, what did Fenianism do for Ireland ? To those who ask the question I would answer that no honest effort for liberty has ever been made in vain. If Fenianism did nothing else, it kept alive the tradition and the spirit of freedom among Irishmen, and handed them on to the next generation. In so far as the men who took part in it were unselfish, were whole-souled lovers of their country, and prepared to risk life and liberty for their country's sake—and I think with pride of the thousands of such men I knew or knew of— then the whole Irish race was ennobled and lifted up from the mire of serfdom.

But it did more than merely make martyrs. Its strength, its spontaneity, and the devotion of its adherents were such that they undoubtedly awakened not merely some alarm, but also some sense of justice in England.

Gladstone admitted that what first prompted him to set in motion the movement for the dis-establishment of the Irish Church was " the intensity of Fenianism." But the result did not end there. For many an Englishman was moved to the belief that surely there must be something wrong with a system which provoked such a movement, some-thing not wholly bad about a cause for which men went with calm, proud confidence to the felon's cell or the scaffold. And, even to-day, England—with all her secret service facilities—does not know one-half of the danger from which she escaped ; nor can I repeat much of what I myself could say of Fenianism in England.

There are men who have made large fortunes in business ; there are eminent men in many of the professions, whose former connection with Fenianism is unsuspected, who, at the time, if the call had been made upon them, would cheerfully have thrown aside their careers and taken their places in the ranks.

Once again " a soul came into Ireland," and men were capable then of high enterprises which to-day seem to belong to another age.

Even for myself, I have many times marvelled how light-heartedly in those days I took the risks of conspiracy—how little it troubled me that there were dozens of men who bore my liberty, and perhaps my life, in their hands. But I never doubted them—and I was right !

CHAPTER XI.

THE HOME RULE MOVEMENT.

It now becomes my business to record the formation and progress of another organisation—one which appealed to me precisely on the same grounds as Fenianism, namely, first, that it was based on justice ; and, secondly, that it was practicable.

This was the constitutional movement for what was known as Home Rule. My principles have never altered, and I can see nothing inconsistent in my adapting myself to changed conditions. I and those who thought like me were driven into Fenianism because it seemed likely to achieve success, and what was call " constitutional agitation " seemed hopeless. Now the position was reversed. On the one hand Fenianism had collapsed, and on the other there seemed a prospect, partly owing to the change wrought by Fenianism, that a constitutional movement might succeed.

This constitutional movement had been going on for some six years previous to the rescue of the military Fenians, having been inaugurated at a meeting in the Bilton Hotel, Dublin, on the 19th May, 1870, five days after the arrest of Michael Davitt, and his disappearance for a season from the stage of Irish history.

In the pages which are to follow I shall have occasion to introduce some of those who took part in that first Home Rule gathering in Dublin. It was a hopeful beginning, as there were assembled men who were of various creeds and politics— Catholics, Protestants, Fenian sympathisers, Repealers, Liberals, and Tories—but all of whom had in view the happiness and prosperity of their common country. There they established the " Home Government Association of Ireland," the first resolution passed being :—

This Association is formed for the purpose of attaining for Ireland the right of self-government by means of a National Parliament.

The fact was that the " intensity of Fenianism " had forced thinking men of every shade of opinion to realise that government of Ireland by outsiders was an abject failure. Even Englishmen themselves began to realise that they were engaged in an impossible task, or, at all events, one in which they were quite at sea. A humorous story is attributed to Mr. T. W. Russell on this point. It is that a certain Englishman, who was appointed Chief Secretary for Ireland, went to an English official of experience in Dublin, and said—

" You know what I mean to do first of all, is to get at the facts—the facts—then I shall be on sure ground."

" My dear sir," said the official wearily, " there are no facts in Ireland."

The conclusion was not a surprising one for a man

who had for years been in touch with the " official
sources" of information.

While all honour is due to the men who initiated
the new movement, the names of those who carried
on the constitutional struggle during the years that
preceded this date should not be forgotten.   Of all
the men I ever came into contact with in the course
of my experience of constitutional agitation, I think
the Sullivans—especially T. D. and A. M.—deserve
the most credit, for they kept the flag flying in the
columns of the "Nation" and in other ways during
all the gloomy years that followed after Charles
Gavan Duffy left the country in despair.   I am
always proud to have reckoned these two men among
my dearest and most trusted friends.

Another great admirer of the Sullivans was
Alfred Crilly, brother to Daniel Crilly, and father
of Frederick Lucas Crilly, the present respected
and able General Secretary of the United Irish
League of Great Britain.   Alfred was one of the
most brilliant Irishmen we ever had in Liverpool,
and no man did better service for the cause in that
city during his lifetime.   It was always a pleasure
to me to work in harness with him, as I did on many
public occasions ; for whatever was the national
organisation going on in Ireland for the time being
we two—Alfred Crilly and myself—always did our
best to have its counterpart in Liverpool.   Indeed it
became the case that for many years our people there
invariably looked to us to take the initiative in
every national movement.   Whenever A. M.
Sullivan came over to our demonstrations it did

not need our assurance to convince him that every pulsation of the national heart in Ireland was as warmly and as strongly felt on this side of the Channel as though we still formed part of our mother island. Indeed, the evidence of his own eyes, the enthusiasm he saw when he came amongst us, caused him to declare at a vast gathering in the Amphitheatre that he felt as if he were not out of Ireland at all, but on a piece cut from the " old sod " itself.

I felt proud when two young men of my training, John McArdle, who had been with me on the "Catholic Times" ; and afterwards Daniel Crilly, on the " United Irishman,'' were appointed to the literary staff of the "Nation," for which they were well fitted, seeing that, with their brilliant gifts, they had, from their earliest days, been imbued with the doctrines of that newspaper.

T. D., like his brother, often came to Liverpool, and used to be equally delighted with the enthusiastic receptions he got from his fellow-countrymen. On one occasion he said to me he was at a loss how to show his appreciation. I told him how to do this. " Write us a song," I said. He did so ; and with that admirable tact which is so characteristic of him he chose for his theme—" Erin's Sons in England," a song which, written to the air of " The Shamrock," has, for many years, been sung at our Irish festivals in Great Britain. As a personal favour to myself he wrote it for one of the penny books of my " Irish Library.

I need make no apology for introducing T. D.

Sullivan's song here. It will be seen that he sings
our praise with no uncertain note ; and, in return,
I may say on their behalf that he had no warmer
admirers than among the Irish of England.

ERIN'S SONS IN ENGLAND.

Air—" Oh, the Shamrock."

ON every shore, the wide world o'er,
 The newest and the oldest,
The sons are found of Erin's ground
 Among the best and boldest.
But soul and will are turning still
 To Ireland o'er the ocean,
And well I know where aye they glow
 With most intense devotion.

CHORUS :—Over here in England,
   Up and down through England,
    Fond and true and fearless too,
   Are Erin's sons in England.

Where toil is hard, in mill and yard,
 Their hands are strong to bear it ;
Where genius bright would wing its flight,
 The mind is theirs to dare it ;
But high or low, in joy or woe,
 With any fate before them,
The sweetest bliss they know, is this—
 To aid the land that bore them.

CHORUS :—Over here in England, &c.

By many a sign from Thames to Tyne,
 From Holyhead to Dover,
The eye may trace the deathless race
 Our gallant land sent over.
Midst beech and oak, midst flame and smoke.
 Up springs the cross-tipped steeple
That, far and wide, tells where abide
 The faithful Irish people.

CHORUS :—Over here in England, &c.

And this I say—on any day
　That help of theirs is needed,
Dear Ireland's call will never fall
　On their true hearts unheeded
They'll plainly show to friend and foe.
　If e'er the need arises
Her arm is long, and stout and strong,
　To work some strange surprises !

CHORUS :—Over here in England, &c.

It will be remembered that T. D. never allowed himself to be bound by conventionalities. There was always a refreshing thoroughness and heartiness in what he did. For instance, when he was Lord Mayor of Dublin, he on one occasion " opened " a public bath by stripping and swimming round it—the Town Clerk and other officials following his example.

I have mentioned the good work done in Liverpool by Father Nugent, and that I had the pleasure of co-operating with him in some of his undertakings. At the time of the Home Rule movement connected with the name of Isaac Butt, and for some years previously, I had been brought into still closer contact with him, first, as secretary of his refuge for destitute and homeless boys, and then as manager and acting editor of the "Northern Press and Catholic Times," after that paper had come into his hands. I also assisted him in the temperance movement which he started in Liverpool.

When Father Nugent asked me to take charge of the "Catholic Times," I entered upon the work literally single-handed, like some of the editors we read of a generation or so ago in the Western States of America ; for, when he left me for a nine months' tour in the States, I constituted in my own person the whole staff. We afterwards had some able men on the paper. Among these was John McArdle, who left us, as I have said, to join the "Nation." He became later a well-known dramatic author, his chief works being burlesques and panto-mimes. We also had James Lysaght Finigan, of whom I speak elsewhere.

While Father Nugent was in America, we used to get great help from a fine old Jesuit priest and good Irish Nationalist, Father James McSwiney, then of St. Francis Xavier's, Liverpool. He was never happier than when smoking his short pipe by the fire in our inner office. With his help we created a much admired feature in the "Catholic Times" in our "Answers to Correspondents." With the view of drawing on real enquiries, he used to concoct and then answer questions on points of doctrine, etc. Some people were astonished at the profound knowledge—and others at what they considered "the impudence"—displayed by Jack McArdle and John Denvir in answering any theological posers that might be put to us, never dreaming we had behind us one of the ablest theologians of the Jesuit order.

When Father Nugent took the paper in hands, the readers had such confidence in it that, from being merely a local paper, we were able before long to make it a leading Catholic organ for the whole country.

The reverend father was chaplain of the Liverpool

Borough jail.   He was respected by all classes,
Protestant as well as Catholic, not only for what
he did for the unfortunate creatures who came under
his ministrations, but as a public-spirited citizen
and benefactor of the town.   It would be wrong
if I did not pay a high tribute to the splendid service
done by him in Liverpool towards elevating the
condition of our own people.   I would be ungrateful,
too, if I failed to recognise the great educational
work he did in giving opportunities for culture to
many Liverpool Irishmen, myself among the number,
which afterwards aided their advancement in the
battle of life.   That is why I never regretted that I
gave Father Nugent, when conducting the "Catholic
Times" for him, three of the best years of my life.
I never regretted my experiences in connection
with that paper, particularly in the reporting
department, for they were often very pleasant ones.
Among these was my having been introduced to the
great Archbishop MacHale, when I went to St.
Nicholas's to report his sermon.

I have many vivid remembrances arising out
of my connection with the "Catholic Times."

It was during the time I was in charge of it that
we started the Irish national organisation on this
side of the Channel—the Home Rule Confederation
of Great Britain, formed at our first annual convention held in Manchester, at which I was elected
as the first General Secretary of the organisation.

I was at the same time secretary of the Liverpool
Catholic Club, and in that capacity I assisted in
entertaining the Canadian Papal Zouaves when

passing through Liverpool on their way home, after
their gallant but unsuccessful struggle to uphold
the power of the Pope against the revolutionaries.

In the same way it became my duty as secretary
of the club to organise the Catholic vote in Liverpool on the occasion of the first School Board
Election.   The Irish and those of Irish extraction
in Liverpool being reckoned as about one-third of
the population, the Catholic body is correspondingly
numerous.   We surprised both friend and foe in
the results.   There were fifteen members to be
elected, and we asked our people to give three votes
for each of our five candidates.   They were not only
elected, but the votes actually given for them—on
the cumulative principle—could have elected eight
out of the fifteen members of the Board.

Father Nugent, though immensely popular with
all classes, was not, I think, a *persona grata*, any
more than myself, with Canon Fisher, the Vicar-
General of the diocese, who was very anti-Irish, and,
so far as he could, prevented anyone connected with
the "Catholic Times" coming into personal contact
with Bishop Goss, who was a typical Englishman
of the best kind.   The bishop had a blunt, hitting-out-
from-the-shoulder style of speaking in his sermons
that compelled attention.   But you could hardly
call them sermons at all ; they were rather powerful
discourses upon social topics, which, from a newspaper point of view, made splendid "copy."
Accordingly, during the year before his death, I
followed him all over the diocese to get his sermon
for each week's paper.   There is no doubt that Dr.

Goss's sermons helped materially to put a backbone into the "Catholic Times" and greatly to increase its circulation.

In one of the rural districts the bishop was giving an illustration of the meaning of " Tradition," and very much to my embarrassment, I found him taking me for his text. He said—" So far as I know, there were no newspapers in Our Lord's days ; there was nobody taking down *His* sermons, as there is to-day taking mine ; so that *His* teaching had to be by word of mouth, and much of it has come down to us as Tradition."

In the interest of the paper, Father Nugent was anxious that I should be introduced to the Bishop. But he knew, as well as I did, that the difficulty in the way of this was what might be called the Grand Vizier, Canon Fisher. " You should push forward, Denvir," Father Nugent would say, " after Mass is over, and ask to see the Bishop." Over and over again I did so, but was always met at the vestry door by Canon Fisher, with his suave smile. " Well, Mr. Denvir, what can I do for you ? " " I would like to see his lordship," I would say. No use. The Canon would say—" No, no ; don't trouble the Bishop; I can give you all the information you want ; " and so it went on, and I was baffled in my attempts.

I ought to say that, though Canon Fisher was able to keep me from coming into personal contact with Bishop Goss, Father Nugent was too strong for him in the end ; for, eventually, we got into communication with the Bishop regularly every week on the subject of his sermons. Each Monday as soon as my copy was set up, we sent him a proof, which he would read and correct and return. But his "corrections" often included the addition of altogether new matter, which made the sermon the more interesting and valuable to us. Indeed, on several occasions, we used his new .matter, with slight alterations, as leaders. The very week he died we had one of these leaders in type, and it appeared in the same issue which announced his death.

When Cardinal Vaughan became Bishop of Salford, Father Nugent succeeded in getting his support and influence for the "Catholic Times," a most valuable thing for us, seeing that Manchester, though with a smaller Catholic population than Liverpool, was of more importance from a publishing point of view, as from that city can be more readily reached a number of large manufacturing towns, of which it is the centre. Again it was—" Denvir, you must see the Bishop." But this time there was no difficulty, as an appointment had been made for me. Accordingly, by arrangement, I reached Manchester one morning between six and seven o'clock, that being the most convenient time for him that Bishop Vaughan could give me, and together we discussed the best means of forwarding the interests of the paper in the diocese of Salford. I found him, besides being a man of courtly presence, as we all know, most broad-minded and genial, and keenly alive to the influence which a good newspaper would have upon his people.

Whenever I see the "Catholic Times," I feel gratified at its very existence, as a proof that my three years with Father Nugent were not altogether spent in vain. For when he placed its control in my hands on his departure for America, I found it with a very small circulation, and anything but a paying concern ; whereas, when I yielded up the trust into his hands, I had the satisfaction of handing over to him a substantial amount of cash in hand, a statement of assets and liabilities showing a satisfactory balance on the right side, and a paper with a largely increased and paying circulation.

For many years previous to his death, I did not come into contact with him. Indeed it was only the year before he died that I had the pleasure—and it was all the more a pleasure as we had differed strongly during previous years on some points—of meeting him at his house in Formby. This was before his last visit to America, where he contracted the illness which terminated in his death soon after his return to England.

CHAPTER XII.

THE FRANCO-PRUSSIAN WAR—AN IRISH AMBULANCE
CORPS—THE FRENCH FOREIGN LEGION.

WHEN the Franco-Prussian War broke out, the
sympathy of Ireland was naturally, for historic
reasons, on the side of France.   It was not surprising, then, that many young Irishmen who had
served in ·America, or in the ranks of the Papal
Volunteers, or had borne a share in the Fenian
movement, were anxious to show their sympathy
in a practical way, and at the same time to gratify
the national propensity for a fight

—in any good cause at all.

I happened to number among my friends some of
these young Irishmen, of whom I may mention
Captain Martin Kirwan, James Lysaght Finigan,
Edmond O'Donovan, Arthur Forrester, Frank
Byrne, and James O'Kelly.   There was a strong
feeling in Ireland to send a considerable body of
men to France, but the law stood in the way.   It
was evaded by the formation of an Ambulance
Corps, and for this generous subscriptions flowed
in, along with numerous applications from volunteers.   These were all medically examined, as if for
a regular army, and in this way as fine a body of

young men as ever left Ireland was picked from
those who had volunteered. The ambulance service
was equipped in the most perfect manner, and presented to the French nation. On arriving in France,
there were (as was, of course, intended) more men
than were required for the ambulance duties, and
these at once volunteered for service as soldiers.
They were formed into a company under the command of Captain Kirwan, one of the sergeants
being Frank Byrne, who was afterwards Kirwan's
colleague as an official of the Irish constitutional
organisation in Great Britain. The company might
have developed into a regiment, and even into a
brigade, had the movement started earlier to get
men over to France by various means. This could
have been done, notwithstanding the Foreign
Enlistment Act ; and towards the end of the war,
French agents were in this country providing for
the sending over of large numbers of men to France,
when the capitulation of Paris caused the collapse
of their arrangements.

The men of the Irish Ambulance Corps did their
work so well as to show that not only did Irishmen
make good soldiers. but that, possessing the
sympathetic Celtic nature, their services were highly
appreciated by the wounded who fell to their charge.
Captain Kirwan's company fought bravely, sus-
taining the credit of their country through the whole
campaign, and, under Bourbaki, were among those
who actually struck the last blow the Germans
received on French soil.

Arthur Forrester, who joined the French Foreign

Legion, was severely wounded in the foot.   After
the war he came into the office of the "Catholic Times,"
when I was manager and John McArdle editor of
that paper. We welcomed him, of course, not only
as an old friend and brother journalist, but as one
who had been fighting for France.

In his "Camp Fires of the Legion" written for my
"Irish Library," James Lysaght Finigan tells of
his adventures in the war. He found his way to
Lille, in the north of France, and, with several hundreds of other Irishmen became enrolled in the
ranks of the Foreign Legion. In Lieutenant Elliott
he was delighted to recognise Edmond O'Donovan,
who had figured so prominently in the Fenian
movement, and whose incarceration in Ireland and
exile in America were fresh in his memory. "The
Legion," Finigan says, "showed itself worthy of its
predecessors, the Irish Brigades of former days,
during the reverses that constantly befel the armies
of France." He gives graphic accounts of the
battles they were engaged in, and how, in the
defence of Orleans, he and a number of his comrades
were taken prisoners, among those being his friend
O'Donovan, who had been wounded by a piece of
shell.

The Foreign Legion must have borne the brunt of
the fighting. The fourth battalion was cut to
pieces at Woerth, Gravelotte, and Sedan ; the fifth
battalion was reduced from 3,000 to some 300 ;
the sixth battalion retook Orleans, was compelled
to abandon it, and covered itself with glory at Le
Mans and elsewhere ; and the seventh was interned

with Bourbaki in Switzerland until the end of the war.

Although I often heard from him afterwards, the last time I met Edmond O'Donovan, if I remember rightly, was in a North Lancashire town, in which John O'Connor Power had been lecturing the same night. I forget exactly who else of the " boys " were there—I think William Hogan was one—but there were some some choice spirits, and we made just such an Irish night of it as Finigan describes they had when he and O'Donovan fought in the Foreign Legion.

Edmond O'Donovan was the son of the famous Irish scholar and antiquary, John O'Donovan, the translator from the Gaelic—with O'Curry and Petrie—of that great Irish history, "The Annals of the Four Masters," and other manuscripts. The elder O'Donovan had made the acquaintance of Sir Thomas Larcom, when both were young men together on the staff of the Ordnance Survey. John O'Donovan appointed his friend Larcom to be guardian of his children in case of his death.

It was Larcom's duty, as an official of the Government, to hunt down the Fenians, both native and foreign, so that he had undertaken a serious and perplexing charge. For O'Donovan's elder sons were strong Nationalists and Fenians ; so that, on the death of his old friend, Larcom was like an old hen having charge of a brood of ducklings who could not be kept from the troubled waters of Fenianism. There is no doubt that Larcom's influence kept them from or saved them from a lot of trouble. The O'Donovans were an accomplished family, the one I knew best, besides Edmond, being Richard, who has held a responsible mercantile position for some years, and who furnished me with much valuable information about his father, when Thomas Flannery—one of our best Gaelic scholars—was writing a life of Dr. John O'Donovan for my " Irish Library " series.

Besides being thoroughly acquainted with several languages, Edmond O'Donovan had an excellent scientific training, which was brought into requisition in connection with the projected Fenian military movements in Ireland. While a thorough classical scholar, the poems he liked best were the songs of Thomas Davis and the Young Irelanders. He was slender of figure and had a handsome oval face. In speaking, whether in private or before an audience, he had an animated and expressive manner, with a good deal of gesture, such as a Frenchman or Italian would use. I have heard him singing songs like " Clare's Dragoons " with much fire and fervour, throwing his whole soul into it in a way I can never forget.

In 1877-1878 he was a special correspondent in the Russo-Turkish war with the Turkish army, and he sent home powerful and graphic accounts of every battle and siege.

His intimate knowledge of Arabic stood to him in these and in the Egyptian campaigns in which he afterwards took part. In 1879 he went through Russia to the shores of the Caspian Sea, travelled through the north of Persia and the adjacent territory of Khorassan, to the land of the Tekke Turcomans, and to Merv, thus penetrating the mysteries of Central Asia as no European traveller had ever done so perfectly before. In 1881 he returned to England, and published his book, " The Merv Oasis," and afterwards read a paper before the Royal Geographical Society on " Merv and its surroundings."

Finally, in 1883, he went as special correspondent to the Soudan, and there this brilliant Irishman perished with the whole of Hicks Pasha's army. No tidings ever came of how Edmond O'Donovan met his death, but those who knew him best feel that he must have yielded up his gallant spirit to its Creator with a courage and fortitude worthy of an Irishman.

In January, 1906, I had occasion to call upon his brother Richard in Liverpool, and asked if they had ever got any trace of Edmond. Nothing had been heard of how he had actually perished, but an authentic relic of him had fallen into the hands of a priest in the Soudan. This was a blood-stained garment, which was proved beyond doubt to have belonged to him.

I have mentioned another name in connection with the Franco-Prussian War—that of James O'Kelly. His career, like that of O'Donovan, had been stormy and adventurous. I had previously met him in connection with the Fenian movement.

He had been in the French army, and served in the campaign which was so disastrous to the Mexican Emperor Maximilian. His adventurous tempera-

ment led him again to join the French service during
the Franco-Prussian war.   He was employed on the
confidential mission of raising a force of Irishmen
for the war.   I have described the formation of the
company under Kirwan, which was the outcome of
the Ambulance Corps.   It will be seen, too, that
there were a considerable number of Irishmen in
the Foreign Legion.   But, after all, these did not
amount to a number sufficient to have much
appreciable result on the ultimate fortunes of the
war.   The French military authorities, knowing
what splendid fighting materials Irishmen would
make, commissioned O'Kelly to raise a large force.
For this purpose he made Liverpool his headquarters, and I was pleased to see him again when
he called upon me at the office of the " Catholic Times "
My sympathies were strongly with France, and I
gave him what assistance I could in furthering the
object of his mission.   At my suggestion, therefore,
he took up his abode at the hotel opposite our
office, at the corner of Moorfields and Dale Street.
A large number of volunteers were got from among
the advanced element in Liverpool and surrounding
towns, who wanted to learn the use of arms in real
warfare—their ultimate object I need not mention.
From other quarters in Ireland as well as England
there were volunteers for the French army.   I had
arranged through an emigration agent, Mr. Michael
Francis Duffy, a much respected and patriotic
Irishman of singular culture, for the charter of two
steamers to take the men to Havre ; but just then
Paris fell, after a long siege; the war ended, and the
Irish Legion project collapsed.

In 1872 James O'Kelly turned his attention to journalism as a profession. He got his first opening on the "New York Herald," partly through his thorough knowledge of the military profession, but still more by that singular tact that never failed him under the most trying circumstances.

Some years after, he called on me again in Liverpool, and I heard from him of some stirring incidents in his career. Amongst those were his perilous experiences in connection with the fighting in Cuba, from which he narrowly escaped with his life.

Since then he has entered Parliament. He was a staunch supporter from the first of Mr. Parnell. When the unfortunate "split" came, he took the side of the "Chief," but none is more pleased than he to be a member of the now re-united Irish Party.

In connection with the Franco-Prussian war I may be allowed to refer here to a non-combatant, who, with his brother priests, remained at their post during the terrible siege of Paris, ministering to the sick and dying. This was my cousin, Father Bernard O'Loughlin, Superior of the Passionist Order in Paris.

And yet, notwithstanding their noble services to humanity on this and other occasions, the Passionist Fathers have since been driven out of the country by the French Government. The announcement of the danger of this, when it was first threatened, caused consternation in the foreign Catholic colony of Paris, to whom the Passionist Fathers had endeared themselves by their labours on behalf of needy and stranded English-speaking people, and their devoted spiritual ministrations.

The Passionist mission in Paris was founded some forty years ago by Father Bernard, with his friend, Father Ignatius Spencer, also a Passionist, and uncle of the present Earl Spencer.

The Archbishop of Paris had invited the Passionists to establish a church in Paris, on account of the number of Irish, American, and English Catholics requiring religious ministrations, few of the French clergy being able to speak English. Father O'Loughlin first commenced his labours in the Church of St. Nicholas, in the Rue Saint Honoré, where be remained three years. After this a sum of 200,000 francs was subscribed, chiefly by Irish, American, and English residents, for the site and building of a church. Father Bernard was soon joined by several other members of the order sent from England, and there were always four or five Passionist Fathers attached as chaplains to the church. The following distinguished prelates have preached in this Church—Cardinal Manning, Cardinal Newman, Cardinal Richard, Archbishop Ireland, Archbishop Spalding, and Archbishop Passadière.

Mrs. Mackay was the most generous of the supporters of the order in Paris ; and, in 1903, when the fathers found themselves unable to pay the tax created by the French " Loi d'accroissement," she paid down the 20,000 francs required to save the church.

Their devotion in remaining faithful to their flock during the long and terrible siege of Paris in 1870 ought to have recommended them to the sympathies of all patriotic Frenchmen. The Passionists not only ministered to the spiritual but to the temporal wants of those coming under their charge. They visited the sick and poor, relieved the age in need, provided for orphans, and assisted stranded Irish and English governesses, irrespective of creed, who had come to Paris in search of situations. Those who suffered most from the withdrawal of the Passionists were the poor and afflicted.

The Cardinal Archbishop of Paris, the American Embassy, and the British Ambassador, addressed the French Government on their behalf, pointing out that the services of the Passionists were indispensable—but in vain. It is humiliating that the government of what is supposed to be a great Catholic nation like France should be appealed to in such a cause, fruitlessly, by the ambassador of non-Catholic England.

Father Bernard O'Loughlin's name in the world was John, after his father, my mother's brother, John O'Loughlin. The elder John was a brewer's traveller, and often came to our house in Liverpool, bringing his violin with him. He had a wide knowledge of old Irish airs, and to his accompaniment we had many a genuine Irish night, singing the stirring songs then appearing in the "Nation."

CHAPTER XIII.

THE HOME RULE CONFEDERATION OF GREAT BRITAIN.

In the previous chapter it will be seen that I have somewhat anticipated the course of events described in this narrative in order to give brief sketches of some of my friends who took part, in various capacities, in the Franco-Prussian war, and incidents arising out of it. I have also, for the sake of compactness, briefly touched on their subsequent careers.

I shall here now resume my recollections of the Home Rule movement from its inception in 1870.

From the first everything pointed to Isaac Butt as its leader. His splendid abilities, even when ranged against us in the celebrated debate in the Dublin Corporation with O'Connell, excited the admiration of his fellow-countrymen ; but now, when he had come over to the popular side, he was welcomed with acclamation, the more so that his genial and loveable nature was bound to win the hearts of a susceptible people like ours. Moreover, his joining the popular side was due to the impression made upon him by the Fenian leaders, so many of whom he defended in the trials from '67 onward ; and he has left on record a remarkable testimony to the purity of their principles and the nobility of their ideals.

He was lacking in certain qualities, the want of which in his character prevented him being such a strong leader as O'Connell or Parnell. But, all the same, while he led he gave splendid services— which can never be forgotten—to the cause.

As I have said, Alfred Crilly and I were generally expected to take the initiative in any new Irish movement in Liverpool. Accordingly, towards the end of 1871, we were asked to make a move in connection with the new organisation in Ireland. We formed a small committee, and invited Isaac Butt to our projected opening demonstration. He was not able to come to our first gathering, but we had many opportunities during the years that followed of making his acquaintance; and, personally, I received many kindnesses at his hands. With Alfred Crilly I was sent to Dublin by the Committee to find influential speakers for our public inaugural Liverpool demonstration, to be held on the 3rd of January, 1872, our association having been opened some months previously. We secured the services of Mr. A. M. Sullivan and Professor Galbraith of Trinity College.

When we returned to Liverpool it became our duty to find a chairman for our meeting worthy of the occasion. Mr. Charles Russell, who was first asked, suggested that we should get some one of more influence than himself. "Why not ask Dr. Commins?" he said.

Dr. Commins was a barrister on the same circuit as Charles Russell. We did ask him. He cheerfully consented, and from that hour he was for a long

time the leading figure in the struggle for Home
Rule in Great Britain, being for several years
President of the organisation.   There is no more
homely and unassuming man, ever accessible to
the humblest of his fellow-countrymen, than " the
Doctor," as his friends affectionately call him.

He had a brilliant university career, and was a
man of such wide attainments that I think there
was a general belief amongst Liverpool Irishmen
that he knew *everything*.   Accordingly, they used
frequently to go to him to settle some knotty point
beyond the ordinary conception, and they seldom
came away unsatisfied.

Dr. Commins is an accomplished poet, and was
for many years a contributor to the columns of the
"Nation" and the " United Irishman" (of Liverpool).   In 1876 he was elected as a Home Ruler to
represent Vauxhall Ward in the Liverpool Town
Council.   He has ever since been a member of that
body, being now an Alderman of the city.   In due
time he became a member of the Irish Parliamentary
Party, of which several other Liverpool Irishmen
have been members.

Liverpool was not alone in forming its Home
Rule Association ;   most of the large towns had
them in due course, but for some time there was no
bond of union between them.   This, however, was
formed in due time, the man to take the first step in
bringing us together being John Barry, then residing
in Manchester, and the chief man in our organisation
there.

John was, therefore, practically the founder of the

great organisation which, under its various names—
of the Home Rule Confederation of Great Britain.
Irish National Land League of Great Britain, Irish
National League of Great Britain, and United Irish
League of Great Britain—has been in existence since
1873, working in accordance with and taking the
name of whatever has been the recognised organisation for the time being in Ireland.

John Barry, who had borne an active share in
the struggle for self-government—irrespective of the
methods being constitutional or unconstitutional—
was a man of attractive personality and an indefatigable worker and organiser. He was the Secretary of the Manchester Home Rule Association,
and, seeing the want of some body in which the
various associations in Great Britain would be
represented, he, in the name and with the authority
of his branch, issued invitations to the associations
then known to exist to send delegates to a Convention
to be held in Manchester. To give importance to the
occasion, and the necessary authority, Isaac Butt
was invited to preside, and to attend a great demonstration in the Free Trade Hall, on the night of the
Convention, January 18th, 1873.

Although I bore an active part in the organising
of that first Home Rule Convention of Great Britain,
it is only a short time since, after a lapse of over
thirty years, that I heard from John Barry himself
the difficulty he had in securing the presence of the
Home Rule leader. It was a long time since we had
seen each other, but I found him the same cheery,
warm-hearted, generous, and patriotic John Barry

as ever. It was in the office of his firm in London
we met, and took advantage of the opportunity to
fight our battles over again ; and he reminded me
of the sort of inner circle of the I.R.B. to which he
and I, and others who have since been prominent
in Irish politics, belonged.

He was always, however, a practical patriot, and
would use every legitimate method to serve Ireland.
That was why he threw himself with such ardour
into the Home Rule movement.

He told me of how he went over to Dublin to
secure the promise of Isaac Butt to preside at the
projected Convention, and to attend the demonstration in the evening. He got the requisite promise,
and the announcement was made in all good faith in
Manchester. So far all looked promising ; but what
was his alarm to hear, within three days of the event,
that Isaac Butt's professional engagements would
prevent his being able to attend. Added to this
he had heard that Butt, who was of a somewhat
irresolute temperament, was being warned that he
was falling into the hands of a " Fenian gang."

Barry spent all the money he had in sending to
the Irish leader a telegram as earnest, hot, and
forcible as he was capable of, beseeching him to
come, and pointing out to him the serious consequences to the Cause in Great Britain of his failure
to do so. This telegraphic budget reached Butt in
Court ; and, as he turned over leaf after leaf of the
message, he said to a friend sitting alongside of
him—" This man's in earnest, at any rate," and
immediately wired back—" Will go, if alive."

Apart from the offensiveness of styling us a
" gang," those who had warned Butt of the hands
into which he was falling may not, probably, have
been far astray as regards some of those from whom
he had received the invitation ; seeing that when
the organisation for Great Britain was duly formed,
John Barry, John Ryan, John Walsh, and myself
were elected on the Executive ; but, at all events,
Isaac Butt turned up.

Some twenty Home Rule Associations responded
to the invitation by sending delegates to the
Convention. There is a remarkable contrast between
this, the first of these Conventions, and those held
every year since ; for, at some of those, several
hundreds of branches have been represented—
showing the growth of the organisation since 1873.

At this Manchester Convention, at which Mr.
Butt presided, it was resolved to form a central body
from the existing local associations, to be called the
Home Rule Confederation of Great Britain.   Isaac
Butt himself was elected the first President.   I was
elected the first General Secretary, and it became
my duty to find out the existing associations which
had not sent delegates to Manchester, and to invite
them, as well as those who had been represented
at the present gathering, to a supplementary
convention.   It was decided to hold this in
Birmingham, to complete the arrangements made
in Manchester for the future working of the organisation.

On the night of the Manchester Convention
Mr. Butt was the chief speaker at the public

demonstration. Mr. John Ferguson, of Glasgow, was our Chairman. He was a sterling Ulster Protestant Nationalist. Many used to think he was a Scot. Indeed, I thought at one time myself he must be of Scottish extraction at all events, there being, I thought, more Scottish Fergusons than Irish. Speaking to him on the subject, I was reminded by him of the Irish king, Fergus, the founder of the Scottish monarchy; and he claimed to be of genuine Irish descent.

He often used to call on me when I was conducting the "Catholic Times." At that time he was travelling for his firm of Cameron & Ferguson, who published a good many popular works on Irish subjects. We were both pleased to hear of the initiative John Barry had taken towards the formation of the Irish organisation of Great Britain. If I remember rightly, John Ferguson was in Liverpool at the time, and we went to Manchester together to attend this our first Annual Convention.

After the Manchester Convention, I found there were considerably more Home Rule Associations in existence than had been represented at our first gathering. As a consequence we had a much larger and more representative attendance at our adjourned Convention in Birmingham. Mr. Butt presided in the morning and Mr. A. M. Sullivan in the afternoon.

The Chairman at the public demonstration at night was Father Sherlock, one of the finest specimens of the good old "soggarth aroon" type it has ever been my privilege to meet. Several years afterwards, when I was organiser for the League in

the Birmingham district, I was right glad to have the
opportunity of renewing my acquaintance with
him. The very contact with Father John Sherlock
was elevating and inspiring, so transparent were
the simplicity and purity of his life. Here was a
saint, I thought, if ever there was one on earth.

In my experience I have generally found that the
men who have taken the lead in most places have
been professional men rather than traders. This
was true of Birmingham as well as elsewhere. There
were no men who did better service than Hugh
Heinrick, an able journalist (who afterwards became
editor of the "United Irishman," the organ of our
Confederation), and Professor Bertram Windle. I
was glad to see in the newspapers the announcement
of such a genuine Irishman as Dr. Windle being
appointed President of the University College, Cork.

Professor Windle is an honour to his new position,
and is as devoted to the cause of creed and country
as he was when one of the Professors of the Queen's
University, Birmingham.

During the years when I was organiser for the
League in Birmingham, I became intimately acquainted with him. I found him not only a man
of great learning, but an earnest Catholic and devoted
Irish Nationalist. No man in our organisation did
better service, and he was always ready to go at a
moment's notice to speak or lecture wherever
required.

As a further illustration of what I have said about
the aid given to the cause by professional men, I
ought to mention Dr. James Mullin, of Cardiff. He

was a leading and active man in his district when I travelled in South Wales as an organiser. His talent as a poet has made him well known in Wales, and his accounts of travels in many lands have found many admiring readers. His heart is as warm as his brain is active, which is saying much.

CHAPTER XIV.

BIGGAR AND PARNELL—THE " UNITED IRISHMAN "—
THE O'CONNELL CENTENARY.

THE General Election of 1874 was remarkable as the first since the Union which had clearly and distinctly returned a majority of Irish members of Parliament as Home Rulers. Previously most of them had been returned as Liberals or Tories. It is memorable in my eyes, as it was the occasion when two of my personal friends, Alexander Martin Sullivan and Joseph Gillis Biggar, first entered Parliament. It was in the year after he was elected that Mr. Biggar made his *debut* as an " obstructionist."

Charles Stewart Parnell having been, in the spring of 1875, elected as successor in the representation of Meath to " honest John Martin," it was not long before the famous " Biggar and Parnell " combination, which was destined to revolutionize the whole system of Parliamentary procedure, was created.

Feeling the necessity for a newspaper representing the views of the Home Rule Confederation and chronicling its work from week to week, the Executive promoted the formation of a limited liability company for the purpose, and the outcome was the issue of the " United Irishman," the first number of which appeared on June 4th, 1875. I was appointed manager, and was also the publisher, the paper being produced at my place of business, 68 Byrom Street, Liverpool. The following were the Directors—Andrew Commins, LL.D., Chairman ; and John Barry, Joseph Gillis Biggar, M.P., John Ferguson, Richard Mangan, Bernard MacAnulty, and Peter McKinley. William John Oliver was Honorary Secretary, with Hugh Heinrick as Editor at the commencement, and Daniel Crilly afterwards.

The newspaper was fortunate in its Honorary Secretary, for William John Oliver was one of the most enthusiastic workers we ever had in the Home Rule movement. He was at this time engaged in commerce in Liverpool, having previously been an officer in the Royal Navy. He was ever willing to be " the man in the gap " in case of an emergency, and that was how he became for a time the Honorary General Secretary of the Home Rule Confederation. He was always a cheery and, at the same time, an eminently practical man. He took a leading part in our local elections in Liverpool from the time we began to fight them on Home Rule principles—when the necessity arose, as I have elsewhere explained, to have public men who were not afraid to identify themselves with the national cause.

Hugh Heinrick, our editor, was a brilliant writer, who had, for several years, been a strenuous worker in the Home Rule cause. He was a frequent contributor of poetry to the " Nation " and other national journals, generally over the signature of " Hugh Mac Erin." He was born in the County Wexford in 1831. Before taking up the editorship of the " United

Irishman " he was for many years resident in Birmingham, where he was a schoolmaster. He died in 1887.

Daniel Crilly, one of the most active and eloquent advocates of the Irish cause in Liverpool, succeeded him—this being his maiden effort in journalism. He was afterwards on the staff of the "Nation," and also did good service while a member of the Irish Parliamentary Party.

Among other contributors to the "United Irishman" were Isaac Butt, Dr. Commins, Frank Hugh O'Donnell, Michael Clarke, Captain Kirwan, and Frank Byrne. Our poetry was a strong point with us—Dr. Commins, Frank Fox, John Hand, Patrick Clarke, Heber MacMahon, and Miss Bessie Murphy being among the contributors.

When the "United Irishman" was started, the offices of the Home Rule Confederation, which had previously been in Manchester, were for convenience removed to my place of business. As the executive meetings and the meetings of the newspaper directors were held there, I frequently had the pleasure of meeting under my own roof Irishmen who either then were or afterwards became prominent members of the Irish Parliamentary Party, including Isaac Butt, Charles Stewart Parnell, and Joseph Biggar.

Mr. Biggar and I were always great friends. He had the reputation of being close-fisted and penurious ; but that this was not so I knew from many circumstances, though it is quite true he would not allow himself to be defrauded of a penny.

He became a Catholic in his later days. Though such

of us as were of the household of the faith welcomed
him into the fold, his conversion did not increase his
value in our eyes—indeed, from a political point of
view, he was of more service to the cause as an Irish
Protestant, there being too few of them in our ranks.
He had a fresh, pleasant, shrewd-looking face, and
spoke with a decided northern accent, which had
somewhat of a metallic ring. Some of his brother
Members of Parliament thought his " obstruction "
methods highly ungentlemanly, but he believed in
fighting England with her own weapons. If good
Irish measures were not allowed to pass, he would
throw every obstacle in the way of English measures
being carried. The tempest of rage that assailed
him in the " House " only added to his popularity
outside. Not only was he an immense favourite
amongst Irishmen, but with democratic Englishmen
also ; and at great mass meetings of English miners
and agricultural labourers he could always get
resolutions carried by the honest, hard-handed sons
of toil in favour of the restoration of Ireland's
rights.

Biggar used to get many letters approving of the
attitude he and Parnell had taken up in Parliament.
One in particular, from a warm admirer, he used to
show to his friends with great glee. It was a song
in the old " Come-all-ye " style. A few lines I can
remember sang in words of high commendation of—

——Joseph Biggar,
That man of rigour,
Whose form and figure
Do foes appal !

My place being the head-quarters of the Confederation at this time, the fact of my being known
to be generally on the spot made me a kind of
" man in the gap," to fill up engagements likely to
fall through for want of a speaker. In this way I
was often rushed off to distant parts of the country
at the shortest notice.

The most important Irish event in 1875 was the
celebration of the O'Connell Centenary in Dublin,
on Friday, August 6th. Our Confederation was
well represented in the processions, there being, as
might be expected from its proximity, a large
contingent from Liverpool. So great was the rush
to cross the Channel for the celebration that we
chartered several of the fine steamers of the City of
Dublin Company, and kept them for several days
fully employed in crossing and recrossing.

The pity of it was that there should be two processions—the magnificent display organised by the
official Centenary Committee and the procession got
up by the Amnesty Association.

The speeches of Messrs. Butt, Sullivan, and
Power on the platform erected in what was then
Sackville Street, when the outdoor display broke
up, explained why the Amnesty Committee and
their friends considered that a protest was necessary
and justifiable—hence the second procession. The
chief objections to the action of the official committee
were that, while all honour was to be paid to the
memory of O'Connell as the Liberator of his Catholic
fellow-countrymen, his services as the champion of
the political freedom of the Irish people were being

kept in the background.   Also—and that was why
the Amnesty Association for the release of political
prisoners took the initiative in the protest against
the action of the Centenary Committee—because,
on a great national occasion like this, the very
existence of the martyrs for freedom, who were
suffering in English prisons, appeared to be forgotten.   Such forgetfulness was considered at the
least highly inappropriate.

There was much indignation, too, that Lord
O'Hagan should have been chosen to speak the
panegyric on O'Connell, seeing that he had actually
sentenced some of those very prisoners.

The Irish organisation in Great Britain sym-
pathised with these views, and the various
branches sending contingents showed their feelings
by throwing in their part with the Amnesty Association.

The contingent from Great Britain was, on the
proposition of Mr. Patrick Egan, given the place
of honour in front of the amnesty procession which,
on the morning of the Centenary celebration, the
6th of August, 1875, started from Beresford Place,
near the Custom House. The banners of the three
Liverpool branches were a picturesque feature in
the procession, as also was the Sarsfield Band,
a body of fine young Liverpool Irishmen who
headed our contingent.

CHAPTER XV.

HOME RULE IN LOCAL ELECTIONS—PARNELL SUCCEEDS
BUTT AS PRESIDENT OF THE IRISH ORGANISATION
IN GREAT BRITAIN.

IT was at the Liverpool Municipal Elections of
1875 that we first introduced the question of Home
Rule into local politics. When we were holding
our inaugural meeting to establish the Home Rule
organisation in the town, we could not get any of
our Irish public men to take the chair. The reason
was that these had not been elected as Irishmen
but as Liberals. As a matter of fact, we had in
Dr. Commins a man immensely superior to any of
them. But we thought that men who had been
elected to public positions mainly by Irish votes
should not refuse to identify themselves with the
national movement, and to help it by whatever
influence they possessed. We therefore decided to
make some public men. In Scotland and Vauxhall
Wards we had a clear majority, but though the
Irish vote in these wards was expected for Liberal
candidates, who were not Irish or Catholic, in no
other ward could a Catholic or Irishman be elected.
We, therefore, commenced to make a change by
putting forward for Scotland Ward one of our own
men, Lawrence Connolly, as a Home Ruler, and

elected him *as such*. He afterwards sat in the Imperial Parliament for an Irish constituency. His election was followed in succeeding years by that of other Home Rulers, so that there was soon a considerable Nationalist Party in the City Council, and no lack of public men to do the honours for the Irishmen of Liverpool when any distinguished fellow-countryman came amongst them. Their civic utility was very great.

Though I have been over twenty years out of Liverpool, I have never lost sight of what has been going on there, and I am pleased to find that the younger generation—men whom we, the elders, have borne some share in training—have improved upon our work, and that there are now considerably more aldermen and city councillors than in our time.

That they are doing good work I am well satisfied, and nothing gives me greater pleasure than to read from time to time in the papers such items as a recent one—the presentation of a congratulatory address from the local branches of the United Irish League to Councillor Thomas Burke on the occasion of his being made a magistrate of the city of Liverpool. I am somewhat proud of Tom Burke. I remember having charge of some election that was going on, and his coming to me, a very small boy, from Blundell Street, to offer his services. I put him in harness at once, and he has been at work in the Cause ever since, and it is with pleasure that I recognise the fact that he is a good type of numerous Irishmen who were either born in Liverpool or spent most of their lives in that city.

There was a dear old *Soggarth* at St. Joseph's who did good service for us in our first municipal election in Scotland Ward. He had, previous to this, been a fellow priest with my uncle, Father Bernard O'Loughlin, in the Isle of Man. As Father Peter McGrath was a good Irish scholar, he was soon able to make himself understood by such of the Manx people as still retained their native speech, its basis being, like the language spoken in the Scottish Highlands, practically—making allowance for provincialisms—the Gaelic spoken in Ireland. This was a great help to him and his brother priest in disarming prejudice.

Before I met Father McGrath in Liverpool I had heard from my uncle of his delightful and saintly character. He was a ministering angel among our people in his district, which was one of the poorest in Liverpool. His charity was unbounded. Going on a sick call and being at the end of his monetary resources—for let his friends give him ever so much he would never leave himself a penny—he had been known to give away his own underclothing, and even to carry away his bed-clothes to relieve some case of abject poverty.

He was a thorough Nationalist, and was delighted when we first raised the banner of Home Rule in Scotland Ward and made honest Lawrence Connolly our standard bearer. As part of the Ward was in his district, he was by far the best canvasser we had. Day by day he used to call on me to hear of the progress we were making. With the active

personal help and the prayers of a saintly man like
Father McGrath how could we lose ?

The return of a Home Ruler at an English
municipal election was the forerunner of a still
greater victory won in the same Scotland Ward,
which as a Division of the Parliamentary Borough
of Liverpool returned to Parliament some ten years
afterwards the only Irish Home Ruler who, *as such*,
sits for a British constituency—Mr. T. P. O'Connor.

At the Annual Convention of the Home Rule
Confederation, held in the Rotunda, Dublin, August
21st, 1876, Dr. Commins in the chair, a vote of
confidence in Mr. Butt was passed. At the same
time what was known as the " Obstruction " policy
was endorsed, though Mr. Butt had given its chief
exponents, Biggar and Parnell, no countenance.
It was also resolved to remove the headquarters
of the Confederation from Liverpool to London.

Although, out of respect for his distinguished
services, Mr. Butt was allowed to remain as the
nominal leader up to the time of his death, it is
quite evident that our people favoured the more
active policy of the younger men.

At a banquet given on the night of this Convention
in the Ancient Concert Room, Mr. Butt, as chairman,
gave the toast of " The Queen, Lords and Commons
of Ireland." It will be seen elsewhere that I have
always objected to join in this toast on the ground
that it implies an acceptance of the existing condition of government in Ireland. Finding it on
the list, I remained away, but I am afraid my friends,
who knew my views, were scandalized at seeing in

the newspaper report my name given as having been present. How it occurred was through the reporter, desiring, no doubt, to save himself the trouble of making out a new list, giving the names of those who had been present at the Convention as having attended the banquet. I had a somewhat similar experience at a Newcastle-on-Tyne Convention— sixteen years later. The Newcastle men, in the interval between the Convention and the banquet, asked my opinion about the toast list. I gave them a sketch of what I thought a good one, but said, " Don't have the Queen." They said they wouldn't, and I went to the banquet. I was surprised to hear the chairman giving " The Queen, Lords and Commons of Ireland." There was nothing for me to do but walk out.

In Mr. Parnell Mr. Biggar found a colleague after his own heart in working the " Obstruction " policy. From the time when I made the acquaintance of Parnell, when he came amongst us, a shy-looking young man, under the wing of Isaac Butt, we were drawn towards each other—he because he looked upon me, from my life-long experience of them, as an authority upon our people in this country, and I because I was impressed by the terrible earnestness that I soon recognised underlying the young man's apparently impassive and unemotional exterior. I was one of the first he came in contact with in this country, and I believe he unbent himself and showed more of his really enthusiastic nature to me than he did to most men. He used to speak unreservedly to me. He knew my views as to

Irishmen taking the oath of allegiance and entering the British Parliament, of which he was at that time a member. He knew that, holding these views, I could not enter the British Parliament myself, though he would have liked to see me there. With me it was a matter of conscience ; I could not take an oath of allegiance to any but an Irish Government. At the same time, I have always been practical, and willing to fight Ireland's battles with the weapons that come readiest to my hand. I, therefore, always gave what support I could to the Irish Parliamentary Party, who could conscientiously enter the House of Commons, and to the recognised Irish organisations for the time being.

It is not to be expected that every Irishman, even every Irish Nationalist, will be of one mind as to which way his duty lies in serving his country. After all, a man who can honestly say " I am an Irishman and I love my country " is already nine-tenths of the way to being a Nationalist. If such a man tries to do his best, according to his lights, for Ireland, he is entitled to all possible sympathy from even those who are working on other lines.

On one occasion, when Parnell had returned from a special mission to America, I had a long discussion with him on these points, and was bound to admit that the British Government would have been much better pleased to encounter an insurrection in Ireland, which they could easily put down, than the policy of the so-called " Obstructionists " in Parliament. Again, I said, there was another fact which I recognised. This was that his

being sent on a mission to America, whence he was
then returning, showed the value of having a man
holding such a well-recognised position as a member
of Parliament, elected by the votes of his fellow-
countrymen, in case we had to send a representative
to speak in the name of Ireland to some other nation,
a circumstance which had happened before and
might again. I said this, even taking into account
the apparent failure of the mission to America,
from which he was returning, for circumstances
might arise in which the head of a State might be
glad to recognise an embassy like theirs. He told
me that was exactly how he viewed the subject.

It was in Dr. Commins' office that we had this
conversation, and at our request Mr. Parnell post-
poned his departure to Ireland in order to attend
a celebration we were having that night of Home
Rule victories we had achieved in two wards of
the town, in Vauxhall by the return of Dr. Commins
to the Town Council, and in Scotland Ward by the
election of Dr. Alexander Bligh. Parnell's appearance at our festival, which was held on Monday,
November 13th, 1876, was a pleasing surprise to
those present, who were not aware of his return from
America, and this added to the intensity of the
outburst of joy and enthusiastic applause which
greeted him.

One of the most important of our Annual Conventions in Great Britain was that held in Liverpool
on 27th August, 1877. Everything showed that,
while our people in Ireland and here still loved the old
leader, they favoured the policy of " Obstruction."

At this Convention there was no intention of displacing Mr. Butt from his position as President of the organisation. They would have retained him on account of his distinguished services and eminently lovable character. But the old man himself could see plainly enough that the people wanted to move faster than he was willing to lead, and, notwithstanding the appeals made to him, insisted upon resigning his position. The Convention being compelled to accept his resignation, Charles Stewart Parnell was elected President of the organisation in his place. This was an indication of what was likely to follow, for though Mr. Butt retained the nominal leadership of the Irish Parliamentary Party up to the time of his death, Parnell was the real leader, and eventually, after a short interval, when Mr. Shaw held the office, became the Chairman of the Irish Parliamentary Party.

John Ferguson was, I think, the first man publicly to indicate Parnell as the probable successor of Butt. But so great is the dread in our people of even the semblance of disunion, that many, myself among the number, expostulated with him for this. Events, however, showed he was right, and Mr. Butt himself plainly felt that it was inevitable. But at the Convention, when Butt had distinctly refused to hold the office of President any longer, nothing could be finer than the tribute paid to our retiring leader by Mr. John Ferguson in proposing the election of Mr. Parnell as his successor. As I was asked to take the official account of that Convention, and have kept a record of it, I here

give a few words of his and some of the other
speeches. He said :—

It is my intention to propose Mr. Parnell as the head of
the Confederation. At the same time I feel the greatest
possible regret that our grand old chieftain who, in trying
times, raised the Irish banner, who has so long guided us,
and who has been with us in so many hard fights, is to
retire from amongst us. We are grateful to Issac Butt for
leading us so far, but we are going to try a more determined
policy, and Mr. Butt holds views different from those we
are determined to carry out. I hope, though, he will take
counsel with the true and earnest men of the Party, and
that, after a time, he will return to lead us at this side
of the water.

Mr. John Barry, Mr. Biggar and others spoke in
the same strain.

So also did Mr. Parnell, who, concluding his
speech seconding the vote of thanks to Mr. Butt,
said :—

I must confess to not having Mr. Butt's confidence in
English justice and sense of right. It is not too late for
him to see a way to deal with England that will obtain
freedom for our country—a way that will show England
that, if she will dare to trifle with Irish demands, it will be
at the risk of endangering those institutions she feels so
proud of, but which Irishmen have no reason to respect.
To Mr. Butt is due a debt of gratitude by the Irish people
which they can never repay, for he has taught them self-
reliance and knowledge of their power. If I have felt it my
duty to put myself in antagonism with Mr. Butt I hope he
will forgive me. If I have said or written harsh things I
have never said more nor less than was due to the gravity
of the occasion.

Mr. O'Donnell, who expressed a wish that the
next session might find Mr. Butt at the head of a
United Irish Party, supported the vote of thanks

to Mr. Butt, which was carried unanimously, and with all sincerity and depth of feeling.

Mr. Butt replied, saying he would be ashamed of himself if he were unmoved by that vote, and the manner in which it had been passed. He hoped that the wish expressed by Mr. O'Donnell might be realized, and it would not be his fault if they had not a United Irish Party in the House of Commons. After expressing his good wishes for the Home Rule Confederation of Great Britain, which he hoped might long continue to assert the power of the Irish people in this country, he took his farewell.

Mr. Parnell was then elected President.

The Convention of 1877 ended with the adoption of a resolution, on the motion of Mr. Peter Mulhall (Liverpool), seconded by Mr Ryan (Bolton) :—

That this Convention of the Home Rule Confederation of Great Britain hereby endorses the vigorous policy of the Home Rule Parliamentary Party who are termed "Obstructionists."

Mr. Mulhall just mentioned was an active worker in the National ranks in Liverpool, and even a more valuable adherent a little later was his younger brother James, one of the most thorough, sincere, and upright of our young men, who never spared himself when there was good work to do.

Before the venerable figure of Isaac Butt disappears from the scene, let me say a few words about his eminently agreeable personality.

There was not an atom of selfishness about him.

I remember his making little of the difficulties some people used to raise in connection with the planning of a Home Rule Bill, and saying, " Three men sitting round a table could in a short time draw up a plan of Home Rule for Ireland that would act, providing people all round meant honestly."

He used to tell us humorous anecdotes of his experiences in the courts, of which I can recollect the following one : " A man came before a magistrate to have a neighbour bound over to keep the peace, In his deposition he stated after the usual preamble : ' That said Barney Trainor at said time and place threatened to send said deponent's soul to the lowest pit of Hell, and this deponent veribly believes that had it not been for the interference of the bystanders the aforesaid Barney Trainor would have accomplished his horrible purpose.' "

Another story that I remember him telling was as to the origin of " Bog Latin." A sheriff's officer was sent to serve a writ, but the object of his search took refuge in a bog. The sheriff's officer, determined to do the thing properly, endorsed his writ " Non comeatibus in swampo," and in Irish legal circles the term " Bog Latin " was thereafter used to describe any mode of caricature of the ancient tongue.

In something less than two years after Charles Stewart Parnell had succeeded him as our President, Isaac Butt died, on the 5th of May, 1879, mourned by Ireland as one of the most brilliant, patriotic, and self-sacrificing men she had ever nurtured.

Of the members of Parliament and embryo

members present at the 1877 Convention, I should
say a word of Tim Healy, by which name he is most
frequently known, who, since then, has been on
many occasions one of the most prominent figures
in Irish politics.

From the day when I first met him, a keen, quick-
witted, enthusiastic Irish lad of about 18, from
Newcastle-on-Tyne, until this 1877 Convention
and later, he did good work for the Cause. Great
as is my affection for him, my pain at his attitude
in recent years has been as great.

From the time we began to work together in
the Home Rule movement I should say that Timothy
Healy had not left his native place, Bantry, more
than a couple of years.

He is related to the Sullivan family, the connection
being still closer from the fact that his wife is a
daughter of our veteran poet, T. D. Sullivan, for
whom I have always had the warmest admiration.

Like myself, Healy had a leaning towards journalism, and we had a common ground in our admiration
of the " Nation " newspaper, not only the " Nation "
of O'Connell and the Young Irelanders, but of the
Sullivans.

Nothing, therefore, could be more congenial to
him than to fill the post of London letter writer to
that paper.

He made his mark at once, as being a worthy
scholar of the " Nation " school, both past and
present, and no one recognised this more quickly
than Charles Stewart Parnell. It was no doubt
this appreciation that prompted the new Irish

leader to ask Tim Healy to become his private secretary.

Parnell possessed in a remarkable degree a gift which was of great service to him during his political career as the successor of Isaac Butt. This was the faculty of weighing up the special qualities of the various members of the Irish Party and using them accordingly. Without attempting for a moment to underrate Parnell as a great leader of men, I must say that there were members of the Party far abler in many respects than he was, and, no doubt, in looking around for someone to supply the qualities in which he, himself, was wanting, he could see that Healy was the very man for his purpose.

When he was in America he wired to Tim offering him the post, which offer was at once accepted, and, in the shortest possible time, Parnell's new secretary had crossed the Atlantic, and was by his side ready to be put in harness at once. It was an excellent combination, and there can be no doubt but that, during the time that the connection existed between them, Parnell owed much towards the successful carrying on of the national struggle to his young secretary's inspiration.

Michael Davitt, in his " Fall of Feudalism," pays a high tribute to Healy's splendid service in connection with Gladstone's Land Act. Undoubtedly his was the credit for what became known as the " Healy Clause," which provided that no rent should be payable for land on improvements made by the tenant himself or his immediate predecessor. Not only was this credit conceded to him of being the author of this clause by distinguished fellow-countrymen like Michael Davitt and Lord Russell of Killowen, but by Mr. Gladstone himself.

As I have referred to the opinions expressed on Healy in Michael Davitt's book, perhaps I may be forgiven if I go out of my way somewhat in referring to another passage in the same book, in which he pays a well-deserved tribute to a noble Irishman, Patrick Ford, of the New York " Irish World," with which, in common with Irish Nationalists the world over, I cordially agree. There are some men whom you may never have seen in the flesh, but whom you feel, through correspondence with them and in other ways, that you know none the less thoroughly all the same. Such a man is Patrick Ford. It is nearly forty years since I first made his acquaintance, and the years that have passed have only increased my regard for him.

I had the pleasure of welcoming in the columns of the " Catholic Times," which was then under my direction, the first number of the " Irish World." I could feel at once that the paper and the man who edited it had for me a congenial ring about them. I am deeply indebted for the kindly and generous interest which Patrick Ford has so long personally and in the columns of the " Irish World " shewn in the success of my Irish publications, and I am delighted to have the opportunity of joining in the tribute paid to him by Michael Davitt.

CHAPTER XVI.

MICHAEL DAVITT'S RETURN FROM PENAL SERVITUDE
—PARNELL AND THE "ADVANCED" ORGANISA-
TION.

IN the year following the Liverpool Home Rule
Convention of 1877, I had the pleasure of welcoming
back to freedom my old friend, Michael Davitt, after
he had been in penal servitude close upon eight
years. He had been released, along with other
Fenian prisoners, and, with Corporal Chambers,
came on April 28th, 1878, to a gathering we organised
and held in the Adelphi Theatre, Liverpool, for
the benefit of the liberated men, John O'Connor
Power being the lecturer for the occasion, and Dr.
Commins our chairman.

Michael Davitt, on rising to speak, was received
with a terrific outburst of cheering, again and again
repeated.

I was sitting immediately behind him on the
platform, and I noticed, while he was speaking, a
constant nervous twitching of his hand, which he
held behind his back, and he was evidently in a
state of highly-strung excitement. I was not
surprised when we had that day a painful proof of
how the prison treatment had undermined his
constitution. After the gathering we brought the

released prisoners and the principal speakers to be entertained at the house of Patrick Byrne, a warm-hearted, patriotic Irishman, and were much alarmed when Davitt fell into a deep faint, from which he only recovered through the ministrations of one of our most respected Liverpool Nationalists, Dr. Bligh, who fortunately was present. For a few moments it seemed as if he never would revive.

There is no doubt but that their treatment during their long term of penal servitude seriously affected the health of several of the Irish political prisoners. It was only three months previous to his visit to us in Liverpool that Davitt reached Dublin, with three others of the released prisoners—Sergeant McCarthy, Corporal Chambers, and John O'Brien. To the consternation of his friends, McCarthy died suddenly at Morrison's Hotel, on January 15th, the cause, it was believed, being heart disease. This caused such a shock to Chambers that his life, too, was put in danger. I was pleased to see him restored to health after this when he called on me in Liverpool with his brother, with whom I was well acquainted. The shock of the sudden death of his friend McCarthy must have affected Michael Davitt too, as we found from the report of our friend, Dr. Bligh, in what a precarious state of health he must have been at the time. It will be remembered that Rickard Burke became insane, it was thought, and stated in Parliament, owing to his treatment while in Chatham Prison.

Following our Liverpool gathering, we had on Sunday, May 5th, a meeting in the St. Helens

Theatre for the same object. At this Parnell as well as Davitt was present. Speaking that day by desire of our St. Helens friends, I called attention to the appropriateness of our addressing the assembly from the boards of a theatre on which there had been the mimic representation of many a stirring drama. But no play the audience had ever witnessed on those boards could exceed in dramatic interest the life of the released convict, Michael Davitt. Nay, more, the grudging terms on which he had been released enabled him to appear that day in the real living character of a " Ticket-of-Leave-Man," which, no doubt, they had seen impersonated on those boards by some clever actor in the play of the same name.

I am reminded of that St. Helens meeting by a passage in Michael Davitt's book " The Fall of Feudalism in Ireland." I travelled from Liverpool to St. Helens to attend the meeting in the same carriage with Mr. Parnell. As I could always speak unreservedly to him I knew that though he would not actually join the advanced organisation, he regarded it as a useful force behind the constitutional movement. In the carriage, which it so happened we had to ourselves, we discussed the probabilities of the result of a resort to physical force for securing Irish freedom, should circumstances justify such a course, for Parnell would not have shrunk from taking the field if there had been a reasonable hope of success. Singularly enough, I find in Michael Davitt's book that he himself, on the day of that same St. Helens meeting, made an

advance to Parnell with a view to getting him to
join the revolutionary organisation, should the
conditions be somewhat modified. Up till then I
had seen more of Parnell than Davitt had and had
enjoyed his full confidence. I had, therefore, come
to the conclusion, from my conversations with him,
that he was of far more service to the Irish cause
as he was than if he had actually joined the
revolutionary movement. I am not surprised, therefore, at Parnell's answer to Davitt : " No, I will
never join any political secret society, oath bound
or otherwise. My belief is that useful things for
our Cause can be done in the British Parliament."

Nevertheless, I remember one public utterance of
his which always struck me as most statesmanlike.
After a frank statement that he was in favour of
constitutional Home Rule, he, with equal frankness,
declined to subscribe to the entire finality of that
solution of the Irish problem. How, he asked,
could he or any man put bounds to the progress
of a nation ?

Seeing that Gladstone gave as one reason for
the disestablishing of the Irish Church " the intensity
of Fenianism," so, in the same way, no one recognised
more than Parnell did that the existence of a physical
force movement was a strong argument for those
engaged in the moral force agitation. Therefore
he was always anxious to conciliate and even
cultivate the advanced element. Of this I will
here give one illustration, out of many I could
mention, and this in connection with the custom of
drinking what was called " the loyal toast," which

at one time used to be observed at some Home
Rule celebrations. It is a matter on which I have
already explained my point of view.

On one occasion Mr. Parnell was invited by the
Liverpool branches to a St. Patrick's Day banquet
at the Adelphi Hotel, where the drinking of the
" loyal " toast was part of the programme. With
the rest of the committee I met him at the railway
station on his arrival, and came with him to the
hotel. After some conversation I was bidding
him " good-night ! " when he asked, as he took
my hand, " Where are you going, Denvir ? Are
you not going to stay for the banquet ? " I had
not intended mentioning it, but as he asked me so
pointedly, I felt bound to tell him my objection to
being present. He did not attempt to controvert
what I said, but still asked where I was going. I
then told him I had been invited to a St. Patrick's
celebration where the toast was *not* to be drunk,
the gathering being one of our advanced Nationalist
friends.

He at once said " I should like to go there." I
told him I was sure they would be delighted to see
him, and that, as theirs was a dance, and it would
be kept up pretty late, I would come back for him
after the banquet, and take him to the other celebration. Our friends were well pleased at his wish to
attend, and asked me to go back and bring him to
where a hearty *cead mile failte* awaited him. In
due time I brought him over, and they gave him
an enthusiastic reception, he being quite as delighted
to be present as they were to receive him, and they

were still more pleased when he addressed a few words to them.

But that was as far as Parnell would go, and his answer to Davitt that day at St. Helens pretty well indicated the course he intended to pursue in connection with the cause of Ireland.

Indeed, it is on record that in later years Michael Davitt altered his own view to such an extent that he would no longer have made that proposition to Parnell.

There was no man whose regard I more valued than that of Michael Davitt. Amongst all the vicissitudes of Irish politics our friendship was an unbroken one. He was little more than a boy when I first met him at a small gathering to which none but the initiated were admitted. From the first I was strongly drawn towards that tall, dark-complexioned, bright-eyed, modest youth, with his typical Celtic face and figure. He was in company with Arthur Forrester, who was a fluent speaker and writer, and who on this occasion did most of the talking, Davitt only throwing in some shrewd remark from time to time. We know since that he had in him the natural gift of oratory, though it was not that so much as other qualities which gave him the commanding position in Irish politics which he afterwards reached.

He had then spent several of the best years of his life in penal servitude for his connection with the physical force movement. Thinking long and hard in the solitude of his prison cell, Davitt resolved that the first vital need of Ireland was to plant firmly in the soil of Ireland the people who were being uprooted—in other words, the land system must be changed.

The result of his convictions was the formation of the Irish National Land League, which dated its birth from the great meeting projected by Davitt and held at Irishtown in April, 1879. Mr. Parnell was elected President of the new organisation, Mr. Patrick Egan treasurer, and Michael Davitt was one of the secretaries. He has been justly called the " Father " of the Land League.

One of the earliest acts of the Land League was to endeavour to stop the tide of emigration from Ireland. In this connection, as certain emigration schemes had been set on foot in England, a branch of the League was founded in Liverpool at my request by Parnell and Davitt.

In consequence of the prevailing distress and impending famine, Mr. Parnell was asked by the Irish National League to go to America to get the assistance of our people there, and Mr. John Dillon was asked to accompany him.

Though there was little done by the Government to relieve the distress, the Irish people could always get coercion without stint, and Messrs. Davitt, Daly and Killen were arrested for " seditious " speeches in connection with the Land League agitation.

To protest against this, Mr. Parnell, previous to his departure for America, attended a great open-air demonstration in Liverpool. The gathering was held in the open space in front of St. George's

Hall, and it was computed that about 50,000 people were present. When the meeting was publicly announced, there was a proclamation from the Orange Society, calling upon the brethren to put down the " Seditious gathering." Upon this our committee took the precaution of enrolling stalwart " stewards " to preserve order. Among those who offered their services were a large number of the Irish Volunteer Corps, under the command of Sergeant James MacDonnell, a County Down man of fine proportions and shrewd brain. To him was entrusted the direction of the whole body of our men on the day of the meeting. The advanced party also gave their services, and non-commissioned officers and men of the other volunteer corps besides the Irish, skilled in military movements, gave valuable help. Round the platform were a select body of nearly a thousand men, many of them carrying revolvers in their pockets, ready for action.

The Orange body must have heard of our elaborate preparations, and finding " discretion the better part of valour," they countermanded their proclamation to break up the meeting.

The authorities of the town made full preparations to cope with possible disturbances, and inside St. George's Hall they had, carefully kept out of view, a large body of the town police, armed with revolvers in addition to their batons. In a window of the North Western Hotel, overlooking the meeting, was the chief constable, and with him were magistrates, prepared to read the Riot Act if necessary.

It was arranged that as I was at that time probably

the best known man in the Irish body in Liverpool,
I should be stationed on a prominent part of the
platform, which consisted of two lorries, in view of
all, and alongside me, our general, Sergeant
MacDonnell. As showing how well in hand was
that immense body of people it was remarked that
when the carrage of Dr. John Bligh, whose guest
Mr. Parnell was, drew up in the street, facing the
platform, and when I made a motion with both
hands, to show where a passage was to be made
for Mr. Parnell from the street to the platform, how
quickly and accurately the opening was made in
that dense and apparently impenetrable body of
people.

In Ireland, at this time, men were being prosecuted
for what were termed " seditious " speeches. When
Mr. Parnell stood up to speak he stepped upon a
chair, that he might be the better seen, and said
" I am going to make a seditious speech." A strong
motion was passed at this meeting condemnatory
of coercion in Ireland. On the same evening a
great demonstration was held in the League Hall.

The authorities must have considered the St.
George's Hall meeting a very serious business, and
it was evidently made note of by the police for use
afterwards.

At the " *Times* Forgeries Commission," Mr.
Parnell was questioned about this gathering, and
about several on the platform who were mentioned
by name. Asked if this one or that one were connected with the Fenian movement, he generally
answered he did not think so. When my name

was put to him by the Attorney-General (now the
Lord Chief Justice), who was cross-examining him,
he replied " He might have been."

In a short time after the Liverpool demonstration
Messrs. Parnell and Dillon went to America, as
had been arranged. They were everywhere received
with enthusiasm, and obtained sympathy and
substantial help as the ambassadors of Ireland.

CHAPTER XVII.

BLOCKADE RUNNING—ATTEMPTED SUPPRESSION OF
" UNITED IRELAND "—WILLIAM O'BRIEN AND
HIS STAFF IN JAIL—HOW PAT EGAN KEPT
THE FLAG FLYING.

" UNITED IRELAND suppressed " was the chief
headline in the morning papers on the Friday
before the Christmas of 1881.

In point of fact, what had happened was that
the detectives, acting under the extraordinary
powers given by the special " law " in force in
Ireland, had invaded the offices of the Land League
organ the night before, and seized all the copies
of the paper found on the premises.

It was a bungled job, for the country·edition had
already gone out, including the supplies for England
and Scotland, so that the only copies seized were
those intended for Dublin and the suburbs.

Nothing indicated the intensity of the struggle
going on between the government and the people
more than the dead set which was being made against
" United Ireland." Its editor was in jail, its sub-
editor was in jail, most of its contributors were in
jail, even the commercial and mechanical staffs
had been seized, one by one, and in the paper each
week the names and descriptions of the victims

appeared, prominently set out in tabular form, in the place where the first leading article had previously been printed.

But, in spite of these difficulties, the paper appeared regularly each week, its fiery spirit not a whit abated, and its outspoken exposure of Mr. " Buckshot " Forster and his methods in no way curtailed. Confronted with this open failure, the government swallowed the last vestige of its regard for appearances, and made the bold attack on the liberty of the press involved in the seizure and attempted suppression of " United Ireland."

It was not the first time (nor has it been the last) in Ireland that a national organ was thus attacked. From the days of the United Irishmen, towards the close of the 18th century, to those of 1867, there had been a long series of suppressions, of which, perhaps, John Mitchel's " United Irishman " (1847) and the Fenian " Irish People " are the best remembered instances.

In this case, however, the leaders of the popular movement determined that they would not be put down, but would use all " the resources of civiliza- tion "—to quote Mr. Gladstone's famous phrase— to keep the flag flying. I am very proud of the fact that they invited me to be their instrument.

What happened was that two members of the printing staff, Mr. Edward Donnelly, foreman, and Mr. William MacDonnell, assistant foreman, escaped to England, taking with them stereo plates of the " suppressed " issue. From these plates, my own jobbing machines not being big enough to print

a full-sized newspaper, I got a local firm to print
sufficient copies to cover the Dublin supply, which,
as I have explained, had been the only part of the
issue which fell into the hands of the police. A
quantity of these papers, made up in innocent
looking parcels, my son, then a schoolboy, took
over with him in the steamer from Liverpool to
Dublin, as personal luggage. He was to take them
to the address which had been given to him of a member of the staff who was then " on his keeping." I
was alarmed the following morning, Christmas
Eve, 1881, to read in the newspapers of the arrest
of this gentleman, and feared that my son would
also fall into the hands of the police. But he had
acted with wariness. Leaving the luggage behind
him in the steamer, until he found how the land
lay, he saw the people of the house, heard of the
arrest, and at once made his own arrangements for
supplying the Dublin newsagents, in which task he
received invaluable help from two gentlemen on the
"Nation" staff, Daniel Crilly and Eugene O'Sullivan.

Thus the *whole* of the issue of the " suppressed "
number actually reached its destination. For future
issues arrangements were made between my old
friend Mr. Patrick Egan, Treasurer of the Land
League, who was then in Paris, and myself. Our
letters were never addressed direct, but always
through third persons, the intermediary in Paris
being Mr. James Vincent Taaffe, and, in Liverpool,
Miss Kate Swift. Mr. Egan had been sent to Paris
to keep the League Funds out of the hands of Dublin
Castle, and to maintain intact the machinery of

the League, for, it must be remembered, Parnell, Davitt, William O'Brien, and most of our prominent men were at the time in jail.

Although illegal in Ireland, there was nothing in the ordinary law to prevent the printing and circulation of " United Ireland " in Great Britain. Arrangements were, therefore, made with the Metropolitan Printing Works, London, for the future production of the paper. For several weeks the papers were printed by that firm, and sent to my place of business in Byrom Street, Liverpool.

As I had, in ordinary course, to supply the whole of the newsagents in England, Wales and Scotland, the police, by whom my place was, by day and night, closely watched, could not know if in the quantity sent to me from London I was getting a supply for Ireland.

The parcels for Ireland I could not send direct from Byrom Street, as they would be followed by the police and traced. Therefore, for packing and forwarding to Ireland, we used a fish-curing shed, not far from Byrom Street, lent for the purpose by a patriotic Irishman, Patrick De Lacy Garton, at that time a member of the Liverpool City Council.

With so many friends in Liverpool willing to assist, it was not difficult to get the parcels of papers, through one channel or another, into our depot each week.

I engaged the services of Mr. Michael Wolohan, to go to Ireland, and act as forwarding agent. It was his task to get people in various parts of the country to receive parcels of " United Ireland," the papers being packed in such fashion as to correspond with the business of the person to whom each consignment was made.

For instance, the edition for the week ending December 31st was packed in hampers provided by Mr. Garton, who advised me to send the lot as dried fish, and found a reliable consignee for them in Ireland. The " dried fish " arrived safely, and then the most arduous part of Michael Wolohan's work began. For it was difficult to get the actual parcels of " United Ireland " into the hands of the agents and sub-agents unknown to the police, but this he did with consummate address, and on the whole very successfully.

On one occasion Michael wrote me he had a good consignee for " woollen goods." Nothing easier, for here was Edward Purcell, a clothier, one of our own young men, who afterwards became a city alderman, having a good business in Byrom Street, Liverpool. Besides helping actively with the " blockade running " in other ways, he at once gave us the necessary wrappers in which he had got his own goods from his woollen merchants, and assisted in packing our " woollen goods " in the correct fashion. Needless to say, these safely reached the consignee in Ireland.

Although there was no illegality in printing " United Ireland " in London, the printers were perpetually harassed by the police to frighten them into giving up the job. The parcels for the British newsagents could not legally be stopped, but with the watchful eye of the police all over Ireland on the look-out for the proscribed paper, it is not surprising that individual parcels fell into their hands. For that reason we took care to send the various kinds of goods in the names of mercantile firms whose loyalty was unquestionable. I should say that to this day these firms have no idea of the large Irish trade they were doing at this particular time.

But Liverpool became much too suspicious a place to send from. I therefore adopted the plan of sending parcels, made up as various kinds of merchandise, to friends in Manchester, from which city there was regular communication with inland towns in Ireland, and these friends sent on the parcels to their destinations more safely than if going direct from Liverpool.

This scheme was working smoothly enough, but eventually the London printers were frightened into giving up the contract, and the printing had to be transferred to Paris.

It is needless to say that, during this time, Michael Wolohan, our agent in Ireland (whose name had for the time being become Brownrigg), had the utmost difficulty in escaping the attention of the police. Some parcels he was sending by the Broadstone terminus were detected and seized. What troubled him most was that, as he paid a considerable sum for carriage on these, and as the railway company had not forwarded them, he was entitled to have the money returned, But the police were on the look out for the so-called Brownrigg, and it was thought best that he should not venture near the station. It happened that week that my son arrived in Dublin with some more of the kind of luggage he had brought over at Christmas, and, with the recklessness of youth, he went to the station, and, as Brownrigg, got the money returned.

" United Ireland " for the week ending January 28th, 1882, was printed in Paris, in a section of a printing office rented by Patrick Egan, and sent, addressed to me, for circulation in Ireland and Great Britain. The parcels were seized on their arrival at Folkestone and Dover, and though the seizure was illegal and I applied for the parcels as being my property (a question being also asked in Parliament) we could get no satisfaction.

But, notwithstanding the seizures made from time to time, it was determined to keep the flag flying, and no matter what might be the difficulty encountered in the production of " United Ireland," not an issue was missed. Of course, as a natural consequence of these difficulties, the paper was sometimes hard to be got, so that, taking advantage of this, some of the newsvendors and all the news-boys in Dublin were reaping a rich harvest, as, owing to the anxiety of the people to get copies, they were frequently sold on the streets of the cities and towns in Ireland at from 6d. to 2s. 6d. a copy. The continued presence of the paper all over Ireland did perhaps more than anything else to keep heart in the people. Accordingly, it must be kept going at all hazards. The type for the paper continued to be set up in Paris, and, after a certain quantity had been printed off each week,

for transmission by post and otherwise, the matrices
from the type were brought over to me by carefully
selected agents from Paris. From these stereotype
plates of the pages were cast. As my own machine
was not big enough, I arranged with a Liverpool
firm of printers to machine the paper for me each
week. Accordingly, they printed the papers for
the week ending February 4th, and delivered the
bulk of them to us, so that we got our parcels for
that week sent off.

The police must have got one of the copies being
sold by the Liverpool agents, and finding it had
no imprint (which was illegal) went to the printers
referred to, who, on this being pointed out, handed
over to them the few remaining copies.

As every printing firm was now afraid to touch
" United Ireland," it only remained for me to
endeavour to print it with my own somewhat
limited appliances. It was now, therefore, reduced
in size to four pages. Every week, as before,
the matrices were brought to me, and, from the
castings taken from these, I printed the papers
on my own small machine, and sent them to their
various destinations.

And so the fight with the police went on with
varying fortune. It was true, as regards size,
half our flag had in a manner been shot away,
but we still kept it flying, and the Government,
with their standing army of police, were never
able to suppress " United Ireland."

As I expected, I was prosecuted for printing
and publishing without an imprint. Mr. Poland,

Q.C., chief prosecuting counsel to the Treasury, was sent down to conduct the case against me for the technical breach of the law involved in the matter of the imprint, and I was fined a sum amounting with costs to £25. I announced my intention in court of continuing the publication, so the Government got very little satisfaction out of their action.

Of the various editions of the paper produced in Ireland at this time I shall not speak in detail, as in this narrative I only describe what came within my own personal knowledge. Mr. William O'Brien in a later issue referred to the mysterious and unconquerable fashion in which one town after another saw its edition of " United Ireland " appear, and then, when police and spies were hot upon its track, as mysteriously pass away. This was, of course, a picturesque exaggeration, but it had a considerable basis of truth. The paper was actually printed more than once in the old office in Dublin under the noses of the police, and on one occasion Mr. Wolohan set up a printing machine in a private house in Derry, and, assisted by my son, actually worked off the copies of the paper next door to the house of the resident magistrate.

Ultimately, there came the period of the " Kilmainham Treaty," and most of the political prisoners were released. The issue of " United Ireland " for March 11th did not appear as on previous occasions. I produced an issue, which I sent in charge of my son to Dublin, putting it at the disposal of Mr. O'Brien. It was not, however, published, though I received a long and interesting letter from Mr. William O'Brien—still in Kilmainham jail—expressing the appreciation of the Irish leaders for the work I had done in these words :—

We are all deeply sensible of your extraordinary energy and courage in this matter.

I am prevented from giving this letter, which explains the reasons for the stoppage of the paper, as Mr. O'Brien has endorsed it " Private and Confidential."

A few weeks later " United Ireland " appeared in its old publishing office in Abbey Street. Mr. O'Brien was set free on April 15th, Messrs. Parnell, Dillon and O'Kelly were released on May 2nd, and Michael Davitt and others soon afterwards.

CHAPTER XVIII.

PATRICK EGAN.

IT will be seen that when " United Ireland " was
" on the shaughraun " during the time that William
O'Brien was in prison, though he was able to send
communications out regularly, the direction very
largely devolved upon Patrick Egan, who had taken
up his quarters in Paris for that and other purposes
of the Land League. I may say that I have been
in frequent communication with Mr. Egan ever
since, and it is but recently that I got a letter from
him touching upon this matter. In making some
valuable suggestions as to the contents of this book,
he says, " There just occurs to me as I write, a
point that you might introduce as an added feature,
namely—all the leading articles that appeared in
' U. I.' during those fateful months (or almost all
of them) were written by William O'Brien *in Kilmainham Prison, smuggled out by the underground
railroad, which ran upon regular scheduled time,*
and were despatched by trusty messengers to me
in Paris, which messengers brought back on their
return journey the matrices to which you refer for
the next issue of ' United Ireland.'

" There were four messengers, in order to avoid
attracting attention—two of them the Misses

Stritch, whose father had been a resident magistrate in Ireland. They were fine patriotic girls, and active members of Miss Anna Parnell's Ladies' Land League. Both are now dead."

After a time Patrick Egan returned from Paris to Ireland, calling upon me in Liverpool on his way home.

On more than one occasion he has visited me at my home in Liverpool. It was always with sincere pleasure that I saw the alert figure, the keen yet smiling eyes, the trim moustache and beard, which were the first impressions one got of his personality. His unvarying suavity and politeness might have deceived a casual observer into supposing that he was not a man of abnormal strength of character ; they were only the silken glove to conceal the hand of iron. Emphatically a man of determination and practical common sense, he united to these qualities a remarkable degree of tact. In addition to much routine matter, which need not be specified here, although grave enough at the time, our meetings were concerned with important work in which we were engaged, as, for instance, the O'Connell Centenary, the political prisoners, and combating the measures being taken to swell the tide of emigration from Ireland.

In dealing with the eventful career of Patrick Egan may I be allowed to go both backward and forward in my dates, in order to bring the story of his life into, as far as possible, one consecutive narrative.

Born in County Longford, he was brought to

Dublin by his parents when quite young. His shrewd business qualities enabled him to make his mark early in life, and his fine administrative abilities admirably fitted him for the post he attained as managing director to the most extensive flour milling company in Ireland.

He has always been a practical patriot, always ready to work for Ireland by every honourable means that came to his hand, whether the means were those of moral or physical force. Consequently, he was an active worker in the ranks of the Irish Revolutionary Brotherhood from the early sixties. He was one of the founders of the Amnesty Movement for the release of the political prisoners of '65 and '67.

When the Home Rule movement was started in Ireland he entered into it heartily, and was elected a member of the Council. He enjoyed the confidence of Butt, John Martin, Justin McCarthy, and all the other leaders of the movement, besides being trusted by Nationalists of all shades of opinion. Like most of us, without abating in the least his love and esteem for Isaac Butt, he soon recognised the coming leader in Charles Stewart Parnell, who used to refer to him in private conversation as his " political godfather " on account of the prominent part he had played in securing his first election to Parliament for the County Meath, in succession to John Martin.

During the early part of the Land League agitation he was three times nominated, for King's County, Meath, and Tipperary, for Parliament, but he refused

election, on the ground of being an advanced
Nationalist. I have more than once talked this
matter over with Pat Egan, and, as I may say in
everything else, we were in complete accord ; we
neither of us could bring ourselves to swear allegiance
to what we considered a foreign power. At the
same time, as practical patriots, we helped every
movement, inside the constitution as well as outside
of it, calculated to benefit Ireland.

When the Land League movement was started in
1879, Egan became at once one of the most prominent
figures in it, and, besides acting as Trustee along
with Joseph Biggar and William H. O'Sullivan, he
was Honorary Treasurer.

In the famous trial of the Land League Executive,
in 1880-1881, he and Mr. Parnell and eleven others
were prosecuted, the jury being ten to two for
acquittal.

In February, 1881, when coercion was so rampant
in Ireland, he left his business in the sole charge
of his partner, James Rourke, and went to Paris,
by desire of Parnell, Dillon and the other leaders,
to keep the League Funds out of the hands of the
enemy. While he was there I was brought into
close relations with him in my endeavours, as I have
already described in this narrative, to carry out
the honourable part allotted to me by our leaders
of keeping " United Ireland " in circulation in
every corner of the land, notwithstanding the
watchfulness of the entire British garrison.

In October, 1882, a National Convention passed
a unanimous vote, thanking him for his distinguished

services and sacrifices as Treasurer of the League, he having given gratuitously to the Cause three entire years of his life, something like a million and a quarter of dollars having passed through his hands during that time. These and many other circumstances that came to my knowledge abundantly prove that no man has more deserved the confidence and gratitude of the Irish race.

In February, 1883, Michael Davitt tells us " In order to avoid the machinations of agents in the pay of Dublin Castle, he left Ireland."

I don't know if I shall ever meet my friend again, and for that reason I shall always remember, as I am sure he will, our last meeting in Liverpool on his return from Paris, when we fought our battles with the forces of the Government over again, and had many a hearty laugh at some of the humorous episodes that cropped up in connection with it. Neither of us then thought that, before long, he would have to leave his home again for another period of exile.

Up to this point I can include the chief incidents in Patrick Egan's career, either directly or indirectly. in my own personal recollections. In order not to break the continuity of this sketch of a noble life, I will briefly speak of his career in America, It will be found, therefore, that in some particulars I have had to anticipate the ordinary course of this narrative.

On arriving in America in 1883, he settled in Nebraska, where he soon established a large and prosperous business in grain.

In 1884, at a Convention in Faneuil Hall, Boston, surrounded by some of the most distinguished of our race in America, he was presented with a service of plate sent from Ireland, with a beautifully illuminated address, paying tribute to the magnificent services he had given to his country, and signed by three hundred of the national leaders in Ireland, including the Lord Mayor of Dublin (Charles Dawson), Parnell, Davitt, Dillon, Biggar. Justin McCarthy, Healy, William O'Brien, Sexton, Harrington and others.

From 1884 to 1886 he was President of the Irish National League of America, during which time 360,000 dollars were collected and sent to Ireland. The salary of the President of the League was 3,000 dollars a year. At the end of his term Patrick Egan returned to his successor in the office 6,000 dollars as his personal contribution to the Fund.

His career in America has been no less honourable than his services to the Irish Cause on this side of the Atlantic. Irishmen everywhere felt proud when he was sent to represent the great American Republic as Ambassador to Chili. They took it not only as an honour to the man himself, but to his nationality. We who knew him best followed with confidence his record during the four years of storm and stress in Chili, the most troublous, perhaps, that country had ever seen.

That our confidence in him was not misplaced was proved by the tribute of admiration paid him by President Harrison in his message to Congress in December, 1891, for the splendid manner in which he had protected the important interests confided to his care, and for his defence of the honour of the flag of the United States, and the rights and dignity of American citizenship.

All this was endorsed in the most emphatic manner by the leading statesmen and naval and military commanders of America, including Secretary of State James G. Blaine, Rear Admiral Evans, Admiral Brown, Rear-Admiral McCann, and numerous other officers of the army and navy.

The strongest eulogies of Mr. Egan's conduct of the Chilian legation were written by the ex-President of the United States, Theodore Roosevelt, who, in 1892, gave a dinner at his home in Washington, D.C., in his honour. In a public letter Mr. Roosevelt said, " Minister Egan has acted as an American representative in a way that proves that he deserves well of all Americans, and I earnestly hope that his career in our diplomatic service may be long, and that in it he may rise to the highest positions."

When I started a new series of my " Irish Library" in January, 1902, I received words of encouragement from John Redmond, from Michael Davitt, and from other distinguished Irishmen, but there was none I valued more highly than the letter of appreciation of my works from Pat Egan. Of these he asked me to send him a set, including my " Irish in Britain."

In a letter he sent me in the May following, I could see the yearning of the exile for news from the " old sod " when he said " Write me a line to say how you are, and how goes the good old cause. I often think with much interest of the last time I had the pleasure of seeing you in Liverpool."

I have made my references to Patrick Egan somewhat lengthy, perhaps, but it is because in no work that I have ever seen has an adequate tribute been paid to his services to Ireland. Unlike other men who are better known, he was little seen and not much heard of in the Land League movement, but his influence in shaping the movement was second only to that of Davitt. He was eminently the practical patriot, and his motto was " deeds not words." If she had had in the past many men like Egan, Ireland would be both free and prosperous to-day.

CHAPTER XIX.

GENERAL ELECTION OF 1885—PARNELL A CANDIDATE FOR EXCHANGE DIVISION — RETIRES IN FAVOUR OF O'SHEA—T.P. O'CONNOR ELECTED FOR SCOTLAND DIVISION OF LIVERPOOL.

THE Franchise and Re-Distribution Acts of 1884 and 1885, besides placing, for the first time, the Parliamentary representation in the hands of the great bulk of the people of Ireland, added greatly to our political power in England, Scotland and Wales. Many thousands of Irish householders obtained votes where formerly, under the restricted franchise, such a thing as an Irish county voter was extremely rare.

At the General Election of 1885, Mr. Parnell made Liverpool his headquarters. The Re-Distribution Act had given Liverpool nine Parliamentary Divisions, in one of which (Scotland Division) we had sufficient votes to return a Nationalist. As Mr. T. P. O'Connor was the candidate chosen, and was, besides, the President of the organisation in Great Britain, he, also, was on the spot.

A central committee room was engaged in the North-Western Hotel, where Mr. Parnell and Mr. T. P. O'Connor were staying. I was detailed to act as secretary to them, and, as the electoral campaign all over the country was directed from this centre, I was kept busy from early morning until late in the night answering the letters which poured in from all parts of the country. Mr. T. P. O'Connor having recently been married, Mrs. O'Connor also was staying in the North-Western. She presided at our luncheon every day, and made a charming hostess.

I have some pleasant remembrances of those days in Liverpool, when I was assisting Mr. Parnell in carrying on the electoral campaign. One day, as we stood together looking out of the window across Lime Street, he pointed to the hotel on the opposite side of the street, reminding me that it was there we first met. This was when he came amongst us, a promising young recruit, under the wing of Isaac Butt. I remembered it well, and the number of questions he asked me about the condition of our people, social and political, in this country, for he knew that I had had opportunities of acquiring a closer knowledge of them than most people. He often afterwards sought from me such information. To me, from first to last, he was always most open and friendly, and I never found him so " stand-off " and unapproachable as was the very common opinion about him.

In the Exchange Division of Liverpool, a Mr. Stephens, the official Liberal candidate, had, for some reason, been replaced by Captain O'Shea, who got the full support of the Liberal party. Following instructions from headquarters, the Irish Nationalists had denounced the candidate of the Liberals, who, when recently in power, had coerced Ireland, and O'Shea was condemned more unmercifully than any of them, as being, besides, a renegade Irishman.

When Parnell himself came on the scene as a candidate for Exchange Division, Captain O'Shea was denounced more fiercely than ever. Mr. Parnell, however, withdrew on the nomination day, and at a great meeting on the same night, much to the astonishment of all, asked, in a very halting and hesitating manner, that O'Shea's candidature should be supported. So great was his power and prestige at the time that, whatever apprehension might be felt, no attempt was made to question his action.

On the morning of the election I went to the North-Western. Mr. O'Connor was somewhat late in getting to work. Parnell, noticing, I suppose, that I seemed uneasy about something, asked, " What's amiss with you, Denvir ? " " We would like to see Mr. O'Connor on the ground in Scotland Division," I said. He shook his head : " Ah, that's the way with him since he got married." I smiled and observed " We'll be losing you that way some time." " No," he replied, as I thought somewhat sadly, " I lost my chance long ago."

All that day Parnell worked with desperate energy for O'Shea. He even took some of our men from Scotland Division to help in Exchange. I expostulated with him, saying, " You'll be losing T. P.'s election for us." As a matter of fact, we won Scotland Division by 1,350 votes.

In point of fact, if O'Shea had got the whole

Irish vote he would have won, but Mr. Parnell's vehement efforts could kindle no enthusiasm among the Irish electors, and there was a small but determined section which—while unwilling to let any public evidence of disagreement with Mr. Parnell appear—absolutely refused to support O'Shea. This lost him the seat.

There was great jubilation in the League Hall that night at the winning of a seat in England by an Irish Home Ruler, elected *as such*, Mr. T. P. O'Connor having been returned that day for the Scotland Division of Liverpool.

Since that time there have been several Home Rulers, Irish by birth or descent, returned to Parliament for English constituencies. These belong to the Labour Party.

Besides T. P. O'Connor, Liverpool has provided for Parliament quite a number of men who at one time or another have represented or still represent Irish constituencies. These are Dr. Commins, Daniel Crilly, Lawrence Connolly, Michael Conway, Joseph Nolan, Patrick O'Brien, William O'Malley, James Lysaght Finigan, and Garrett Byrne.

At the League Hall demonstration on the night of the election, Mr. Parnell appeared to have caught the high spirit and enthusiasm of his audience, and in a more powerful address than I had ever before heard from him, he said :—

Ireland has been knocking at the English door long enough with kid gloves. I tell the English people to beware, and be wise in time. Ireland will soon throw off the kid gloves, and she will knock with a mailed hand.

In this General Election, the Irish vote of Great
Britain, in accordance with the League manifesto,
generally went for the Tories, who came into office,
but with a majority so small that they were turned
out at the opening of the Session of 1886, and Mr.
Gladstone again came into power. Seeing that
85 out of the 103 Irish members of Parliament
had been returned pledged to National self-government, he came to the conclusion to drop coercion,
and no longer to attempt to rule the country against
the wishes of the people. He, therefore, introduced his Home Rule Bill on the 8th of April, 1886,
but, failing to carry the whole of his party with
him, he was defeated on the second reading by
30 votes. His defeat at the polls at the General
Election which followed seemed even more crushing
than his defeat in Parliament, for, of the members
elected, there was a majority against him of 118.

Mr. Gladstone, looking more closely into the
figures of the General Election, was not disheartened,
and as the British public became educated on the
Irish question, bye-election after bye-election proved
triumphantly the truth of his famous saying that
the "Flowing Tide" was carrying the cause of
Home Rule on to victory.

Nor were *we* disheartened, for, counting up the
whole of about two and a half millions of votes
given, we found that the Unionists, as the Tories
and Dissentient Liberals called themselves, had
a majority of less than 80,000 votes at the polls.
During this time I had become general organiser
of the recognised Irish political organisation of

Great Britain, and upon me chiefly devolved the duty of directing the work of registration of our Irish voters. A close study of the local conditions in the various constituencies showed that the mere bringing up of the neglected Irish vote to something approaching its proper strength would *alone* be sufficient to effect the necessary gain. We threw ourselves into the task—and we succeeded.

I shall always remember with pride my share in increasing and organising the Irish vote throughout Great Britain, and its result in bringing Mr. Gladstone back to power, and enabling him to carry the Home Rule Bill through the House of Commons.

It was my duty to visit every part of Great Britain to see that the various districts and branches were kept in a high state of efficiency, and at the end of that period of hard and unremitting work from 1886 to 1892 I was able to show our Executive from the books and figures in our possession that we had accomplished our aim.

CHAPTER XX.

GLADSTONE'S " FLOWING TIDE."

I was present at most of the bye-elections that led up to Gladstone's great victory at the General Election of 1892.

In this way I was brought to many places interesting to us as Catholics as well as Irishmen.

No spot in Great Britain is more sacred to us than Iona, an island off the West coast of Scotland, which our great typical Irish saint, Columba, made his home and centre when bringing the light of faith to those regions. It will, therefore, be one of the memories of my life most dear to me that I had the blessing of taking part in the famous Pilgrimage to Iona on June 13th, 1888. The town of Oban, on the mainland of Scotland, is generally made the point of departure for Iona, which is not far off.

Oban is one of the five Ayr burghs which, combined, send a member to Parliament, and it was singular that, at this time, there was a bye-election going on. As creed and country have always gone together with me, I did not think it at all inappropriate that I should do a little work for Irish self-government while on this Pilgrimage. On the contrary. Was not St. Columba himself a champion of Home Rule, for was it not through his eloquent advocacy of their cause before the great Irish National Assembly that the Scots of Alba, as distinguished from the Scots of Erin, obtained the right of self-government ?

One of the best numbers of my Irish Library was the " Life of St. Columbkille," written for me by Michael O'Mahony, one of a band of young Irishmen, members of the Irish Literary Institute of Liverpool, who did splendid service for the Cause in that city. Michael was, of these, perhaps the one possessing the most characteristic Irish gifts. He has written some admirable stories of Irish life, and is a poet, although he has not written as much as I would like to see from his pen.

There are no Irish residents in Iona itself, but I found a few in Oban, on whom I called to secure their votes for Home Rule.

To hear Mass on the spot made sacred by the feet of our great Irish saint, in the building, then a ruin, erected by his successors to replace that which he himself had raised here as a centre of his great missionary labours, was an experience to treasure until one's latest day. What made the celebration the more memorable was the sermon in Gaelic by Bishop MacDonald of Argyll and the Isles. I had the pleasure, after Mass, of having dinner with him, and some most interesting conversation.

I told him I had read with great interest a pastoral of his, issued some five years before, in which he said that an interesting peculiarity of his diocese,

in respect of which it stood almost alone in the
country, was that its Catholicity was almost exclusively represented by districts which had always
clung to the faith, places where in the Penal days
no priest dared show himself in public, but visited
the Catholic centres in turn as a layman by night
and gathered the children together to instruct
them as far as he was able. This was, he said, of
extraordinary interest on a day like that, when we
were specially honouring the memory of the great
saint who had sown the seeds which had continued
to bear fruit through so many centuries. We also
spoke of the singular fact that he had that day
preached on the spot on which St. Columba himself
had stood, and in the same language that he spoke,
a language which had been in existence long before
the present English tongue was spoken. As showing
that the Scottish and Irish Gaelic were practically
the same, as distinguished from the Celtic tongue
spoken by the Welsh and Bretons, Bishop MacDonald
told me he could read quite easily a book printed
in the Irish characters.

As a bye-election brought me to the sacred
scene of the labours of our great Irish saint, Columba,
so did another bye-election bring me to the spot
where a martyr for Ireland suffered in 1798—Father
O'Coigly. There was a bye-election at Maidstone,
where the martyr priest had been tried for treason,
and near it is Pennenden Heath, where he was
executed, so that both places will for ever be held
sacred by patriotic Irishmen. Besides securing a
pledge for Home Rule from one of the candidates,

and organising the small Irish vote in his favour, I took the opportunity of inaugurating a movement for the erection of a memorial to Father O'Coigly. With the co-operation of the London branches of the United Irish League the movement was brought to a successful issue. On two succeeding years there were Pilgrimages to the spot where Father O'Coigly was executed, at which Mr. James Francis Xavier O'Brien, who himself had been sentenced to be hanged, drawn and quartered, was the chief speaker one year, and Mr. John Murphy, M.P., on the other.

Besides this, chiefly through the exertions of Mr. John Brady, District Organiser, funds were raised, and there have been erected in the Catholic Church at Maidstone a Celtic Cross and three beautiful stained-glass windows, of Irish manu- facture, to commemorate the martyrdom of Father O'Coigly.

A gratifying thing in connection with our Pilgrim- age was, I reminded those I addressed on Pennenden Heath, that a man pledged to support self-govern- ment for Ireland, the Cause for which Father O'Coigly had suffered, had been elected to Parliament for Maidstone.

In the bye-elections about this time, we often got the most satisfactory results from places where the Irish vote was but small. I have before my mind the Carnarvon Boroughs bye election of 1890. Here the seat had been held by a Tory, and the Irish vote in the five towns, all told, was not much more than 50. I was sent to the constituency

by our Executive to use every exertion to get our
people to poll for David Lloyd-George, a thoroughgoing Home Ruler, at that time an unknown man,
though he has since risen to the first political and
ministerial rank. It was then I made his acquaintance, and time has only increased the friendly
feeling between us.

Our meeting happened rather curiously. While
on my round I came across an unpretentious-
looking young man who, I discovered, was also
working on the same side. We had chatted together
for some time when I happened to make some
reference to the candidate. " Oh," he said, with
a laugh, " I am the candidate." It was Mr. Lloyd-
George. We worked together with all the more
ardour being brother Celts. I frequently expressed
to him my admiration for a striking feature in their
great meetings during the election campaign. This
was the singing in their native tongue of songs
calculated to rouse the enthusiasm of an emotional
people like the Welsh, the climax being reached
at the end of each meeting with their noble national
anthem, sung in the native tongue of course, " Land
of my Fathers."

Since that time it is gratifying to realize the
great progress which has been made in the revival
of *our* native tongue through the instrumentality
of the Gaelic League. The success of our friends
in this direction ought to be an encouragement to
us. The old Cymric tongue is almost universal
throughout Wales, side by side with the English, so
that it is not all visionary to think that a day may

come when ours, too, may become a bi-lingual people.

Mr. Edmund Vesey Knox, an Ulster Protestant Home Ruler, who was then a member of the Irish Parliamentary Party, came to assist in the return of Mr. Lloyd-George. At one of their great gatherings he told his audience how much he was impressed by the enthusiasm created by their native music and song. This reminded him, he said, that one of their great Irish poets, Thomas Davis, was partially of Welsh descent, which no doubt inspired one of his noblest songs " Cymric Rule and Cymric Rulers," written to their soul-stirring Welsh air, " The March of the Men of Harlech." After Mr. Knox, more singing, and then came a delightful address from a distinguished Irish lady, Mrs. Bryant, who did splendid service at many of these bye elections. Doctor Sophie Bryant, to give her full title, is a lady of great learning and eloquence, and not only a thorough Nationalist in sentiment, but an energetic worker in the Cause. A literary lady colleague thus sums up her chief qualities : " She is more learned than any man I know ; more tender than any woman I have ever met."

Mr. Lloyd-George was elected by the bare majority of 18 votes, so that without the small Irish vote in the Carnarvon Boroughs he could not have been returned at his first election for the constituency. Nor did he forget the fact. On one occasion we were speaking together in the lobby of the House of Commons when a friend of his came up. " This," said Mr. Lloyd-George, slapping me on the shoulder,

" is the man who brought me here." In a sense it was true, so that I might claim to have assisted in making a British Chancellor of the Exchequer.

I have spoken of the series of bye-elections which Mr. Gladstone described as the " Flowing Tide " which had set in for Home Rule. I remember with special pleasure one of these—that for the Rossendale Division of Lancashire. It was a sample of all the other bye-elections in 1892. The registration had been well done, and we knew to a man the strength of the Irish vote. We had 438 on the Register. This was no mere estimate, and we could give the figures at the time with equal accuracy for most places where we had an Irish population. Every voter of ours living in Rossendale had been visited. If he had removed from place to place inside the district it was noted. If he had gone out of the district he was communicated with, if possible through the medium of the branch of his new location. We knew where to find them all, and it was astonishing from what distant places men turned up to vote on the election day, through the agency of the local branches of the places to which the voters had gone.

In this Rossendale election I had two of the most capable lieutenants a man need wish to have, Patrick Murphy and Daniel Boyle, both then organisers of our League. Dan Boyle (now Alderman Boyle, M.P.) took the Bacup end of the Division ; Pat Murphy took Rawtenstall ; and I made my headquarters at Haslingden, for I had a *grah* for the place, on account of its connection with my old friend, Michael Davitt.

There can be no better test of a man's sterling qualities than the opinions held of him by the friends of his youth. Several times I had had occasion to visit Haslingden, the little factory town in North-East Lancashire, where Martin Davitt, the father of Michael, and his family lived when they came to this country after being evicted from their home in Mayo. Here I met Mr. Cockcroft, the bookseller, who gave Michael employment after he had lost his arm in the factory, and he and his family bore the Irish lad in kindly remembrance. But it was among his own people—those who had been the companions and friends of his youth— that I found the greatest admiration for "Mick," as they familiarly called him. I need scarcely say that they watched with pride the noble career of one who had grown to manhood in their midst.

I was able to turn that feeling to good account on the occasion of this Rossendale election. I asked the Liberal candidate, Mr. Maden, a young and wealthy cotton spinner of Rossendale, who had given us satisfactory pledges on Home Rule, to invite Michael Davitt's assistance. He did so. I backed up the request by a personal appeal, which he never refused if it lay in his power to do what I wished. He came, and words fail to describe his loving and enthusiastic reception by his own people.

I have alluded to the perfect way in which the Irish Vote had been organised. Michael Davitt

came into our committee room one day, and it was
with intense pride he turned over the leaves of our
books to show Mr. Maden, the candidate, how well
we were prepared to poll every Irish vote on the
election day. Davitt was a tower of strength to
us in this election, not only amongst our own people,
but amongst the English factory operatives, who
form the majority in Rossendale. As in other
bye-elections which had preceded it, we won the
Division by a handsome majority.

I was at once amused and amazed some time
ago to hear of a so-called biography of Davitt, the
keynote of which was a suggestion that he was,
first and foremost, an "Anti-Clerical." The idea
is an absurd one. He was an intense lover of right,
and one who scorned to be an opportunist. Consequently, he never hesitated to speak out, no
matter who opposed him, priest or layman. But
none knew better than he that there have been times
when the priests were the only friends the Irish
peasantry had ; and no one knew better than he
that the influence they have had they have, on
the whole, used wisely. If individual clerics have
gone out of their proper sphere of influence it is
certain they would have found Davitt in opposition
to them where he thought them wrong. I have
been placed in the same unpleasant position myself.
but I too have always carefully distinguished
between the individual priest who needed remon-
strance, and his wiser colleague ; and also between
the legitimate use of a priest's influence and its
abuse. So that to classify Davitt as an "Anti-

cleric " deserves a strong protest from one who loved him as well and as long as I did.

As I have said, when I asked him to come to Rossendale to help to further the cause of self-government for Ireland, he never refused a request of mine if it lay in his power to grant it, and, in this way, he wrote for me one of the books of my " Irish Library"—" Ireland's Appeal to America."

Michael has gone to his reward, and there are two things I shall always cherish as mementoes of him. One is a bunch of shamrocks sent to me, with the message :

" With Michael Davitt's compliments,
" Richmond Prison, Patrickstide, 1883."

The other is his last letter to me, written not long before his death. It was dated " St. Justin's, Dalkey, Co. Dublin, 7th March, 1906." In this he said : " I hope you are in good health and not growing too old. I shall be 60 ! on the 25th inst. ! ! ! " Was this a premonition that his end was near ? He died on May 31st, within three months of the time he wrote the letter.

I have spoken of the necessity for our organisation doing registration work at least as effectually as the Liberals and Tories do. It is not always men of the highest intellectual attainments who make the best registration agents. This fact came home to me very forcibly when reading a biography of Thomas Davis. It was stated that in the Revision Court he was not able to hold his own against the Tory agent. It is just what I would have imagined, considering the sensitive nature of Davis. A man with a face of brass, who *might* be an able man, but who, on the other hand, might be some low ignorant fellow, might easily do better than Thomas Davis with his fine intellect and varied learning.

At the same time, I have known men of the highest attainments who have made excellent agents, such a man as John Renwick Seager, who has for many years been connected with the London Liberal organisation. Just such another we have in our own ranks in Daniel Crilly who, before he became a journalist or entered Parliament, was a very successful agent in the Liverpool Courts.

One of the most efficient and conscientious of registration and electioneering agents I ever met was John Mogan, of Liverpool. Besides the annual registration work he was engaged on our side in nearly every election of importance in Liverpool for over 30 years. He was so engrossed in his work that, during an election he would, if required, sit up several nights in succession to have his work properly done ; indeed, I was often tempted to think that John never considered any election complete without at least *one* " all night sitting."

We believed in fighting the enemy with his own weapons. On election days in Liverpool there were shipowners who made it a practice of getting their vessels coaled in the river. As, unlike the Liffey at Dublin or the Thames at London, the Mersey at Liverpool is over a mile wide, and as most of the coal heavers were Irishmen, this move of the shipowners was to keep our men from voting. We were successful, to some extent, in counteracting this, for owing to the patriotism of a sterling Irishman, John Prendiville, the steam tugs which he owned were often used, on the day of an election, to take our men ashore.

Sometimes the Revision Courts gave us the opportunity of teaching a little Irish history. In South Wales most of our people hail from Munster. In one of the Courts there was the case of Owen O'Donovan being objected to, on the ground that he had left the qualifying property, and that *Eugene* O'Donovan was now the occupier. I explained to the Barrister that in the South of Ireland the names of Owen and Eugene were often applied to the same man, Eugene being the Latinized form of Owen. I gave as an illustration our national hero, Owen Roe O'Neill, who, in letters written to him in Latin, was styled Eugenius Rufus. A Welsh official in Court suggested that O'Donovan was anxious to become a Welshman by calling himself Owen. I replied that the name Owen was just as Irish as it was Welsh, coming no doubt from the same Celtic stock, and that, as a matter of fact, our man preferred being on the Register as Owen. The Barrister, being satisfied that both names applied to the same man, allowed the vote, and our voter would appear on the Register as Owen O'Donovan.

In looking up our people to have them put upon the Register, or in connection with an election, our canvassers are often able to form a good judgment of the creed, or nationality, or politics of the people of the house they are calling at by the pictures on the walls. If they see a picture of St. Patrick, or the Pope, or Robert Emmet, they assume they are in an Irish house of the right sort. One of my own apprentices, when I was in business, came across a bewildering complication on one occasion, for on one side of the room was the Pope, which seemed all right, but facing him was a gorgeous picture of King William crossing the Boyne. It was the woman of the house he saw, a good, decent Irishwoman and a Catholic, who explained the apparent inconsistency. Her husband was an Orangeman, "as good a man as ever broke bread" all the year round, till it came near the twelfth of July, when the Orange fever began to come on. (Our people at home in the County Down, as my father used to tell us, often found it so with otherwise decent Protestant neighbours.) He would come home from a lodge meeting some night, a little the worse for drink, and smash the Pope to smithereens. The wife was a sensible body, and knew it was no use interfering while the fit was on him. When she knew it had safely passed away, she would take King William to the pawnshop round the corner and get as much on him as would buy a new Pope. He was too fond of his wife, "Papish" and all as she was, to make any fuss about it, and would just go and redeem his idol, and set him up again, facing the Pope, for another twelve months at all events.

CHAPTER XXI.

THE "TIMES" FORGERIES COMMISSION.

WHEN the "Times" on the 18th of April, 1887 published what purported to be the *fac simile* of a letter from Mr. Parnell, and suggested that it was written to Mr. Patrick Egan in justification of the Phœnix Park assassinations, I at once, like many others, guessed who the forger must be. I had from time to time come into contact with Pigott, and I was satisfied that he was the one man capable of such a production.

When the company was formed in 1875 for the starting of a newspaper in connection with the Home Rule Confederation of Great Britain, there was an idea of buying Pigott's papers, "The Irishman," "Flag of Ireland," and "Shamrock," which always seemed to be in the market, whether to the Government or the Nationalists after events showed to be a matter of perfect indifference to him. Mr. John Barry and I were sent over to Dublin to treat with him. Mr. Barry went over the books and I went over the plant. What he wanted seemed reasonable enough, we thought.

The Directors of our Company did not, however, close with Pigott, but concluded to start a paper of their own, "The United Irishman," the production and direction of which, as I have stated, they placed in my hands.

During these years I had many opportunities of getting a knowledge of Pigott's true character. From time to time money had been subscribed through Pigott's papers for various national funds. Michael Davitt told me that when the political prisoners were released the committee appointed to raise a fund for them, to give them a start in life, applied for what had been sent through the " Irishman " and " Flag," that the whole of the funds subscribed through the various channels might be publicly presented to the men. There was considerable difficulty in getting this money from Pigott, but ultimately it was squeezed out of him.

An employe of the " Irishman," David Murphy, was shot—he survived his wound—in a mysterious manner. This was ascribed, and from all we know of the man, correctly, to Pigott, who, it was thought, fearing that Murphy might know too much about the sums coming into his hands and the sources whence they came, had tried to get him put out of the way. There was a still more serious aspect of this attempted assassination. The revelations of the " Times " Forgeries Commission afterwards proved that all this time Pigott was giving information to the police and getting paid for it. To my own personal knowledge David Murphy held an important position in the advanced organisation, for I once brought a young friend of mine, a printer, a sterling Irishman I had known from his early boyhood in Liverpool, from Wexford, where he was at the time employed, specially to introduce him to Murphy.

From the information given to the police by Pigott, it would soon be found there was some leakage, which would, no doubt, be traced to the " Irishman " office. It would, of course, be Pigott's cue to put the blame on the shoulders of Murphy, hence probably his attempted assassination.

It was not unreasonable, then, in looking round for the actual forger of the famous *fac simile* letter, that I and others who knew him should single out a man with such a bad record as Richard Pigott as the actual criminal.

The collapse of the conspiracy against the Irish leaders, and the suicide of the wretched Pigott on the 1st of March, 1889, are matters of history.

For the complete way in which the conspiracy was smashed up great credit was due to the distinguished Irish advocate, Sir Charles Russell. In his early days I knew him well, and was often thrown into contact with him, when he was a young barrister practising on the Northern circuit, and making Liverpool his headquarters. He was a member of the Liverpool Catholic Club when I was secretary of that body. The Club, before the Home Rule organisation superseded it in Liverpool. generally supported the Liberals in Parliamentary elections, but on one occasion there was, from a Catholic point of view, a very undesirable Liberal candidate, whom it was determined not to support. Pressure had, therefore, to be put upon the Liberals to withdraw this man. They were obstinate, though they had not the ghost of a chance without the Irish and Catholic vote, which formed fully half the strength they could generally count upon. On the other hand, *we* could not carry the seat by our own unaided vote. But, to show the Liberals that we would not have their man under any circumstances, it was arranged that if he were willing we should put Charles Russell forward as our candidate. As secretary it became my duty to ask him to place himself in our hands. He agreed, on the understanding that he was to be withdrawn if our action had the effect of forcing the Liberals to get a candidate more acceptable to us. We succeeded, and, of course, withdrew our man.

When we started the Home Rule organisation in Liverpool, we asked Charles Russell to be chairman of our inaugural public meeting. He had been contesting Dundalk as a Home Ruler, so we thought he was the very man to preside at our meeting, and gave that as our reason for asking him. He received the deputation—my friend, Alfred Crilly and myself—with that geniality and courtesy which were so characteristic of him. As it happened that the three of us were County Down men, who are somewhat clannish, we soon got talking about the people " at home." He knew both our families in Ireland, and had served his time with a solicitor of my name in Newry, Cornelius Denvir, before he had entered the other branch of the legal profession. We also got talking of the barony of Lecale, which he, as well as my own people, had sprung from, and how it had been the only Norman colony in Ulster ;

how many of the descendants of De Courcy's followers were still there, as might be seen from their names—Russells, Savages, Mandevilles. Dorrians, Denvirs, and others, whose fathers, inter-marrying with the original Celtic population, MacCartans, Magennises, MacRorys, and so on, had become like the Burkes, Fitzgeralds, and other Norman clans, " More Irish than the Irish them-selves."

This was all very well, and very interesting, but it did not get us our chairman. Charles Russell was too wary, and, perhaps, too far-seeing, who can tell ? for that. It was quite true, he said, he had contested Dundalk as a Home Ruler, and, of course, he was a Home Ruler, but he advised us to ask Dr. Commins to be our chairman, as being so much better known than himself. We did ask " The Doctor," and, kindly and genial as we ever found him, he at once consented.

Nearly forty years have passed since then, and I really believe that these two, then comparatively young men, practically made choice of their re-spective after-careers on that occasion.

Dr. Commins, who, like Charles Russell, was a practising barrister on the Northern circuit, held for some years the highest position his fellow-country-men could give him as President of the Home Rule Confederation of Great Britain, and became a member of the Irish Parliamentary Party.

Charles Russell, though always a Home Ruler and sincere lover of his country, made a brilliant career for himself as a great lawyer and Liberal statesman. I have often wondered since, if he had become chairman of our meeting in 1872, and had then identified himself with the Home Rule movement, if his statue would be to-day as it is in the London Law Courts, or if he would ever have been Lord Chief Justice of England and Lord Russell of Killowen ? I think not.

The " Times " Forgeries Commission, though got up to do deadly damage to the Irish Cause, had not, even before the final collapse of the conspiracy, had that effect, as bye-election after bye-election proved. For instance, when the Commission appointed to deal with the " Times " charges against the Irish leaders re-opened, after a short vacation at Christmas, the Govan election was going on, and, on the 19th of January, 1889, the Liberal Home Ruler won the seat by a majority of over 1,000.

After the exposure of the plot, Mr. Gladstone's " Flowing Tide " swept on with increased velocity, and, wherever there was a bye-election, there was an enormous demand for our members of Parliament. During this period, when the Irish vote in Great Britain was more fully organised than it ever had been before, I attended most of these elections. It was keenly felt, as had been proved on several occasions, that *no* place, however small the number of Irish voters, should be overlooked, especially at a time when British parties had become once more pretty evenly balanced.

CHAPTER XXII.

DISRUPTION OF THE IRISH PARTY—HOME RULE
CARRIED IN THE COMMONS—UNITY OF PAR-
LIAMENTARY PARTY RESTORED—MR. JOHN
REDMOND BECOMES LEADER.

THERE is nothing more bitter than a family quarrel.

The unfortunate disruption in the Irish Parliamentary Party and the fierce quarrel that arose among the Irish people near the end of 1890, would be to me such a painful theme that I must ask my readers to pardon me if I pass on as quickly as possible towards the happier times which find us practically a re-united people, while the Irish Party in Parliament is a solid working force under the able leadership of Mr. John Redmond.

In accordance with the demands of the branches of the Irish organisation in Great Britain, a special Convention was called and held in Newcastle-on-Tyne on Saturday, 16th May, 1891. Delegates from all parts of Great Britain attended, and elected a new Executive in harmony with the bulk of the League, with Mr. T. P. O'Connor, President, as before.

Provision was also made for carrying on the fight for Home Rule in the constituencies, which had been somewhat relaxed by the unhappy split in our ranks. This was imperative, in view of the necessity for assisting to return to Parliament a sufficient majority to enable Mr. Gladstone to carry his Home Rule Bill through the House of Commons.

The result of the General Election of 1892 was the return to power of Mr. Gladstone. His majority was the best proof to friend and foe of the value of the work done by our organisation during the previous years in adding to the Irish vote in Great Britain. It also showed we had the power and the influence in the constituencies we had claimed. Indeed, the books in the offices of the League could show, by the figures for every constituency, that without the Irish vote Mr. Gladstone would have had no majority at all.

When we come to consider the terrible crisis we were passing through, the result was magnificent.

Although, as we all expected, Mr. Gladstone's Home Rule Bill was thrown out by the House of Lords, the fact that a Bill conferring self-government on Ireland had been passed in the Commons was recognised as a step towards that end which could never be receded from, and that it was but a question of time when the Home Rule Cause would be won.

Moreover, the event proved that our grievance was no longer against the English democracy, but against the class which misgoverned us, just as it, to a lesser extent, misgoverned them.

Most of us have, no doubt, taken part in a family gathering on some joyous occasion when the mother realizes that *all* her children are not around her, and is overcome with sadness. So it was with us. Well might mother Ireland ask why were not *all* her children in the one fold, to be one with her and with each other in the hour of rejoicing, as they had been loyally with her in all her sorrows ? Why was the bitter feud over the leadership of the Irish Party so long kept up ? Why was the happy reconciliation so long delayed ?

While the majority, it is true, were arrayed on one side, the fact remained that on the other side there were men of undoubted patriotism and great ability, not only members of Parliament such as John and William Redmond or Timothy Harrington, but some of our best men all over the country, who had done splendid service for the Cause, and were either in fierce antagonism or holding aloof.

It was during this sad time that I met that distinguished orator, Thomas Sexton, to whom John Barry was good enough to introduce me. Sexton came specially from Ireland on this occasion in the interests of peace. Actuated by the same motive was Patrick James Foley, another member of the Party and of the Executive of the League, who, while holding strongly to his own conscientious opinions, was always most courteous to those differing from him.

I attended the great Irish Race Convention, held in the Leinster Hall, Dublin, on the first three days of September, 1896. The Most Reverend Patrick O'Donnell, Bishop of Raphoe, a noble representative of old Tyrconnell, and a tower of strength to our Cause, presided, and it was, undoubtedly, one of the most representative gatherings of the Irish race from all parts of the world ever held.

Two admirable resolutions were passed with great enthusiasm and perfect unanimity, and there is no doubt but that this Convention was the first great step towards the reunion of the Irish Parliamentary Party, which has been since so happily effected.

It was more than three years after the Race Convention before the long-desired re-union of the Irish Party and the Irish people all over the world was accomplished at a Conference of members of Parliament of both parties held in Committee Room 15 of the House of Commons, on Tuesday, January 30th, 1900.

CHAPTER XXIII.

THE GAELIC REVIVAL—THOMAS DAVIS—CHARLES
GAVAN DUFFY—ANGLO-IRISH LITERATURE—
THE IRISH DRAMA—DRAMATISTS AND ACTORS.

ONE effect of the disturbance in political work
caused by the split seemed to be the impetus given
to existing movements which, so far as politics
were concerned, were neutral ground.   Chief amongst
these was the Gaelic League, which from its found-
ation advanced by leaps and bounds and brought
to the front many fine characters.

Francis Fahy was one of the first Presidents of
the Gaelic League of London, and there is no doubt
but the Irish language movement in the metropolis
owes much to his influence and indefatigable
exertions.

I first made his acquaintance over twenty-five
years ago, when he was doing such splendid Irish
propagandism in the Southwark Irish Literary
Club, of which, although he had able and enthusiastic helpers, he was the life and soul.   He has
written many songs and poems, which have been
collected and published.   What is, perhaps, one
of the raciest and most admired of his songs, " The
Ould Plaid Shawl," first appeared in the " Nationalist " for February 7th, 1885, a weekly periodical

which I was publishing at the time. Several stirring songs of great merit by other members of the society also appeared in its pages. Indeed, the members came to look upon the " Nationalist" as their own special organ, and ably written and animated accounts of their proceedings appeared regularly in its columns. I also published a song book for them, compiled by Francis Fahy, chiefly for the use of their younger members.

An active Gaelic Leaguer, who did much for the success of the movement in London, was William Patrick Ryan. He wrote a" Life of Thomas Davis " for " Denvir's Monthly," a sort of revival of my " Irish Library." This book was very favourably received by the press. The " Liverpool Daily Post " gave it more than a column of admirable criticism, evidently from the pen of the editor himself, Sir Edward Russell. In it was the following kindly reference to myself : " Our present pleasing duty is to recognise the labours of Mr. Denvir—efforts in such a cause are always touchingly beautiful—as an inculcator of national sentiment ; to illustrate the genuine literary interest and value of the first booklet of his new library ; and to wish the library a long and useful, and in every way successful vogue."

Another active man in the language movement in London, whose acquaintance I was glad to renew when I first came to the metropolis, is Doctor Mark Ryan.

It is nearly forty years since we first knew each other in connection with another organisation. He then lived in a North Lancashire town, and was studying medicine, not being at that time a fully qualified doctor. If I remember rightly, our interview had no connexion with the healing art, indeed quite the contrary, for besides qualifying for the medical profession, he was graduating in the same school as Rickard Burke, Arthur Forrester, and Michael Davitt, but, like myself, was more fortunate than Burke and Davitt, inasmuch as he escaped their fate of being sent into penal servitude. Although Mark Ryan was for a long time resident in Lancashire, he there lost nothing, nor has he since, of the fluent Gaelic speech of his native Galway, for I heard him quite recently delivering an eloquent speech in Irish at a gathering of the Gaelic League.

Speaking of Dr. Mark Ryan reminds me of how often I have noticed in my travels through Great Britain, what a number of Irish doctors there are, and also that they are almost invariably patriotic. They are of great service to the cause, for it frequently happens that, in some districts, they are almost the only men of culture, and are not generally slow to take the lead among their humbler fellow-countrymen.

One of the finest Irish scholars in the Gaelic League was Mr. Thomas Flannery. He, too, was a valued contributor to my " Monthly Irish Library," two of the best books in the series, " Dr. John O'Donovan," and " Archbishop MacHale," being from his pen. In fact, he and Timothy MacSweeny I might almost look upon as having been the Gaelic editors of the " Monthly."

I once, when in business in Liverpool, printed a Scottish Gaelic Prayer-Book for Father Campbell, one of the Jesuit priests of that city, for use among the Catholic congregations in the highlands and islands of Scotland. John Rogers, like Timothy MacSweeny, a ripe Irish scholar, called on me while it was in progress, and was delighted to know that such a book was being issued. To Mr. MacSweeny I also sent a copy, and they both could read the Scottish Gaelic easily, showing, of course, how closely the Irish and Scottish Gaels were, with the Manx, united in one branch of the Celtic race, as distinguished from the Bretons and Welsh.

I have always had an intense admiration for the poetry of " Young Ireland." I used to call it Irish literature until I found myself corrected, very properly, by my Gaelic League friends, who maintained that, not being in the Irish tongue, its proper designation was Anglo-Irish literature.

I had the pleasure of making the acquaintance of one of the leading young Irelanders, Charles Gavan Duffy, after his return to this country, when he assisted at the inauguration of our London Irish Literary Society, which has been a credit to the Irishmen of the metropolis. Much of the success of the Society is due to Alfred Perceval Graves, author of the well-known song " Father O'Flynn," a faithful picture of a genuine Irish *soggarth*. Among others of the members of the society who have made their mark in Irish literature is Mr. Richard Barry O'Brien, the President, the author of several valuable works of history and biography.

It was at the opening of our Literary Society that I first met Duffy in the flesh, but I had known and admired him in spirit from my earliest boyhood.

I was greatly pleased when he told me he had been much interested in my publications, not only those issued more recently, but those of many years before. I afterwards had a letter from him in reference to my " Irish in Britain," in which he said : " I saw long ago some of the little Irish books you published in Liverpool, and know you for an old and zealous worker in the national seed field."

His son, George Gavan Duffy, is a solicitor, practising in London, and an active worker in the national cause. His wife is a daughter of the late A. M. Sullivan, and is as zealous a Nationalist as was her father, and as patriotic as her husband.

The first book of National poetry I ever read was one compiled by Charles Gavan Duffy—" The Ballad Poetry of Ireland." I should say that this has been one of the most popular books ever issued. There are none of his own songs in this volume. The few he did write are in the " Spirit of the Nation " and other collections. These make us regret he did not write more, for, in the whole range of our poetry, I think there is nothing finer or more soul-stirring than his " Inishowen," " The Irish Rapparees," and " The Men of the North."

It is unfortunate that we have nothing from the pen of Thomas Davis on the subject of the Irish drama and dramatists, for among the most delightful and valuable contributions to the Anglo-Irish literature of the nineteenth century were his " Literary and Historical Essays."

For students, historians, journalists, lecturers, and public speakers, they have been an inexhaustible mine, since they first appeared week by week in the " Nation " during the Repeal and Young Ireland movements. As sources of inspiration they have been of still more practical value to the Irish poet, painter, musician and sculptor.

Though he was apparently in good health up to a few days of his death, which was quite un-expected, Davis, in giving to his country these unsurpassed essays, might have had some idea that his life would not be a long one, and that, if he could not himself accomplish all he had projected, he would at least sketch out a programme for his brother workers in the national field, and for those coming after them.

A glance at the contents of Davis's Essays will show how fully he has covered almost every field in which Irishmen are or ought to be interested. We have Irish History, Antiquities, Monuments, Architecture, Ethnology, Oratory, Resources, Topo-graphy, Commerce, Art, Language, Our People of all classes, Music and Poetry dealt with in an attractive as well as in a practical manner. Anyone who has ever gone to these Essays, as I have over and over again, for information, has always found Davis completely master of every subject that he touched. His " Hints to Irish Painters " are illustrations of the value of the advice he gives in connection with his varied themes. Those of the generations since his time who have profited by his teaching know best how valuable would have been his views in connection with the Irish Drama.

Knowing as we do how *thorough* Davis was in everything he took up, the reason he did not deal with it was, probably, that he had not had the same opportunities of getting information on this as upon the other wonderfully varied subjects in his Essays.

I have in my mind at this moment one Irish dramatist, Edmond O'Rourke, who would have appreciated anything Davis would have written on the subject, and would certainly have profited by it.

O'Rourke, better known by his stage name of Falconer, was an actor as well as a dramatist. He was "leading man" when I first saw him in the stock company of the Adelphi Theatre, Liverpool, and used to play the whole round of Shakespearean characters, his favourite parts being the popular ones of Macbeth, Hamlet, and Richard the Third. He was a dark-complexioned man of average height, somewhat spare in form and features. Though his performances were intellectual creations, we boys used to make somewhat unfavourable comparisons between him and Barry Sullivan, another of our fellow-countrymen. Barry was by no means superior to Falconer in his conception of the various parts, but he greatly surpassed him in voice, physique, and general bearing on the stage, in which respects I think he had no equal in our times.

After Falconer went to London he became manager of the Lyceum Theatre, where sev ral of his pieces were performed, including the well-known Irish drama, " Peep o' Day," which had an enormously successful run. With this he also produced a magnificent panorama of Killarney, to illustrate which he wrote the well-known song of " Killarney " which, with the music of Balfe, our Irish composer, at once became very popular, as it ever since has been. Madame Anna Whitty, the distinguished vocalist, who first sang " Killarney," was a daughter of Michael James Whitty, of whom I have spoken elsewhere. In going through my papers I have just come across a letter from O'Rourke, dated from the Princess's Theatre, Manchester, August 19th, 1872, in which he tells me of the great success in Manchester of another play of his," Eileen Oge." This also he produced at the Lyceum Theatre, London, where it had a long and successful run. Edmund O'Rourke was a patriotic Irishman, and in this respect I could never have made the same comparison between the partiotism of the two men, Barry Sullivan and him, as I did between them as actors. *Both* were patriotic Irishmen. It will be remembered that in an early chapter of this book I have mentioned that Barry Sullivan once offered himself to our committee as an Irish National-alist candidate for the parliamentary representation of Liverpool.

Dion Boucicault, too, is one, I am sure, who would have profited by anything Thomas Davis might have written on the subject of the drama. I am quite satisfied that though he was severely criticised for the wake scene in his play of " The Shaughraun " at the time it was first produced, the objectionable features in this were more the fault of the actors than of the dramatist ; but the subject was an exceedingly risky one, even for a man like Boucicault, and would have been better avoided altogether.

Besides Barry Sullivan and Falconer, other Irish actors I knew were Barry Aylmer, James Foster O'Neill, and Hubert O'Grady. They were impersonators of what were known as " Irish parts," and being genuine Irish Nationalists, as well as actors, did much to elevate the character of such performances. For with them, all the wit and drollery were retained, while they helped, by their example, to banish the buffoonery that used to characterise the " Stage Irishman."

I am reminded by a criticism on one of his pieces in a London daily paper that we can claim, as a fellow-countryman, perhaps the most brilliant writer at the present time for the British stage— George Bernard Shaw. From a conversation I had with him once, I would certainly gather that he was a patriotic Irishman.

I have done something in the way of dramatic production myself, one of the pieces I wrote being at the request of Father Nugent, to assist him in the great temperance movement he had started in Liverpool. He engaged a large hall in Bevington Bush, where every Monday night he gave the total abstinence pledge against intoxicating liquors to large numbers of people. I was then carrying on the " Catholic Times " for him, and he asked me to be the first to take the pledge from him at his public inauguration of the movement. Although, as he was aware, I was already a pledged teetotaler to Father Mathew, I was greatly pleased to agree to assist him all I could in his great work.

He believed in providing a counter-attraction to the public house, and each Monday night, in the Bevington Hall, he provided a concert or some other kind of entertainment ; giving, in the interval between the first and second part a stirring address and the temperance pledge. As there was a stage and scenery in the hall, we often had dramatic sketches. The drama I wrote for Father Nugent had a temperance moral. It was called " The Gormans of Glenmore." It was played several Monday nights in succession, and was well received.

Some years afterwards I made it into a story, calling it " The Reapers of Kilbride." This appeared over a frequent signature of mine, " Slieve Donard," in the " United Irishman," the organ of the Home Rule Confederation.

Singularly enough, I found that part of it had been changed back again into the first act of a drama by Mr. Hubert O'Grady, the well-known Irish comedian.

That gentleman was giving a performance for the benefit of the newly released political prisoners at one of our Liverpool theatres. Being somewhat late, I was making my way upstairs in company with Michael Davitt, and the play had commenced. I could hear on the stage part of the dialogue, which

seemed familiar to me, and, sure enough, when I
took my seat and listened to the rest of the act,
the dialogue was pretty nearly, word for word, from
"The Reapers of Kilbride." The compiler of the play
being acted had also drawn upon another drama of
mine for his last act, "Rosaleen Dhu, or the Twelve
Pins of Bin-a-Bola." The play we were witnessing
was very cleverly constructed, for Mr. O'Grady, with
his strong dramatic instincts and experience, could
tell exactly what would go well, and could use
material accordingly. The transformation of the
story as it appeared in the "United Irishman"
back again into a play would be easily effected, as,
leaving out the descriptive part, the dialogue itself,
with the necessary stage directions, told the story.
This, no doubt, Mr. O'Grady had perceived.

Later still, I carried out a similar transformation
with another of my own productions. I have a
piece in three acts which, as a play, has never been
published or performed. It is called "The Curse
of Columbkille." This drama I changed into a
story, which has appeared in the series of 6d. novels
published by Messrs. Sealy, Bryers and Walker.
The most striking character in it is Olaf, a Dane,
who believes himself to be a re-incarnation of one
of the old Danish sea rovers. A member of the
firm, the late Mr. George Bryers, a sterling Irishman,
called my attention to the opinion of the professional
reader to the firm that it would be advisable to call
the story "Olaf the Dane ; or the Curse of Columbkille." I accepted the suggestion, and accordingly
the book has been published with that title.

I have seen with much interest the movement inaugurated by the Irish Theatre Company in Dublin, and have been present at some of their performances in London. In spite of some false starts and a tendency to imitate certain undesirable foreign influences, the movement should certainly help to foster the Irish drama.

CHAPTER XXIV.

" HOW IS OLD IRELAND AND HOW DOES SHE STAND ? "

SUMMING up these pages, how shall I answer the question asked by Napper Tandy in " The Wearin' of the Green " over a hundred years ago—" How is old Ireland, and how does she stand ? "

Let us see what changes, for the better or for the worse, there have been during the period—nearly seventy years—covered by these recollections.

Catholic Emancipation had, five years before I was born, allowed our people to raise their voices, and give their votes through their representatives in an alien Parliament.

I am not one to say that no benefit for Ireland has arisen through legislation at Westminster, but the system that allowed our people to perish of starvation has always been, to my mind, the one great justification for our struggle for self-government by every practicable method. It has been a struggle for sheer existence.

If Ireland had had the making of her own laws when the potato crop failed, not a single human being would have perished from starvation. That I am justified in introducing the terrible Irish Famine and its consequences into these recollections as part of my own experiences I think I have shown

in my description of its effects upon our people
when passing through Liverpool as emigrants or
as settlers in England.

I have always endeavoured to look upon the
most hopeful aspects of the Irish question. But
with the appalling tragedy of the Famine half way
in the last century, with half our people gone and
the population still diminishing, one is bound to
admit that the nineteenth century was one of the
most disastrous in Irish history.

Is it surprising that, during my time, driven
desperate at the sight of a perishing people in one
of the most fruitful lands on earth, we should have
made two attempts at rebellion ?

In 1848 the means were totally inadequate.

In 1867 the movement looked more hopeful in
many respects. The revolutionary organisation had
a large number of enrolled members on both sides
of the Atlantic. Among them were hundreds in the
British army, and many thousands of Irish-American
veterans trained in the Civil War, eager to wipe off
the score of centuries in a conflict, on something
like equal terms, with the olden oppressor of their
race.

But the real hope of success lay in the prospect
of a war between America and England, which at
one time seemed imminent, and justified the action
of the Fenian chiefs in their preparations.

It was, however, the very existence of Fenianism
which, more than any other cause, prevented war.
For none knew better than far-seeing statesmen
like Mr. Gladstone (who declared that he was

prompted to remedial measures for Ireland by " the intensity of Fenianism ") that within a month of the commencement of a war between America and England, Ireland would be lost to the British crown for ever. That is why English statesmen would have grovelled in the dust before America, rather than engage in a conflict with her.

The generous way in which the Irish exiles in America have poured their wealth into the lap of their island mother, and the determination they have shown to shed their blood for her just as freely, should the opportunity only come, are the features which to some extent counterbalance the tragedy of the Famine. For that terrible calamity, by driving our people out in millions, raised a power on the side of Ireland which her oppressors could not touch, a power which is no doubt among the means intended by Providence to hasten our coming day of freedom.

Nevertheless, emigration, the most unanswerable proof of English misgovernment, is a terrible drain on our country's life-blood, and no entirely hopeful view of Ireland's future can be held until this is stopped.

What, however, are the reflections which bring encouragement ?

One is that the time cannot be far distant when some statesman of the type of Gladstone will try to avert the danger threatening the British empire throug' an ever-discontented Ireland, by conceding to her at least the amount of self-government possessed by Canada and Australia.

To this one section of Englishmen will say
"Never!" Students of history have many times
heard the "Never" of English statesmen, and know
how often it has proved futile. Before I was born
they were saying "Never" to Catholic Emancipation. Later on they said "Never" to the demand
for tenant-right. A few years ago, when fighting
the Boers, they said "Never" to the suggestion
that the war should be ended on conditions. Even
now economic causes and the competition of rival
powers are at work in such a way that it is plain
that the existence of the British Empire is at stake.
England's one chance lies in the possibility of the
friendship of the free democratic commonwealths
which are at present her colonies—and of Ireland.

The establishing of County Councils in Ireland
and Great Britain was an acceptance of the principle
of Home Rule. Their successful working has
caused the belief in that principle to gain ground.
Their administration in Ireland has shown that in
no part of the British empire does there exist a
greater capacity for self-government. All creeds
and classes there have found the material benefit
arising from them, for instead of their finances being
managed by irresponsible boards, the money of
the people is now wisely spent by their elected
representatives.

Moreover, if there is one thing that is certain,
it is that the *future* is on our side. In my own
time I have seen a most startling change come over
the attitude of the working classes of England
towards Ireland as they progressed in knowledge

and political power themselves. They are the certain rulers of England to-morrow, the men whose democratic ideals are our own, and who have in fact largely been trained by us. Their rise means the fall of the system that has mis-governed Ireland. Thus every day brings nearer the triumph of our ideal, the ideal of freedom, which will probably be worked out in the form of Ireland governing herself and working harmoniously with a democratic self-governing England.

The unquestionable growing desire among the people of Wales and Scotland to manage their own affairs proceeds largely from their having felt the benefits of *local* self-government in their County Councils. Their prejudice against *National* self-government for Ireland, and for themselves, too, should they desire it, is rapidly breaking down. In this connection, too, we must never forget what an enormous power we have in the two millions and more of Irishmen and men of Irish extraction in Great Britain, and that, under ordinary circumstances, they hold the balance of power between British parties in about 150 Parliamentary constituencies.

With regard to the Irish land question, we have every reason to be hopeful of the final and complete success of the great movement commenced by the organisation founded by Michael Davitt.

We have had, since the days of Strongbow, many conquests and confiscations and settlements, the main object of each being the acquisition of the land of Ireland. Is it not marvellous, notwithstanding all the attempts to destroy our people, how they have clung to the soil and so absorbed the foreign element that you still so often find the old tribal names in the old tribal lands ? Apart from this, we have, in the descendants of the various invaders, what would be a most valuable element in a self-governing Ireland, for whatever be the creed or the race from which men have sprung, it is but natural that all should love alike the land of their birth. As a result of Michael Davitt's labours, that land is to-day more nearly than it has been for centuries the property of the people, and it seems now, humanly speaking, impossible that they should ever be dispossessed of it again.

Then there is the improvement in education. At one time it was banned and hunted along with religion and patriotism. Then it was permitted, with a view of turning it into a lever against the other two elements. Concessions have so far been wrung from the British parliament that there is now a university to which Irish youths can be sent. Here there is a great factor for good, for while, on the one hand, knowledge is power, on the other hand the thirst for knowledge has always been ineradicable in the Irish character. There are also the beginnings of technical training so long badly needed. Under self-government we should have been a couple of generations earlier in the race than we are, but it is not too late.

Lastly, in reckoning up the conditions from which we can take hope and comfort there is this : In the darkest hour we have never lost faith in ourselves and our Cause. To find a parallel for such tenacity in the pages of the history of any land would be difficult.

We come of a race that, through the long, dreary centuries, has never known despair, nor shall we despair now. I am assured that, before long, the drain on our life blood that has gone on for sixty years will stop, and that we shall stand on solid ground at last, ready for an upward spring.

And so, to the young men of Ireland I would say : Be true to yourselves ; hold fast to the ideals which your fathers preserved through the centuries, in spite of savage force and unscrupulous statecraft. The times are changing ; new impulses are constantly shaping the destinies of the nations ; have confidence in God and your country ; and who shall dare to say that the future of Ireland may not yet be a glorious recompense for the heroism with which she has borne the sufferings of the past.

THE END.

INDEX.

———❖———

A.

Alabama Claims, 75.
Allen, Larkin, and O'Brien condemned and executed, 104.
Ambulances, Irish, for Franco-Prussian War, 160,161.
Amnesty Association and O'Connell Centenary, 183.
Ancient Fenians, 52.
Anderson, Arthur, resembled Corydon, 85.
"Annesley's Mountain, Lord," 31, 47.
Answers to Correspondents, 154.
Antrim, my birthplace, 2.
Archbishops Crolly and Murray support the Bequest Act, 30.
Archdeacon, George, 52.
Architectural Drawing and Surveying, employed at these, 54.
Arms for Rising of 1867. Inadequate supply, 94.
Arrest and rescue of Kelly and Deasy, 95.
Aunt Kitty, my godmother, 2.
———— Mary, 38.
———— Nancy, 15.
Aylmer, Barry, adopts the stage as profession, 119.

B.

Ballad Poetry of Ireland, 260.
Ballymagenaghy, my mother's birthplace, 31.
———— rocky soil, 31.
Ballymagenaghy, "Papishes to a man," 31.
——— cottage industries, 33, 34.
———— large families, 33.
Ballymagrehan, 36.
Ballywalter, my father's birthplace, 2.
Ballinahinch, Battle of, 38, 39.
Banbridge, weaving industries by steam, 34.
Bannon, Oiney, 31.
Barrett, David, examines the Lia Fail, 110.
"Barney Henvey" and the Fairies, 35, 36.
Barry, John, 8, 127.
——— calls us together to form Home Rule Confederation of Great Britain, 173.
Barry Sullivan, a great Irish actor, 22.
Beers, Lord Roden's agent in Dolly's Brae massacre, 45.
Beecher (Captain Michael O'Rorke), "The Fenian Paymaster," 78, 79.
Belle Vue Prison, Manchester, near the scene of rescue, 101.
Benedictines, 4.
Biggar, Joseph, 180, 181, 193.
——— Catholic, becomes a, 181.
——— "Obstruction," enters upon, 182.
——— Parliament, enters, 179.
——— Parnell, combination with, 179.
Birmingham, supplementary Convention, 176.

" Black North," The, 15.
Bligh, M.D., Alderman Alexander, 200.
Bligh, M.D., John, 207.
Blockade, running of " United Ireland," 209, 215.
Boer War, The, 271.
" Bog Latin," Mr. Butt gives the origin of it, 195.
Boucicault, Dion, 263.
Bourbaki, our men in Foreign Legion with him struck last blow in Franco-German War, 161.
Boyle, M.P., Alderman Daniel, 239.
Brady, John, 236.
Breslin, John, 76.
—— aids in escape of military Fenians, 140.
Breslin, Michael, " on his keeping," 77, 123.
Breslin, Michael, narrowly escapes arrest, 124.
Brett (sergeant of police) shot in Manchester rescue, 101.
" Brian, Tribe of," 28.
Brian O'Loughlin in '98, 38.
Brotherhood of St. Patrick, the forerunner of Fenianism and Irish Revolutionary Brotherhood, 87.
Bryant, Mrs. Dr. Sophie, 238.
Bryers, George, 266.
" Buckshot Foster," 210.
Burke, Rickard, meets a notable company, 93.
—— purchases arms, 105.
—— Clerkenwell explosion an attempt to rescue him, 106.
—— sent to penal servitude, 106.
—— returned to America, 112.
Burke, Thomas, J.P., of Liverpool, 186.
Bushmills, Co. Antrim, my birthplace, 2.

Butt, Isaac, presides at the first Annual Convention of the Home Rule Confederation of Great Britain, and becomes its first President, 173.
—— a contributor to " United Irishman," 181.
—— gives no countenance to obstruction, 188.
—— 1876 Convention votes confidence in him, 188.
—— resigns presidency of organisation, and succeeded by Parnell, 192.
—— his death, 195.
Byrom Street, Liverpool, my house for a time the headquarters of Home Rule Confederation of Great Britain, 181.
—— frequently met Butt, Parnell, Biggar, and other leaders there, 181.
Byrne, Daniel, Richmond Prison warder, 77.
Byrne, Frank, 160, 181.
Byrne, M.P., Garrett, 230.
Byrne, Patrick, 199.

C.

Cahill, Rev. Dr., a great preacher, 59.
Camp in Everton, in view of expected rising in Liverpool, 55.
Campbell, Richard, a humorous Irish singer, 120.
" Camp Fires of the Legion," by James Finigan, 162.
Carlingford Lough, vies with Killarney in beauty, 27.
Carnarvon Borough election, where I first met Lloyd George, 237.
Carraig Mountain, 31
Cassidy, Tom, " a flogger," 67.
Castlewellan, Eiver Magennis its member in King James's Parliament, 29.

Castlewellan, a Nationalist centre for South Down, 47.

" Catalpa " carries off the military Fenians, 140.

—— lands them safely in New York, 145.

Catholic Emancipation, 268.

Catholic Hierarchy, Restoration of, 58.

Catholic Institute, 54.

" Catholic Times," I review in it " Life of Robert Emmet," by Michael James Whitty, 21.

—— carrying it on single-handed, 153.

Celtic Race, the Catholics of Ulster the most Celtic part of Ireland, 30, 57.

Chambers, Corporal, 200.

Chester Castle, plot to seize, 81.

—— I volunteer for the raid, 82.

Christian Brothers, The, 14, 27.

Churches, increase rapidly in Liverpool, 6.

Clampit, Sam, a good, honest Protestant Fenian, is arrested, 108.

Clan Connell War Song— O'Donnell Aboo " 115.

Clan na nGael, 36.

Clarence Dock, Liverpool, 3.

—— where the harvest men landed, 35.

Clarke, Michael, 180.

Clarke, Patrick, 180.

Clarkhill, Co. Down, 47.

Coming over from Ireland, 3.

Commins, Dr. Andrew, his record, 172.

—— becomes head of Home Rule Organisation in Great Britain, 171, 172.

Conciliation Hall, Dublin, 16.

Condon, Captain Edward O'Meagher, 93.

Condon, plans rescue of Kelly and Deasy, 96.

—— is himself arrested, 102.

Condon, his defiant shout in the dock of " God save Ireland," 104.

—— returned to America, and has been since helping the Cause there and here, 106, 107, and 112.

Confederates, Irish, 55.

Connolly, Lawrence, 185.

Connaught, 35.

Convention of 1876 votes confidence in Isaac Butt, 188.

Copperas Hill Chapel, 5.

—— Schools, 13.

Cork, " No sin in Cor-r-r k," 26.

Corydon, the informer, what he was like, 85.

—— throws off the mask, 85.

Cottage Industries in Ulster, 33.

Council of Fenian Leaders, 93.

Cousens, a Liverpool detective, 131.

Cranston, Robert, escaped military Fenian, 141.

Crilly, Alfred, a brilliant Irishman, who did good service for the Cause, 150, 171.

Crilly, Daniel, brother of Alfred, 150, 211.

—— on staff of " Nation," 151.

—— registration agent, 243.

—— editor of " United Irishman," 180.

— — Member of Parliament, 180.

Crilly, Frederick Lucas, General Secretary of United Irish League of Great Britain, 150.

Crimean War, The, 65.

Crosbie Street, mostly spoke Connaught Irish, 15.

Crowley, Thade, the Cork pork butcher, 25, 26.

Cumberland, 33.

Curragh of Kildare, I help at the building of camp there, 65.

D.

" Daily News," The, describes the rescue of Kelly and Deasy, and acknowledges the courage and skill of the rescuers, 101.

" Daily Post," Liverpool, 21.

Darragh, Daniel, brings the arms from Birmingham for Manchester Rescue, 96.

—— dies in Portland Prison, 126.

—— Hogan brings his remains to Ireland, and Condon visits his grave, 127.

Darragh, Thomas, escaped military Fenian, 141.

Davis, Thomas, as registration agent, 242.

—— his " Literary and Historical Essays," 261.

Davitt, Martin, father of Michael, 240.

Davitt, Michael, takes up Forrester's work of supplying arms, 132.

—— is arrested and convicted on Corydon's testimony, 136.

—— returns from penal servitude, 199.

—— formation of the Land League, 205.

—— his " Fall of Feudalism," 197.

—— tries to get Parnell to join advanced movement, 202.

" Dear Old Ireland," T. D. Sullivan's Song, 38.

Denvir's " Monthly " and " Irish Library," 257.

De Courcy, 27, 29.

Denvir, Bishop, Bible, 30.

—— see Father O'Laverty, 30.

—— I met him with my father, 3 .

Denvir, General Denver's daughter enquires after him, 41.

Denver City, the Capital of Colorado, named after General James William Denver, descended from Patrick Denvir, a '98 Insurgent. 40.

Desmond, Captain, one of the rescuers of the military Fenians, 140.

Devoy, John, he aided the escape of James Stephens, 76, and of the military Fenians, 140.

Dillon, John, M.P., 205.

Distinguished Irishmen I have met, 10.

Disestablishment of the Irish Church prompted by Gladstone's recognition of " the " intensity of Fenianism," 147.

Disruption of the Irish Party, 252.

Doctors and other professional men excellent helpers in the National Cause, 177, 258.

Dock labourers' love of learning, 19.

Dolly's Brae Fight, 44.

—— massacre, 45.

Donnelly, Edward, foreman printer of " United Ireland," brings me the stereos, 210.

Doran, Arthur, an Irish newsagent, becomes bail for Forrester, 135.

Dowling, chief constable of Liverpool, dismissed, 60.

Down, County, 2, 29, 47.

—— cottage industries, 33.

Drumgoolan, my uncle's parish, 28.

Dublin Castle wires warning of Manchester Rescue—too late, 97.

Duffy, Michael Francis, 166.

Duffy, Sir Charles Gavan, loses heart for a time, 62.

Duffy, Sir Charles Gavan, his
old hopes revive, 62.
Dundas, General, routed by the
Kilcullen pikemen in '98.
Dundrum Bay, 32.

E.

Egan, Patrick, 184.
—— sustains "United Ire-
land" against attempted
suppression, 215.
—— his life story, 219.
—— always a practical
patriot, 221.
—— attitude towards Par-
liament, 221.
—— President of Irish
National League of America,
224.
—— American ambassador
to Chili, 224.
—— President Harrison's
tribute, 224.
Elizabethan days, 5.
"Emerald Minstrels," The,
115, 116, 117.
—— inspired by "Spirit
of the Nation," 118.
"Erin's Hope," with Irish-
American officers, arms, and
ammunition, reaches Sligo
Bay, 94.
—— returns to America, 95.
"Erin's Sons in England,"
racy song by T. D. Sulli-
van, 152.

F.

Fahy, Francis, poet, 137
Falconer (Edmond O'Rourke),
a famous Irish actor and
dramatist, author of " Peep
o' Day," " Killarney," etc.,
52, 263.
Famine, The great Irish, 6.
—— heroism of the clergy,
53.
—— the greatest disaster
in Irish history, 269.

"Felon Repeal Club " in New-
castle-on-Tyne, 56.
Fenian Brotherhood,The, 52,73.
—— the two wings, 123.
—— Conference in Paris,
Michael Breslin attends, 123.
—— gathering, which Par-
nell attends at my invitation,
203.
" Fenian Paymaster " (Captain
O'Rorke), known as
" Beecher," 78.
Fenian leaders in England take
counsel, 93.
Fenianism.—What did it do
for Ireland ? 146.
Ferguson, John, assists at
foundation of Home Rule
Confederation of Great
Britain, 176.
—— indicates Parnell as
future leader, 192.
—— director of " United
Irishman," 180.
Finigan, James Lysaght, his
adventurous career, 124.
—— in the Franco-German
War, 160.
Finn MacCool and the ancient
Fenians, 52.
Flannery, Thomas, an able
Irish scholar, 164, 258.
Flood, John, and the Chester
raid, 82.
" Flowering," girls employed at
34.
" Flowing Tide,'' 233.
Foley, Patrick James, 254.
Ford, Patrick, Michael Davitt's
tribute to him, 198.
—— I welcome the " Irish
World" in the " Catholic
Times," 198.
Forrester, Arthur, he brings me
revolvers, 131.
—— I am visited by detec-
tives, 131.
—— they can make out no
case against him, and he is
released, 135.

Forrester, Arthur, he joins the French Foreign Legion, 134, 160, 162.

Forrester, Mrs. Ellen, comes with Michael Davitt, 133.

—— like others of her family, she wrote poetry, 134.

Fox, Frank, one of our poets, 181.

"Fount of patriotism," 11.

Franco-Prussian War, 160.

Freemantle, rescue from of the military Fenians, 139.

"Frolics of Phil Foley," a sketch by John F. McArdle, 121.

G.

Gaelic characters, the, 11.

Gaelic League Revival, 256.

Gaelic Prayer Book (Scotch), printed by me for Father Campbell, S.J., for use in the Highlands and Islands of Scotland, 259.

Garton, Patrick De Lacy, Stephens escapes in his hooker, 78.

—— he helps the blockade-running of "United Ireland."

"Georgette," passenger steamer, pursues the military Fenians, 143.

—— fires a round shot across the bows of the "Catalpa," in which they are escaping, 143.

Gilmore, Patrick Sarsfield, a distinguished Irish-American composer and musician, 114.

Gilmore, Mary Sarsfield, his daughter, an able contributor to "Irish World," 114.

Gladstone, William Ewart, introduces Home Rule Bill, 231.

—— "Flowing Tide," 233.

—— returned to power through aid of Irish vote, 232.

"God Save Ireland," Condon gives us a rallying cry and a National Anthem, 104.

"Gormans of Glenmore," The, 265.

Goss, Bishop, a typical Englishman of the best kind. Blunt-hitting-out-from-the-shoulder style of speaking, 156.

Grattan's Parliament, 41.

Graves, Alfred Perceval, 138, 259.

Gunboats in river Mersey in view of expected rising in Liverpool, 55.

H.

"Hail to the Chief" (from the "Lady of the Lake"), 118.

—— played as salute to Parnell, 117.

Halpin, General, a scientific soldier, 90.

—— in command at the rising, 90.

—— gives us lecture on fortifications and earthworks, 91.

—— arrested at Queenstown, 91.

"Hamlet" played by Falconer, 262.

Hand, John, one of our poets, 181.

Hanlons, Hughey and Ned, 51.

Harrington, Martin, escaped military Fenian, 141.

Harvestmen from Connaught and Donegal, a hardy lot, 35.

Haslingden, the home of Davitt, 84.

Hassett, Thomas Henry, escaped military Fenian, 141.

Healy, T. M., when I first met him, 196.

—— becomes Parnell's secretary, 197.

Heinrick, Hugh, editor of "United Irishman," 180.

Hibernians, Ancient Order of, strong in Liverpool, and stout champions of country and creed, 16.

—— a bodyguard for the priests in penal days, 17.

—— their stronghold in northern Irish counties and counties adjoining, 18.

—— in America, Rev. Thomas Shahan pays tribute to the Order, 16, 17.

"Hidden Gem," a play by Cardinal Wiseman, 63.

Hierarchy restored, 58.

Highlands of Scotland, the Gaelic spoken there, 187.

Hints from Thomas Davis to Irish painters, students, historians, lecturers, journalists, public speakers, and others, 261.

Hogan, the Irish sculptor, crowns O'Connell with Repeal cap, 49.

Hogan, Martin Joseph, escaped military Fenian, 141.

Hogan, William, a friend of Captain John M'Cafferty, 87.

—— helps Darragh to get the revolvers for Manchester rescue, 96.

—— is arrested for this, tried, and acquitted, 124, 125.

Holyhead, wagons and carriages for there to be seized, 81.

Holy Cross Chapel, Liverpool, as it was, 58.

—— the chief of police countenances the getting up of a panic there, 60.

Holland, of the submarine, 145.

Home Rule Organisation, formation in Ireland, various sections assist, 148.

—— John Barry calls us together to form Home Rule Confederation of Great Britain, 173.

Home Rule Organisation, I become its first secretary, 155.

Hyde Road, the scene of the Manchester rescue, 99.

Hymans, Jewish admirers of Thade Crowley, 25.

I.

Igoe's publichouse at the Curragh, 67.

"Inishowen," noble song by Charles Gavan Duffy, 260.

Insurrection in Ireland considered easier to put down than "Obstruction," 190.

Iona Pilgrimage, 233.

Irish-American officers to leave Ireland for England, 79.

Irish Brigade of Liverpool, 92.

"Irish Library," I start it, 35.

"Irish in Britain," The, 78,102.

Irish National League organiser, Edward M'Convey, 33.

Irish Parliamentary Party, disruption and reunion of, 252.

Irish Race Convention, 254.

"Irish Rapparees," by Gavan Duffy, 260.

Irish Revolutionary Brotherhood, 73, 74.

Irish of Great Britain compact and politically important, 2.

"Irish World," The, 198.

Isle of Man, 32, 187.

J.

Jack Langan, an Irish boxer, 4.

"Jigger Loft," where our men work, 7.

Journalism, 21.

Johnson, my classical teacher, 28.

K.

Kehoe, Inspector Lawrence.— Did he shut his eyes in my case? 129.

Kelly, Col. Thomas, his personal appearance, 92.
—— directs rescue of James Stephens, 76, 77, 78.
—— I meet him in Liverpool, 92, 93.
—— his arrest in Manchester with Captain Deasy, 95.
—— rescue, 100, 101.
—— how he escaped from the country, 105.
Kildare, gallant fight of the men of Kildare in '98, 69.
King Edward VII., plot for his abduction when Prince of Wales, 88.
Kirwan, Captain Martin Walter, in the Franco-Prussian War, 160.
—— afterwards general secretary of Irish organisation in Great Britain,
Knox, Edmund Vesey, a Protestant Member of Parliament, who did good service at Lloyd George's election and elsewhere, 238.

L.

Lambert, Michael, makes key to fit James Stephens' cell, 78.
"Lancashire Free Press," 91.
Land League, The, its formation in April, 1879, with Davitt recognised as its "Father," 205.
Larkin, Michael, 103, 104.
Lecale, Celtic and Norman admixture since De Courcy's time, 27.
Leitrim Chapel, where I served Mass for my uncle, 32.
—— band of fiddles, flutes, and clarionets, 37.
Lia Fail (Stone of Destiny), 1c9, the stone to be stolen, 110,

Lia Fail, David Barrett, League organiser, tries to test its weight. Is stopped by its guardians, 111.
Liberator, The (O'Connell), frequently passed through Liverpool, 43.
Lloyd–George, David, Chancellor of the Exchequer, I help in his first Election, 237.
London Irish Literary Society, 259.
Lost opportunity for Irish tongue, 15.
Lover, Samuel, painter, poet, musician, composer, novelist, and dramatist, 10.
—— his patriotism, 10, 11.
—— his wit, 12.
Loyal toasts, 188, 189, 203.
Lumber Street Chapel, 4.
Lynch, Daniel, translates "God Save Ireland" into Irish, 113.

M.

McAnulty, Bernard, a strong Home Ruler and Fenian sympathiser, 34, 56, 180.
McArdle, John, 15, 16.
McArdle, John F., the most brilliant of the Emerald Minstrels, 118.
McCann, Michael Joseph, author of "O'Donnell Aboo," I make his acquaintance, 114, 115.
McCafferty, John, had fought for the South in the American Civil War. His plot to seize Chester Castle, 81.
—— his scheme (as Mr. Patterson) to abduct the Prince of Wales, 88.
McCartans, The, 29.
McCarthy, Sergeant, his sudden death, 2c0.
M'Cormick, Father, of Wigan, men on way to Chester raid go to Confession to him, 82.

McDonald, Bishop of Argyll and the Isles, preached at Iona in Gaelic on the life of St. Columbkille, 234.

McDonnell, Sergeant James, 206

McGrady, Owen, conference at his house to arrange for reception of expedition then on the sea, 93.

McGrath, Father Peter, 187.

McGowan, James, my god-father, 2.

McHale, Archbishop, I report his sermon, 155.

McKinley, Peter, 180.

MacMahon, Father, of Suncroft, gives the Curragh men a good character, 70.

—— he tells us of St. Brigid's miraculous mantle, 69.

—— and of the gallant Kildare men in '98, 69.

McMahon, Heber, 181.

MacManus, Terence Bellew, 49, 52.

McNaghten, Sir Francis, 2.

McSwiney, Father, S.J., and the "Catholic Times," 154.

"Macbeth" played by Falconer, 262.

Magennis, Eiver (see Castle-wellan), 29.

Maguire, the marine, wrongly charged at Manchester, 104.

Manchester, first Convention of Home Rule Confederation held there, 173.

Manchester Martyrs, place of rescue confounded with place of execution, 99.

Mangan, Richard, 180.

Mass in Penal times, 5.

Massacre at Dolly's Brae, 45.

Mathew, Father, Apostle of Temperance, what he was like, 13.

Maughan, Peter, recruiting agent for the I.R.B. among the British soldiery, 72, 86.

Mazzinghi, Count, composer of "Hail to the Chief," 115.

Meany, Stephen Joseph, a journalist, 91.

—— in Young Ireland movement, 22.

—— starts "Lancashire Free Press," 91.

—— imprisoned for Fenianism, 91.

"Men of the North, The," stirring ballad by Charles Gavan Duffy, 260.

Military Fenians, their rescue, chiefly by John Breslin, going from America, and John Walsh from this side, 139 to 145.

Millbank Prison, M'Cafferty writes from there to William Hogan, 87.

Mogan, John, a capable man at registration and electioneering, 243.

Monroe, General, a Presbyterian leader, hanged at his own door in '98, 41.

Mourne Mountains, 27, 32, 57.

Mulhall, Peter and James, 194.

Mullaghmast, 49.

Mullin, Dr. James, 177, 178.

Murphy, Bessie, 181.

Murphy, Captain, 93, 112.

Murphy, David, supposed to have been shot by connivance of Pigott, 247.

Murphy, Patrick, 239.

Murphy, William, sent to penal servitude for attack on the van at Manchester, though not there, 102.

Murray, Archbishop, 30.

N.

"Nation" newspaper, readings from it, 15.

—— "O'Donnell Aboo" appears in it, 115.

" Nation once again, A," 36.
National Anthem of "God Save Ireland," Condon's defiant shout in the dock the origin of it, 104.
" Nationalist " The, 256.
Naughton, Miss, 132.
" Ninety-eight" memories, many of the leaders Presbyterians, 41.
" No Popery" mob, A, 4.
" No Popery" mania over " Papal aggression," 58.
Normans in Ireland, The, 27.
" Northern Press and Catholic Times," 72.
Norse settlements, 27.
Nugent, Father, and the Catholic Institute, 63.
—— St. Patrick's celebrations, 64.
—— proprietor of " Catholic Times," which I conducted for him, 91.
—— after a long interval, am pleased to meet him just before his death, 159.

O.

Oates, Tom, of Newcastle, 94.
Oath of allegiance, Parnell and my view on this, 112.
" O," the prefix, 33.
O'Brien, Captain Michael, is hanged at Manchester, 104, 112.
O'Brien, John, released prisoner, 200.
O'Brien, James Francis Xavier, introduces me to O'Donovan (Rossa), 73.
—— No more gallant figure among the Fenian leaders than J. F. X. O'Brien. In all things *straight*, 89, 90.
O'Brien, M.P., Patrick, 230.
O'Brien, Richard Barry, 259.
O'Brien, William, 212, &c.

" Obstruction," the 1877 Convention endorses the policy, 104.
O'Coigly, Father, Pilgrimage, 235.
O'Connell Centenary, 183, 184.
O'Connell in Liverpool, 48.
—— a faithful son of the Church, 48.
—— enormous attendance at his meetings, 49.
—— Orange attack repelled by McManus and his friends, 49.
O'Connell, John (son of the Liberator, Daniel O'Connell), a British militia officer at the Curragh; gives good example to his men by going to Holy Communion, 68.
—— he wrote fine verses, 68.
O'Connell, Maurice, wrote " Recruiting Song of the Irish Brigade," 69.
O'Connell Centenary, 183.
O'Connor, M.P., T. P., the only Home Rule Member of Parliament for Great Britain elected *as such*, 24, 188, 230.
O'Donovan, Edmund, son of John O'Donovan, 90.
—— in French Foreign Legion, 160, 162.
—— special correspondent in Russo-Turkish War, 164.
—— Merv, 165.
—— perishes in the Soudan, 165.
O'Donovan, Jeremiah (Rossa), 73.
O'Donovan, John, the distinguished Irish scholar, 163.
—— memoir of him by Thomas Flannery, 164.
O'Donnell, Bishop, 254.
' O'Donnell Aboo " as our national anthem ? 114, 115.
—— no claim, 116.

O'Donnell, F. H., 181, 193.

O'Grady, Hubert, 265.

O'Hagan, Lord, 184.

O'Hanlons, The, the Ulster standard bearers, 51.

O'Kelly, James, in Mexican campaign, 165.

—— recruits for the French army until fall of Paris, 166.

—— adopts journalism, 167.

—— enters Parliament, 167.

"Olaf, the Dane, or the Curse of Columbkille," 266.

Oliver, William John, 180.

O'Laverty, Father, historian of Down and Connor, 29, 30.

O'Loughlin, Brian, 38.

O'Loughlin, Father Bernard, my uncle, 33.

—— Father Bernard, Passionist, of Paris 169.

—— John, my uncle, 169.

—— Michael, Father, my uncle, 28, 33.

—— Margaret, my mother, 33.

O'Mahony, Michael, writes "Life of St. Cólumbkille" for me, 234.

O'Malley, M.P., William, 230.

Opening of a bath by swimming in it, by T. D. Sullivan, when Lord Mayor of Dublin, 153.

Orangeism, 19, 20, 22, 23.

O'Reilly, John Boyle, his "Life" in our Library, 86.

—— helps escape of the military Fenians, 140.

O'Rorke, Captain Michael (Beecher), the Fenian paymaster, 78, 79.

O'Rourke, Edmund (Falconer), actor and dramatist, 52, 263.

O'Shea, Captain, a candidate for Parliament, 228.

O'Sullivan, Eugene, 211.

—— Eugene or "Owen," a Welsh registration case, 244.

P.

Packmen from Ulster, Oiney Bannon, Bernard McAnulty, 34.

"Pagan O'Leary," "Beggars and Robbers," 80.

"Papal aggression," 58.

Papal Volunteers, we entertain them, 155.

"Papishes," 19.

Parnell, Charles Stewart, enters Parliament, 179, 181.

—— becomes chairman of Irish Parliamentary Party, 192.

—— could weigh men's capabilities, 197.

—— Davitt cannot induce Parnell to join the advanced organisation, 202.

—— Parnell and the I.R.B. men, 203.

—— with Dillon, goes to America for relief of Irish distress, 208.

—— collapse of the "Times" Forgeries against Parnell, 248.

—— disruption in the Party, 252.

—— reunion, January 30th, 1900, 255.

"Patriot Parliament of 1689," by Thomas Davis, 29.

Patterson, Mr. (Captain McCafferty), calls on me, 88.

"Peggy Loughlin's wee boy," 32.

Penal days in Liverpool, 4, 5.

Phœnix movement and trials, 73.

Pictures at election times, "the Pope," "Robert Emmet," "King William," 245.

Plantation of Ulster, 31, 39.

Power, John O'Conror, lectures at Davitt's meeting, 199.

"Punch" and "Times" seemed to gloat over probable extinction of Irish race, 53.

"Punch's" caricature of O'Connell, 54.

Purcell, Edward, helps blockade running of "United Ireland," 213.

Prendiville, John, his steamers used to bring voters from the river, 244.

"Presbyterian Government," was there a call for this at Ballinahinch ? 39.

Price, Father John, S.J., 4.

"Protestant Ulster" chiefly an importation, 30.

Q.

"Quare man doesn't know his own mother's name," 33.

R.

Race Convention in Ireland, 254.

Rails to Chester to be taken up, 81.

"Rapparees, The Irish," Charles Gavan Duffy's fine song, 260.

Readings from the "Nation," 15.

"Reapers of Kilbride," 265, 266.

"Rebel, An Old," 1.

Red-haired woman stops the growth of the Curragh, 69.

Redmond, John, 3, 252.

Redmond, Sylvester, 86.

Refugees of the '67 Rising, 92.

Repeal Hall, 52.

"Repeal Cap," 49.

Rescue of Kelly and Deasy. Incidents of the arrest and rescue described in page 95 and following pages.

Reunion of the Parliamentary Party, January 30th, 1900, 255.

Revisiting Ireland, 27.

Revolvers for Manchester, 96.

Revolvers from Forrester, 131.

Reynolds, Dr., 52.

Ribbonmen, 23.

Richards, Richard ("Double Dick"), 109.

Richardson, John, 5.

"Richard III." played by Falconer, 262.

Rising of 1848, drilling to oppose it, 55.

Rising of 1867, 89.

Roden, Lord, 32.

——— Dolly's Brae massacre, 45.

"Roderick Vich Alpine Dhu," 115.

Rogers, John, a Gaelic scholar, 259.

Roney, Hughey, his house threatened by Orangemen, 15, 20.

"Rory O'More," by Lover, 11.

——— a scene from it re-enacted, 12.

"Rosaleen Dhu," 266.

Rotunda, Dublin, 155.

Round Towers, Kildare, &c., 70.

Russell, Lord John, his Ecclesiastical Titles Act, 58, 61.

Russell, Charles (Lord Russell of Killowen), willing to become our candidate for Parliament to induce Liberals to withdraw objectionable man. This has desired effect, 249.

——— we ask him to take the chair for our first Home Rule meeting. He advises us to get Dr. Commins, 171.

Russell, Sir Edward, of "Liverpool Daily Post," 21, 257.

Ryan, John (Capn. O'Doherty), calls on me ; I join the I.R.B., 74.

Ryan, John (Capn. O'Doherty), —— he describes to me the escape of Stephens, in which he assisted, 77, 78.
—— now dead many years, 68, 112.
Ryan, Wm. James, his "Life of John Boyle O'Reilly," 86.
Ryan, William Patrick, 257.
Ryan, Dr. Mark, an Irish scholar, 257.

S.

Sadlier, John, his suicide, 62.
Sadlier-Keogh gang, their betrayal of the cause of the Irish tenants, 61, 62.
Saintfield, battle, in '98, 38.
Salford Gaol, 99.
Santley, Sir Charles, 5.
Sarsfield Band, 184.
Saturday Evening Concerts, 10.
School Board Election, Liverpool, our votes enough to elect 8 out of the 15 members, 156.
Schoolmaster, The, 93, 111.
Scone, 110.
Scott, Sir Walter, author of "Hail to the Chief," 115.
Scotland Ward and Division in Liverpool, an Irish stronghold, both Municipal and Parliamentary, 24, 185.
Seager, John Renwick, 243.
Servant girls, Irish-American, 111.
Sexton, Thomas, 254.
Shahan, Father, on "Hibernianism," 16, 17.
"Shan Van Vocht," on the "Curragh of Kildare," sung by the "Emerald Minstrels," 71.
Shaw, George Bernard, 264.
"Shemus O'Brien," 121.
Sherlock, Father, a saintly man, presides at our first Birmingham Convention demonstration, 175, 177.

Slieve Donard, 32, 265.
Slieve na Slat (Mountain of rods "), 31.
Sloops from Ireland, 3.
Smyth, George, 52.
"Spirit of the Nation," 11.
Stephens, James, his escape from Richmond, 76, 77.
St. Brigid's mantle, Father MacMahon tells the legend of, 69.
"Stage Irishman," discountenanced, 119, 264.
Strongbow, 272.
Saint Columbkille, 233.
St. George's Hall, Liverpool, great gathering addressed by Parnell, 206.
St. Helens meeting, Parnell and Davitt attend, 201.
St. Mary's, Lumber Street, 4.
St. Nicholas's, Liverpool, 4, 6.
St. Patrick's effigy, as if addressing our people from Ireland, 3.
St. Patrick's Day processions, 22, 24, 64.
—— celebrations, 64, 65.
Steamers for O'Connell Centenary, 183.
Sullivan Brothers, 150.
Sullivan, A. M., becomes proprietor and editor of the "Nation," 63.
—— presides at adjourned initial Convention of Home Rule Confederation of Great Britain, 176.
Sullivan, T. D., author of our national anthem, 113.
—— he writes, 'Erin's Sons in England" for me, 152.
Supernatural, Irish faith in the, 13.
Swift, Miss Kate, 211.

T.

Taaffe, James Vincent, 211.
Tenant Right Agitation, 62.
"Terence's Fireside," 115.

" Thrashers," The, 42.

" Times " Forgeries Commission, 207, 246.

Tollymore Park, seat of Lord Roden, 45.

Tribal ñames still in tribal lands, 27, 273.

" Tribe of Brian," 28.

Tragedy of the Famine, The, 6.

U.

Ulster Catholics, the most pure-blooded Celts in Ireland, 30.

Ulster, plantation of in King James I.'s time, 39.

" United Ireland," attempted suppression, 210.

—— sent out as " dried fish," 212.

—— not an issue missed, 215.

—— I am prosecuted by Government, 216.

—— printed once in Derry, 217.

—— re-appeared in old office, 218.

Union of North and South destroyed, 61.

" United Irishman," organ of Home Rule Confederation of Great Britain, 177, 181, 265.

United Irishmen of 1798, 11, 41.

V.

Vaughan, Cardinal, Bishop of Salford, I get his support for " Catholic Times," 158.

Vauxhall Ward, Liverpool, 185.

Volunteers of 1782, The, 41.

" Vatican, The Treasures of," 61.

W.

Walsh, John, informs a select gathering how he and a friend from this side helped to rescue the military Fenians, 143.

Warders from Belle Vue Prison interfere in the Manchester Rescue—no use, 101.

Ward, Joseph, 121.

Widow Walsh welcomes her lodgers at the Curragh of Kildare, 66.

Whitty, Michael James, Liverpool head Constable, afterwards editor of the " Daily Post," 20, 21, 22, 91.

Wilson, James, escaped military Fenian, 141.

Wilson, John, a Birmingham gunsmith, 136.

Windle, Dr. Bertram, President of University College, Cork, 177.

Wiseman, Cardinal, " Papal aggression" mania directed against him, 63.

—— his fine play of " The Hidden Gem " given by Father Nugent's students at the Catholic Institute, Liverpool, 63.

Wolohan, Michael, the " blockade runner" for " United Ireland," 212.

" Woollen Goods" (for " United Ireland "), 213.

Y.

" Young Ireland," 11, 52.